M000247989

Law's Imagined Republic

Law's Imagined Republic shows how the American Revolution was marked by the rapid proliferation of law talk across the colonies. This legal language was both elite and popular, spanned different forms of expression from words to rituals, and included simultaneously real and imagined law. Because it was employed to mobilize resistance against England, the proliferation of revolutionary legal language became intimately intertwined with politics. Drawing on a wealth of material from criminal cases, Steven Wilf reconstructs the intertextual ways Americans from the 1760s through the 1790s read law: reading one case against another and often self-consciously comparing transatlantic legal systems as they thought about how they might construct their own legal system in a new republic. What transformed extraordinary tales of crime into a political forum? How did different ways of reading or speaking about law shape our legal origins? And, ultimately, how might excavating innovative approaches to law in this formative period, which were forged in the street as well as in the courtroom, alter our usual understanding of contemporary American legal institutions? *Law's Imagined Republic* tells the story of the untidy beginnings of American law.

Steven Wilf is Joel Barlow Professor of Law at the University of Connecticut. He is the author of *The Law Before the Law* (2008), which examines how legal systems address the problem of existing law prior to a law-giving moment, and numerous articles in law and history. Professor Wilf's research focuses on intellectual property law, historical jurisprudence, and legal history.

Cambridge Historical Studies in American Law and Society

SERIES EDITOR

Christopher Tomlins, *University of California, Irvine*

PREVIOUSLY PUBLISHED IN THE SERIES

Andrew Wender Cohen, *The Racketeer's Progress: Chicago and the Struggle for the Modern American Economy, 1900–1940*

Davison Douglas, *Jim Crow Moves North: The Battle over Northern School Segregation, 1865–1954*

Tony A. Freyer, *Antitrust and Global Capitalism, 1930–2004*

Michael Grossberg, *A Judgment for Solomon: The d'Hauteville Case and Legal Experience in the Antebellum South*

Rebecca M. McLennan, *The Crisis of Imprisonment: Protest, Politics, and the Making of the American Penal State, 1776–1941*

David M. Rabban, *Free Speech in Its Forgotten Years*

James D. Schmidt, *Industrial Violence and the Legal Origins of Child Labor*

Robert J. Steinfeld, *Coercion, Contract, and Free Labor in Nineteenth-Century America*

Michael Vorenberg, *Final Freedom: The Civil War, the Abolition of Slavery, and the Thirteenth Amendment*

Jenny Wahl, *The Bondsman's Burden: An Economic Analysis of the Common Law of Southern Slavery*

Barbara Young Welke, *Recasting American Liberty: Gender, Law, and the Railroad Revolution, 1865–1920*

Michael Willrich, *City of Courts, Socializing Justice in Progressive-Era Chicago*

Law's Imagined Republic

*Popular Politics and Criminal Justice
in Revolutionary America*

STEVEN WILF

University of Connecticut School of Law

CAMBRIDGE
UNIVERSITY PRESS

CAMBRIDGE UNIVERSITY PRESS
Cambridge, New York, Melbourne, Madrid, Cape Town, Singapore,
São Paulo, Delhi, Dubai, Tokyo

Cambridge University Press
32 Avenue of the Americas, New York, NY 10013-2473, USA

www.cambridge.org
Information on this title: www.cambridge.org/9780521145282

© Steven Wilf 2010

This publication is in copyright. Subject to statutory exception
and to the provisions of relevant collective licensing agreements,
no reproduction of any part may take place without the written
permission of Cambridge University Press.

First published 2010

Printed in the United States of America

A catalog record for this publication is available from the British Library.

Library of Congress Cataloging in Publication data
Wilf, Steven Robert.
Law's imagined republic: popular politics and criminal justice
in revolutionary America / Steven Wilf.
p.   cm. – (Cambridge historical studies in American law and society)
Includes bibliographical references and index.
ISBN 978-0-521-19690-1 (hardback)
1. Criminal justice, Administration of – United States – History –
18th century.   I. Title.   II. Series.
KF9223.W534   2010
345.73'05–dc22   2010002831

ISBN 978-0-521-19690-1 Hardback
ISBN 978-0-521-14528-2 Paperback

Cambridge University Press has no responsibility for the persistence or
accuracy of URLs for external or third-party Internet Web sites referred to in
this publication and does not guarantee that any content on such Web sites is,
or will remain, accurate or appropriate.

For Guita

After the leaves have fallen, we return
To a plain sense of things.
It is as if
We had come to an end of imagination,
Inanimate in an inert savoir.

Wallace Stevens
"The Plain Sense of Things"

Contents

Acknowledgments

More than anyone else in the academy, Charles Maier is responsible for my becoming an historian, and thus he bears part of the blame for this book. The original topic emerged out of discussions with Linda Colley, whose work I deeply admire, and I have benefitted considerably from her commitment to a transatlantic history that is simultaneously granular and global. Over the years, John Demos has been most supportive – and most persistent – in pressing upon me his particular views about the importance of storytelling. The use of the micronarrative of the legal case, as opposed to the microhistory of local settlements, reflects our agreements, and disagreements, about how to write history. Jon Butler, David Brion Davis, Thomas Green, Edmund Morgan, William Nelson, Kent Newmyer, John Reid, Avi Soifer, and Carol Weisbrod contributed to the project at important junctures. Robert Gordon and Morton Horwitz have been ideal mentors. Our many wide-ranging discussions over the years demonstrate that conversation, like well-kept wine, only becomes better over time.

Christopher Tomlins has proved to be the consummate scholar-editor. I also would like to thank Eric Crahan, who skillfully guided this book to completion, and the two anonymous readers at Cambridge University Press. As someone working in a neighboring field, I often have had the pleasure of drawing on Richard Ross's broad knowledge of the legal history of the period. My close friend and gifted historian, Judith Miller, constantly reminds me of the importance of true companionship.

Most of the research in printed sources was conducted in the Yale University libraries. I also have benefitted from the collection at the American Antiquarian Society, the John Carter Brown Library, and the various archives and manuscript collections cited in the bibliography. During my fellowship years at New York University Law School and the University of Chicago, I availed myself of their libraries. Lee Sims and his indefatigable research staff at the University of Connecticut Law Library tracked down innumerable sources for me. Under the guidance of Deans Hugh Macgill and Jeremy Paul, the University of Connecticut Law School has become a center for law and humanities research. I appreciate my provocative yet gentle colleagues and the law school's continuing support. It is difficult to imagine a more hospitable pair of institutions than the Law Faculty at Hebrew University and Hebrew University's Institute for Advanced Studies. I truly have cherished my extended stays in Jerusalem.

Even an imagined republic impinges on a real family life. I would like to thank Sara and Laurence, Moses, and Lily for their patience. My parents, Morris and Selma Wilf, and my mother-in-law, Shifra Epstein Goldberg, have been most supportive, as have my various siblings and siblings-in-law, Joel and Sofia Wilf and Henry and Sherry Stein. My father, in particular, has been delighted to discuss the peculiarities of the past. Quite rightfully, my wife, Guita, has not been patient. But she has created the most important of all commonwealths – a tangible place filled with her grace.

Law's Imagined Republic

Introduction

How did Americans imagine law as they sought to establish their own independent sovereignty? This book is about the forging of new conceptions of legalism between the beginning of the Seven Years' War in 1756 and the period of the French Revolution in the 1790s. To tell this story properly means focusing on the intersection of criminal law, politics, and language. Criminal law – not the abstraction of constitutional principles – was often the locus of debates about justice. Its captivating tales from the underworld, its setting into stark relief fundamental issues of proper conduct, and its reliance upon the violence of punishment made it the most talked-about legalism in late-eighteenth-century America's coffee houses and cobblestone streets. Politics was intertwined with law in Revolutionary America. Legal arguments and narratives provided a cultural network for galvanizing a population stretched out along the Atlantic seaboard and westward. The rituals of punishment, such as hanging in effigy, became the rituals of rebellion.

Popular law talk was at the heart of revolutionary law-making and at the heart of the American Revolution itself. It assumed many guises and served many purposes, including the legitimation of resistance against the British, establishing a link between street ritual and print culture, acting as an instrument of political mobilization, and mere entertainment. Historians have uncovered a burgeoning public sphere for political discourse in the end of the eighteenth century across the Atlantic world. This arena is often associated with meeting places such as taverns or new forms of conviviality. But law – an abstraction made tangible through mock executions or contestation over actual cases – was itself a public sphere.

Although the explosion of law talk in Revolutionary America had its origins in the folk rituals of rough justice from early modern England, the particular circumstances of its spread were grounded in the social milieu of a politicized America searching for a common language that would bridge differences in social status and geography. As we shall see, the centrality of legalism in American culture did not begin with the settled jurisprudence of courts. Ironically, however, law's prominent cultural role led to the common designation by the early nineteenth century of America as a country dedicated to the rule of law – what John Adams famously called "a government of laws, not of men." This predisposition is even more surprising when one remembers that this was a people located at the edge of an empire, facing a frontier filled with new immigrants raised in disparate traditions, and that just emerged from a revolution against lawful authority. In every sense of the word, the United States in the end of the eighteenth century was a new democracy. Nevertheless, Revolutionary America had chosen to replace the personal governance of monarchy with an ordered republic of legal norms. Tom Paine summed up this change with a pithy phrase: "In America the law is king."[1]

Most stories of how America became subject to the rule of law focus on framers and justices, on the serious-minded founders of a new nation. The received traditional narrative is quite straightforward. America's Revolution, we have been told, distinguished itself from other political upheavals by elevating law to a dominant position. Rule of law ensures equal protection under a rational legal regime. Through Constitutional decision-making, moreover, it commands obedience to legal doctrine as a central means for resolving societal disputes. There are many different versions of the rule-of-law tradition. But the essential narrative remains much the same. After the American Revolution, popular sovereignty became inscribed in a written form of fundamental law, the Federal Constitution. Its enduring authority has often assured recourse to legal norms rather than factitious politics. In a famous passage, Tocqueville describes how legal language originates with judges and judicial proceedings, extends to lawyers who bring it to bear on public life, and descends to the common people so that "it so to speak infiltrates all society, it

---

[1] Thomas Paine, "Common Sense," in *The Complete Works of Thomas Paine*, ed. Philip S. Foner (New York: Citadel Press, 1945), p. 29; John Adams, "Novangelus" in *Works of John Adams*, ed. Charles Francis Adams, 10 vols. (Boston: Charles C. Little and James Brown, 1851), 4:106.

descends into the lowest ranks, and the people as a whole in the end contract a part of the habits and tastes of the magistrate."[2]

This book suggests a different sort of founding. The subject of this
book is the outpouring of law talk in America between the conclusion
of the Seven Years' War in 1763 and the end of the eighteenth century.
Criminal trials, as in our own time, best captured the public imagination, and many of these were the subject of discussion in taverns and
coffee houses – which might span the gamut from raucous gossip to
serious legal analysis. This expressive legalism was readily communicated across different levels of society and across different geographic
regions. Its symbolic idiom ranged from imagined punishments as a
form of political protest to hanging ballads to serious proposals for
criminal law reform. During the Revolutionary period, Americans did
not simply draw upon law as a language of politics and social criticism,
but also learned to read law differently. While certainly they employed
a panoply of techniques for interpreting legal expression during this
period, one stands out – intertextuality. Cases were read against other
criminal law cases, text was read against the narrative of its political context, and the American legal doctrine was read comparatively
against its English counterpart.

In a certain way, then, it is possible to speak of the criminals at the
core of such stories as founders. These founders – who would have been
surprised to be granted such a title – included petty thieves, over-the-
hill housebreakers, and a motley array of blackguards. In their own,
self-interested ways, late-eighteenth-century criminals were subversive.
Nevertheless, they were reluctant founders of sorts because their stories, often artful-dodger sort of tales – and the debates about justice,
public legal interpretation, and the role of English legal authority that
constitute the connective tissue of American legal debates – depended
upon their punishment. Such stories did not borrow from the "habits
and tastes of the magistrate." Often vulgar, they might be described as the
late-eighteenth-century version of kitsch legalism.

Quite recently, the problem of law's relationship to revolutionary
upheaval has animated a way of thinking about contemporary law,
"popular constitutionalism." As identified by Gary D. Rowe and Larry
Kramer, and presaged by an extensive examination of customary law by
John Reid, this discussion has focused upon the constitutional authority

[2] Alexis de Tocqueville, "On What Tempers the Tyranny of the Majority in the United
States," in *Democracy in America*, eds. Harvey C. Mansfield and Delba Winthrop
(Chicago: University of Chicago Press, 2000), pp. 257–258.

of late-eighteenth-century Americans.[3] Kramer argues that ultimate constitutional authority was once vested in the people, though it increasingly became the purview of Federalist-controlled courts by the early nineteenth century. Seeing constitutional authority as belonging to the people themselves, of course, has important consequences for how we view the current power of the United States Supreme Court, especially judicial review.

Nonetheless, too much of popular constitutionalism has been concerned with the issue of who holds the reins of legal power – the courts or the people. By investing the "people themselves" with the role of judicial review, popular constitutionalism envisions a late-eighteenth-century constitution remarkably like our own, but with the power of courts and people differently calibrated. The very notion of an earlier, unformed common-law constitution would have been familiar to eighteenth-century Anglo-Americans. Imposing the legal category of constitutionalism as seen today, however, is an anachronistic enterprise, which is not terribly helpful for understanding this formative period. It presumes that settled constitutional principles were embodied at the popular level while providing less attention to the diffuse, contradictory, and often maddeningly imprecise ways that law was expressed in a period brimming over with all sorts of law talk.

In contrast, I have focused upon criminal law as language, not upon eighteenth-century debates about governance, because it was this form of law with all its high drama, sometimes vulgar and sometimes elevated, where so much of the creative legalism of the period resides. Occasionally, law at the popular level was articulated in constitutional terms. It was more often simply an intoxicating mix of gossip, politics, sensationalism, tales of murder, and astute attention to the procedural norms that make law matter. As contemporary lawyers periodically rediscover, law is ultimately about stories and language as much as it is about straightforward rules. My hope is that by returning to the well-spring of law talk – recovering how late-eighteenth-century Americans mixed criminal law and politics and used this intoxicating combination as a means to mobilize citizens, both elites and common people, within a revolutionary context – we can elucidate how Americans ultimately transformed the rule of law into a dominant cultural feature of the Early Republic.

---

[3] Gary D. Rowe, Constitutionalism in the Streets, *Southern California Law Review* 78 (2005): 40; Larry Kramer, *The People Themselves: Popular Constitutionalism and Judicial Review* (Oxford: Oxford University Press, 2005). Even Christian G. Fritz's path-breaking study of the importance of notions of the people's collective role in legal decision-making focuses on its particular role in framing revolutionary constitutions rather than on popular

The social history of crime and punishment is also closely related to the themes in this book. Nearly a quarter of a century of historical investigation has uncovered much about the habits of ordinary criminals, the workings of courts, and the patterns of punishment in late-eighteenth-century America and England. Three excellent works on the subject by Daniel Cohen, Louis Masur, and Michael Meranze, for example, reflect the turn toward cultural history. Cohen describes the shifting of execution narratives from Puritan moralism to a genre of popular entertainment. Masur underscores the importance of hidden punishment for an increasingly refined American public culture. Meranze interrogates the ambivalence of liberal reformers to corporeal punishment even as they rely upon a broad array of disciplinary practices.[4] All three books, with their different approaches to the role of literary genre, private and public spheres, and disciplining of the body, seek to chart the broad social transformation from colonial America through the early nineteenth century.

My subject, however, is not the sociological, but the legal. I am interested less in felons and more in law itself – as it is conceived, expressed, and interpreted through different forms of reading. Literary scholars have long drawn the connection between the fictive voice in early modern criminal narratives and the rise of the modern novel.[5] However, hitherto the importance of criminal legal narrative for creating new forms of American law has been ignored. Law, I would contend, is as much about storytelling as it is about constitutionalism, statutes, and sociohistorical understandings of compliance with legal norms.

---

thinking about law. Christian G. Fritz, *American Sovereigns: The people and America's Constitutional Tradition Before the Civil War* (Cambridge: Cambridge University Press, 2008), pp. 11–46.

4 Daniel A. Cohen, *Pillars of Salt, Monuments of Grace: New England Crime Literature and the Origins of American Popular Culture 1674–1860* (Oxford: Oxford University Press, 1993); Louis P. Masur, *Rites of Execution: Capital Punishment and the Transformation of American Culture 1776–1865* (Oxford: Oxford University Press, 1989); Michael Meranze, *Laboratories of Virtue: Punishment, Revolution and Authority in Philadelphia 1760–1835* (Chapel Hill: University of North Carolina Press, 1996).

5 Lincoln B. Faller, *Turn'd to Account: The Forms and Functions of Criminal Biography in Late Seventeenth and Early Eighteenth Century England* (Cambridge: Cambridge University Press, 1987); John Richetti, *Popular Fiction Before Richardson: Narrative Patterns 1700–1739* (Oxford: Oxford University Press, 1992); J. Paul Hunter, *Before Novels: The Cultural Contexts of Eighteenth-Century English Fiction* (New York: W. W. Norton, 1990); Lennard J. Davis, "Wicked Actions and Feigned Words: Criminals, Criminality, and the Early English Novel," *Yale French Studies* 59: 106 (1980); Lennard J. Davis, *Factual Fictions: The Origins of the English Novel* (New York: Columbia University Press, 1983); Frances Ferguson, "Rape and the Rise of the Novel," *Representations* 20 (1987): 88–112; Gladfelder, *Criminality and the Narrative in Eighteenth Century England* (Baltimore: The Johns Hopkins University Press, 2001).

WHY CRIMINAL LAW?

When New York's Assembly in 1773 sought to stem a recent rise in counterfeiting, it envisioned an unusual statute. New paper money would be engraved with forms that would be hard to imitate. Creating something of a triptych representing the execution of counterfeiters, the proposed currency shamelessly borrowed scaffold imagery: an eye in a cloud, an execution cart and coffin, three felons on a gallows, a weeping father and mother with several small children, and a burning pit with human figures being forced into it by fiends. A caption would read "Let the name of a money maker rot." In Connecticut, a half-dozen years and a revolution later, a proposed 1779 bill suggested tattooing the figure of the gallows on the forehead of criminals guilty of robbery, burglary, and maiming. The gallows mark would be indelible.[6]

It is remarkable to think of everyday monetary transactions in New York being paid for with bills depicting the execution of counterfeiters or convicted Connecticut felons walking about with tattooed scaffolds on their foreheads like so many marks of Cain. Neither law was actually instituted. But these were serious proposals that reflected the abundance of execution iconography across the late-eighteenth-century cultural landscape. From the hanging of effigies to execution narratives and ballads hawked on street corners to the spectacle at the scaffold itself, early Americans encountered the predominant symbol of the criminal law: capital punishment.

Most legal actions involved the collection of debt; most criminal prosecutions were for misdemeanors. Nevertheless, popular legal imagination grasped at the symbolism of capital punishment. The nearly three decades from the close of the Seven Years' War in 1763 through the mid-1790s emerged as the high-water mark in Anglo-American scaffold imagery. Why did Americans in the Revolutionary period repeatedly draw upon executions as a political idiom? It might be simple to dismiss this use as simply a matter of convenience. Sanctions, after all, neatly express a rage to punish. But mock executions remain only one small example of the proliferation of criminal legal language and images, debates, and controversies during the last quarter of the eighteenth century. What do these

---

[6] "An Act to Remedy the Evil this Colony is Exposed to from the Great Quantities of Counterfeit Money Introduced to It" (1773) in the *Journal of the Votes and Proceedings of the General Assembly of the Colony of New-York 1766–76* (Albany: J. Buel, 1820), pp. 50–51; "Bill for Adding to Punishment of Atrocious Crimes the Puncturing of Forehead with Design of Gallows" (1779), Connecticut Archives, First Series, 6/100 (Hartford).

representations tell us about how the common people thought about law during this critical period when foundational legal norms were framed? And how did the complex, tangled relationship between punishment and politics change from the 1760s to the 1790s?

To answer these questions requires a different approach. Legal historians tend to confine their work to studies of codes, judicial decision-making, and, perhaps, the mutual influence of law and society. But I became intrigued by what stood outside of official legal boundaries: imaginary punishments, mock executions, stillborn reform proposals, fabular criminal narratives, and the ways that both sophisticated critics and the common people envisioned criminal law. Such a path departs from the traditional conception of law as a hegemonic power of the state. I instead would like to suggest that law as envisioned, formulated, and represented as a cultural artifact by a wide range of historical actors, including the common people, enables its later reinscription in official statutes and institutions.

Take, for example, the 1765 mock execution of a Massachusetts Stamp distributor. After hanging the effigy on the gallows, other punishments were conjured up as well: never-ending incarceration in prison or the invention of a Sisyphean cell where the prisoner has to constantly pump out water or drown. What is striking here is that these species of punishment, confinement and labor, would become the touchstones of legal reform two decades later. This particular fragment, then, hints at what I am trying to suggest. Law is imagined before it is enacted.[7]

Imagining law is the subject of this book. By imagination, I mean something less passive than simply *mentalité*, inherited beliefs, or participation in legal culture. But it is also less ordered than ideology. What

---

[7] My concern here with the imaginative in law is informed by the new historicism in literary criticism. See, for example, such works as Stephen Greenblatt, *Marvelous Possessions: The Wonder of the New World* (Chicago: University of Chicago Press, 1991) and, especially, John Bender, *Imagining the Penitentiary: Fiction and the Architecture of Mind in Eighteenth-Century England* (Chicago: University of Chicago Press, 1987). Steven Wilf, "Imagining Justice: Aesthetics and Public Executions in Late Eighteenth-Century England," *Yale Journal of Law & the Humanities* 5 (1993): 51–78; Peter Fitzpatrick, *The Mythology of Modern Law* (London: Routledge, 1992), pp. 146–211; and, of course, Robert Cover in a number of essays provide excellent discussions of the role of imagination in crafting broader narratives of law. Robert Cover, *Narrative, Violence, and the Law: The Essays of Robert Cover*, eds. Martha Minow, Michael Ryan, and Austin Sarat (Ann Arbor: University of Michigan Press, 1992). I address the methodological approach to the legal imagination in Steven Wilf, *The Law Before the Law* (Rowman & Littlefield, 2008), pp. 11–14.

I discuss here is largely a nonprofessional discourse taking place in the public sphere as opposed to the bounded sphere of courts and codes. This definition is purposefully broad. It includes using punishment as a symbolic language in the context of politics out-of-doors, legal storytelling, transforming trials into political contests, mythopoetic renderings of the origins of legal systems, and – if that were not capacious enough – any imaginative political readings of law or cases where legal norms are seen as representing something more than simply a means of restraining criminality.

Three more points should be made at the outset about legal imagination. First, imagination, is generative. Not only does legal imagining create novel interpretations of doctrine, but it also enlarges the domain where one imaginative notion might elicit another. For this reason, I discuss at length the formation of a public sphere for talking about law as well as the ideas within that sphere. Imagining law, secondly, is syncretic. New interpretations often emerge through appropriating bits and pieces of official rules. The result may be considered simultaneously *of* official law and – since extraofficial historical actors lack the status to establish governing rules – *beyond* or transcending official law. I have tried to avoid overdrawn distinctions between high and low legal cultures. Thirdly, it is important to emphasize the political significance of legal imagination. By its very definition, legal imagination challenges state and professional monopolies over law. In certain historical moments where political authority is contested, such as Revolutionary America, interpreting doctrine, judging cases and controversies, and inflicting punishment must be seen as a radical assertion of sovereign powers.

Stephen Greenblatt makes a distinction between the imagination at play, as mere entertainment, and the imagination at work.[8] The legal imagination described here worked very hard. It did more than simply invent fanciful tales about notorious felons or permit a voyeuristic gazing at fictive or actual executions. In this vein, literary critics see criminal narratives as precursors of the novel. Reading these as legal texts rather than as literary genre, however, uncovers aspirational visions of the law. During the second half of the eighteenth century, I will suggest, questions about legal possibilities became commonplace: What is the purpose of punishment? Who controls the right to judge? And might it be possible to create a legal order founded upon a less harsh regimen of sanctions?

---

[8] Greenblatt, *Marvelous Possessions*, p. 23.

But this was also an imagination at work because it needed to explain a great deal. A new understanding of criminal law emerged around the time of the American Revolution. Criminal justice was seen as a mirror that reflected truths about the surrounding political and social structure. Accustomed to Oliver Wendell Holmes's metaphor of law as mirror, we have forgotten how this might be a truly radical notion. It assigns a significant explanatory burden for a legal system. No longer were the outward guises of criminal law – penal codes, criminal procedure, modes of punishment, and the like – simply instruments for identifying and sanctioning offenders, they were also transformed into representational objects that inscribe and reinscribe a deeper political meaning about themselves.

REVOLUTION AND INTERTEXTUAL READINGS OF LAW

Revolutionary America was a seedtime for imagining the criminal law. This is not an accident. Revolutions are political moments when both critical and inventive faculties are unleashed. Part of the book's purpose is to recapture the excitement of imagining criminal law in a revolutionary period. Americans during this period drew upon a familiar repertoire of punishment symbolism rooted in early modern English popular culture – such as rough justice and the hanging of effigies – in order to create a new legal culture. But there was also a heightened focus on intertextual readings. Intertextuality, a term coined by Julia Kristeva, identifies every text as "the absorption and transformation of another text."[9] For legal texts, this can occur in all sorts of ways: the borrowing or transformation of a prior text such as a statute; court cases can be read with deep referencing of each other; law can be read against politics; or texts can be subject to parody.

At a certain level, moreover, there was a macrointertextual reading of American law against the legal forms of other regimes. The chronological parameters of the book reflect the importance of such comparative interpretive practices. Two sharply defined watersheds in transatlantic political history form its rough boundaries, the American and French Revolutions. It begins in 1763, a year before the Stamp Act Crisis with mounting tension between England and its North American colonies. In the midst of their protest, Americans drew upon the repertoire of legal language as political agitation began to couple criminal justice with

---

[9] Julia Kristeva, *Semiotike* (Paris: Seuil, 1969), p. 146.

popular politics. It concludes at the end of the 1790s when the French Revolutionary regime sentenced to death Louis XVI. Between these two great political upheavals lies the apotheosis of America's making criminal law the lingua franca of popular politics.

Most important, this discourse about law took place outside the boundaries of formal legal structures. It was open to people at all levels of society. Legal language was made simpler and more accessible. Such broad-based discussions reflected the rise of popular politics in the 1760s. Seeking to mobilize the population, American radicals widened the public debate over legal issues and used what might be called vernacular legal culture, such as criminal narratives and mock executions, to garner support. Americans rallied behind a new idea of criminal law with legal transparency and participation of the common people at its core.

During the 1780s Americans launched a full-scale attack on English criminal justice. They chose to critique English law at its most vulnerable point: the capital-laden statutes of the criminal code. Rejection of English law was part of a discourse of legitimization and delegitimization that surrounded the American Revolution. English publicists, as David Brion Davis has shown, dismissed American claims for liberty as coming from slave holders. Americans, in turn, sought to delegitimize England by representing it as a country with Tyburn as its iconographic centerpiece. According to this argument, England's reliance upon capital punishment suggests a social order badly in need of a repressive apparatus. Mid-century colonials praised English due process in contrast to minimal French protections. But now Americans compared England's legal system unfavorably with an idealized version of their own.

The 1780s was a period of legal myth-making. Americans reinvented their own legal past by claiming that England imposed its harsh legal regime upon the colonies against their will. Capital punishment took on remarkably powerful tropes of brutality and repression. Imagining the meaning of punishment, Americans, not surprisingly, turned to recasting their actual criminal codes. Statutes mandated prison sentences, which both replaced sanguinary punishment and curbed judicial discretionary use of pardons. Penal reform created an outward representation of the new republic, playing much the same role as health care or literacy programs for twentieth-century revolutions. The political authority of the nascent republic turned in part upon its remaking of criminal law.

But this emphasis upon a nonsanguinary system of punishment reflects only one facet of revolutionary legal discourse. In fact imagining justice was Janus-faced. On one side, it critiqued the violence implicit

in existing legal regimes. Republican government implied mild sanctions. The other side called for public participation in the implementation of criminal justice. A tension, of course, existed between these two
notions. During the early 1790s, criminal code reform crowded out radical notions of participatory justice. Two consequences of this reform
stood in marked contrast to the earlier ways justice was imagined. First,
prisons shunted aside execution rituals. Punishment was bounded by
space. Interpretive power, secondly, became the sole purview of legislatures and courts.

The early 1790s witnessed the waning of vernacular legal culture, participatory justice, and the kinship of legal discourse with politics. Images
of the guillotine from the French Revolution, moreover, underscored the
dangers of involving the common people in questions of criminal justice.
No longer were Americans comfortable with execution symbolism and
popular politics sharing a common language. Fictive punishment might
evolve into a form all too real. Not surprisingly, no attempt was made to
revive the legal imagination of the Revolutionary period. In the hothouse
atmosphere of the factional politics of the Early Republic, with domestic
as well as transatlantic ideological differences expressed in legal language
and taken to court, Americans stepped back from the mingling of law
and politics.

An interpretive investigation – seeing law as both envisioned and represented, deciphered and inscribed – poses its own methodological difficulties. Scattered, fragmentary, sometimes half-formed texts must be united
into a coherent reconstruction of the representation of criminal law. This
is not an easy task. Not surprisingly, then, I have turned to a wide variety
of sources: hanging ballads, bits and pieces of iconography, pardon petitions, diaries, contemporary accounts of punishment, mock executions
and execution narratives, and descriptions of official execution rituals,
as well as more traditional sources such as learned legal treatises and
court documents. Revolutionary debates about law are scattered through
newspapers and political pamphlets. If one looks carefully in eighteenth-
century America, law is everywhere.

We know remarkably little about what ordinary people thought about
law. In the course of this investigation, I have come to appreciate how
difficult it is to reconstruct even the most basic aspects of the common
people's legal imagination. The unknown social origins of some anonymous sources, the interweaving of different discourses, compound the
task. Because this book is a preliminary study with few precursors, I have
focused upon how imagining justice was shaped by external events and

cross-cultural comparisons.[10] Legal imagination in the Revolutionary period, however, was not monolithic. Regional differences abound. Admittedly, my close readings of legal texts overemphasize those places with the most robust print culture, New England and the middle colonies. More work also is needed on distinctions founded upon class, race or ethnicity, and gender.

Another caveat is in order. To be sure, all criminal law is local. But this study was designed to emphasize the coupling of broader legal and political narratives. It therefore counters the trend toward local studies in both legal and general early American studies through situating itself in a transatlantic context.[11] Americans thought of law in comparative terms. Mid-century myths about Anglo-American common law, for example, were formed around comparison with France's civil law regime. During the 1780s, American legal imagining turned to representations of London's Tyburn. A few years later, debate shifted to focusing upon the popular justice of Parisian crowds. I argue that American criminal law at the very end of the eighteenth century was juxtaposed to these two imaginative constructions. Americans envisioned England's legal regime as bound by the tyranny of custom shaped by counter-majoritarian judges, and revolutionary France's legal regime as bound by the tyranny of unbridled immediacy shaped by an antinomian mob. Both rested upon executions. In contrast, republican America embraced a model of legislative codes and the repudiation of capital punishment.

The origin of American legalism, in short, was a transatlantic process. But how did communities read these broad themes into their local criminal process? How did particular cases and controversies become reimagined as criminal law became coupled with politics? After embarking upon this project, I found myself trying to balance these larger transatlantic issues and the detailed archival work that characterizes local studies. I chose a way of writing that was intended to draw together the insights from three fields – the social history of crime and punishment, the law

[10] Among the innovative work on French and English legal culture with a focus on criminal process, see Lisa Silverman, *Tortured Subjects: Pain, Truth, and the Body in Early Modern France* (Chicago: University of Chicago Press, 2001); Malcolm Gaskill, *Crime and Mentalities in Early Modern England* (Cambridge: Cambridge University Press, 2000). Legal history should learn to cross boundaries. For a superb example of global history that preserves the granularity of the local, see Linda Colley, *The Ordeal of Elizabeth Marsh: A Woman in World History* (New York: Pantheon Books, 2007).

[11] On the local approach to early American law, see Richard Ross, "The Legal Past of Early New England: Notes for the Study of Law, Legal Culture, and Intellectual History," *William & Mary Quarterly* 50 (1993): 28–41.

and literature movement, and the new cultural legal history. To recapture the immediacy of legal imagining, this study includes extended readings of three sets of cases. Each case has been read read as a novella, much as critics might read a fictional work. As microhistorical stories, however, these tales were constructed out of more than one source. Competing authorial voices, their contradictions and rhetorical strategies, add a certain dynamism to the analysis.

The first of these stories takes place in Revolutionary Boston at the beginning of the 1770s. By reading a pair of cases in an intertextual fashion within a milieu awash with popular politics it is possible to see how late eighteenth-century Americans might turn official law upside down. Borrowing vernacular legal culture forms, hanging ballads as well as execution narratives, Bostonians transformed a political opponent into a petty criminal. At the same time, reading this case against the other, a common felon was recast as a victim of a repressive and sanguinary legal regime.

In the second set of stories, two post-Revolutionary Connecticut felons, a rapist and a murderer, drew upon contemporary political and intellectual themes to explain their crimes. The intertextual readings demanded searching for the points of connection between law and race, political economy, and republicanism. Local communities, however, turned these self-justifying narratives against their authors. Fellow citizens appropriated the first-person criminal accounts to create alternative readings of the crimes. The third extended tale tells about a reform statute that mandated postmortem dissection of executed felons. While the statute was silent about its purpose, contemporaries saw it as an instrument of punishment. Partly, this was due to the reading of the American dissection statute against an earlier English sanction that mandated dissection as a further sanction in cases of homicide. All three of these studies are about storytelling of sorts. Yet they prompt us to ask how the myriad of cases – the tales told by offenders, the tales told by authorities justifying the imposition of state violence as a sanction, and the tales told by contemporary observers trying to make sense of it all – fit within our own larger narrative of the origins of American law.

Criminal Law Out-of-Doors

Ebenezer Richardson, Levi Ames, and the Uses of Punishment in Revolutionary Boston

Constitutional scholars and social historians have uncovered two very different languages of law articulated by Revolutionary Americans. Constitutional scholars have engaged in an archeological task, recovering a literary discourse about constitutional issues dealing with patriot theories of rights, the relationship between England and the colonies, and the quest for a balanced government. This enterprise, of course, is related to their interest in the historical foundations of American Constitutionalism. On the other hand, historians have been concerned with a quite different legal language, one which seems hardly legal and, at times, hardly a language at all. In fact, historians have often portrayed the relationship of ordinary Americans in the Revolution as antinomian: launching extralegal attacks on British customs officials, engaging in riots and a broad array of civil disobedience meant to shunt aside official legal norms, not to engage with them.

These two approaches – one focused on a learned elite's articulated claims to higher constitutional authority, the other upon the common people's pragmatic extralegal actions – are portrayed as if, borrowing Disraeli's well-known metaphor, they were two trains traveling by parallel tracks that head in the same direction while never meeting. Such an understanding of these two legal languages, of course, is troubling. On one hand, the American Revolution is described as a sophisticated and somewhat rarified ideological transformation authored by bourgeois radicals, and awaiting its apotheosis nearly two decades later in the Constitutional Convention in Philadelphia. On the other hand, it is a popular insurrection centered in the streets, looking backward to the tradition of Anglo-American popular radicalism, but divorced from the soon-to-emerge law-centered world of the Early Republic.

Instead, this chapter seeks to show through a pair of microhistorical close readings precisely how significant the interaction was between official justice and extraofficial legal public opinion. Common people spoke the language of common law. Citizens of Revolutionary Boston inserted themselves into the process of legal interpretation by evaluating evidence, interpreting doctrine, and determining procedural issues. Instead of an antinomian rejection of legal norms, Bostonians in the Revolutionary period recast those norms. But neither was this popular legalism simply derived from constitutional claims to higher law. It emerged out of interpretations of the technical *règlement* of common-law rules and conflict over the deciding of specific cases.

To fully understand the complexity of revolutionary approaches to law requires close readings of how contemporaries interpret cases. In the two Boston cases we will examine, those of Ebenezer Richardson and Levi Ames, opinions delivered in broadsides, newspapers, and the street overturned official sentences. Ebenezer Richardson, a customs officer who accidentally shot a rioter in 1770, was freed by the authorities. Nevertheless, many Boston citizens thought him guilty of murder. But when a career criminal, Levi Ames, was sentenced to be death for burglary in 1773, there was a popular outcry against the harshness of his punishment. Both began with outrage about a single incident, which later swelled into a broad critique of English justice. In fact, Bostonians intertwined the two controversies by contrasting Richardson's pardon for the more serious crime of murder with the execution of Ames for a property crime.

At the center of popular understanding of law was the notion of placing blame. Revolutionary Americans appropriated both official legal process and popular genres, such as execution narratives, designed to ascribe blame to criminals, and attached that culpability to legal regimes themselves. Establishing their roles as interpreters of legal process, late-eighteenth-century Americans learned to turn upside down legal hierarchies: Judges were judged; codes were shorn of their power. Most importantly, however, through the grappling with cases evolved a language of law that was both norm-centered and radical.

"EXHIBIT AN ATROCIOUS VOLUME"

"If there was even a color of justice in the public opinion," wrote John Adams about Ebenezer Richardson, "he was the most abandoned wretch in America. Adultery, incest, perjury were reputed to be his ordinary crimes. His life would exhibit an atrocious volume." Adams' comment is revealing. Colonial felons awaiting execution would be described in just such a biographical volume – an execution narrative. Cataloging multiple crimes served as a narrative thread of transgression, but it also played a legal role, since being a repeat offender was critical to bolstering a case for capital punishment.

Yet Richardson lacked the trail of felonies that marked the life of most executed criminals. The typical execution narrative depicted a felon's progress from petty theft to highway robbery to murder. Where was Richardson's early life of crime? Moreover, Richardson's offense, a death caused in the midst of a riot, was, unlike premeditated murder, not the stuff of execution narratives. It might, in fact, be mere manslaughter. Popular opinion had the task, then, of constructing a fictive biographical narrative that would justify treating him like any other murderer. It needed to invent a criminal past as well as criminalize the current offense. In short, imagining law meant creating the ultimate legal fiction: a fictive life.[1]

Unlike many of the felons who populated eighteenth-century American execution narratives, Richardson was not raised at the margins of colonial society. Born at Woburn in 1718, he was a direct descendent of the Richardson brothers who helped found the town in the 1640s.

---

[1] Letter of John Adams to Dr. J. Morse, January 20, 1816, in *The Works of John Adams*, ed. Charles Francis Adams, 10 vols. (Boston: Charles C. Little and James Brown, 1851), 10:204–210. On fictive biography, see John Eakin, *Fictions in Autobiography: Studies in the Art of Self-Invention* (Princeton: Princeton University Press, 1985), pp. 181–278 and Marie-Paul Laden, *Self-Imitation in the Eighteenth-Century Novel* (Princeton: Princeton University Press, 1987), pp. 3–29. A number of essays have explored the narrative literature surrounding condemned felons, including execution sermons, pardon petitions, dying speeches, and execution narratives, in England, France, and America: J. A. Sharpe, "'Last Dying Speeches': Religion, Ideology, and Public Executions in Seventeenth-Century England," *Past and Present* 107 (1985): 144–167; Peter Linebaugh, "The Ordinary of Newgate and his *Account*," in *Crime in England 1500–1800*, ed. J. S. Cockburn (Princeton: Princeton University Press, 1977), pp. 246–270; Natalie Zemon Davis, *Fiction in the Archives: Pardon Tales and their Tellers in Sixteenth-Century France* (Stanford: Stanford University Press, 1987), pp. 1–35. Some of this work (such as Daniel A. Cohen, "A Fellowship of Thieves: Property Criminals in Eighteenth-Century Massachusetts," *Journal of Social History* 22 [1988]: 65–92) uses this genre as a source of information about felons without taking into account the imaginative and literary strategies employed in crafting the text. The next chapter will develop more fully the theme of the execution narrative as fictive biography. As John Brewer points out, understandings of criminal motive shifts according to the cultural norms of the period. John Brewer, *A Sentimental Murder: Love and Madness in the Eighteenth Century* (New York: HarperCollins, 2004).

Richardson's father owned eighty acres of Woburn land and another fifty-one acres at Stoneham. He left two-thirds of this land to his son Ebenezer. While the convicted thief Levi Ames spent his youth wandering through New England, for many years, Richardson remained in Woburn as a settled resident with substantial holdings. In 1740, two years prior to inheriting his father's estate, Richardson married a widow twelve years his senior. As the daughter of the town clerk, she was equally connected. Perhaps the only documentary hint of Richardson's contentiousness was the suit, only a year after his marriage, against the estate of his wife's deceased husband for support of her three minor children.[2]

Nevertheless, Richardson would be transformed into what one newspaper called an "old offender."[3] In 1770, at the height of the Richardson affair, a broadside pretending to be a verse confession written in Richardson's words assigned to Richardson a role in what was then a well-known controversy that took place in his native town of Woburn. This fabrication called upon the town of Woburn as a witness to Richardson's earlier criminal life: "Woburn, my native place can tell/My crimes are blacker far than Hell/What great disturbance there I made/Against the people and their head."[4] Adams's comment accusing Richardson of adultery almost certainly alluded to an adulterous affair that tore apart Woburn in 1752. The controversy over the affair was complicated and rooted in long-standing social divisions within the community.

As with many New England towns, the conflict in Woburn centered on the meeting house. In 1728, a young minister newly graduated from Harvard, Reverend Edward Jackson, was hired to assist Reverend John Fox. Resentment over salaries and duties quickly emerged between the two ministers. Backed by different factions, the battle between the ministers came to a peak after the building of the new meeting house. The partisans of Fox threatened succession from the parish. In the midst of this struggle, a widow, Keziah Henshaw, gave birth to an illegitimate child. Henshaw might have been bribed by Fox's supporters, for, shortly afterward, she accused Jackson of being the father.[5]

---

[2] Edward F. Johnson, *Woburn Records of Births, Deaths, and Marriages 1640–1873* (Woburn: Andrews, Cutler & Co., 1890), p. 213; John Adams Vinton, *The Richardson Memorial, Comprising a Full History and Genealogy of the Three Brothers Ezekiel, Samuel, and Thomas Richardson* (Portland: Brown Thurston, 1876), pp. 208, 242–244, and 523–524. Middlesex County Probate Records, January 24, 1742/3, 1918/2.

[3] *Boston Gazette*, February 26, 1770.

[4] *The Humble Confession of Richardson, the Informer* [Broadside, 1770].

[5] *A Council Conven'd at Woburn, upon the Request of the Rev. Mr. Jackson and the First Church in Said Town to Hear and Advise upon the Great and Uncommon Difficulties*

Accepting Henshaw's accusation, Reverend Josiah Cotton charged Jackson was unfit for the ministry. This was clearly a partisan attack. Cotton was acting on behalf of his contentious brother, a schoolmaster in Woburn. Jackson responded by suing for libel. The case dragged through the courts. The Court of Common Pleas decided in Jackson's favor. Cotton appealed to the Superior Court, where the jury overturned the lower court's ruling. Legal fees mounted, and the acrimony between the factions grew intense. Finally, there was a dramatic discovery that ended the case. A letter to Henshaw that showed the charges were false and fabricated by Fox's supporters fell into Jackson's hands. He petitioned the Superior Court. Reversing the ruling one last time, the court found for Jackson.

What was Richardson's involvement in this affair? Edmund Trowbridge, Attorney General of Massachusetts and later a justice at Richardson's trial, wrote that Richardson was "very serviceable to me in detecting a conspiracy to father a bastard child on the parson of a parish." It appears, then, that Richardson was somehow party to the events in Woburn, and his defense of the falsely accused Jackson ironically may have marked the beginning of work as an informer.[6] There is no evidence of Richardson's paternity. Yet a number of oddly coincidental facts might incorrectly suggest otherwise. Not only was Richardson from Woburn, but Keziah Henshaw was his wife's younger sister. It appears that another Ebenezer Richardson, not the one who confronted rioters in Boston, married Keziah Henshaw in 1754. And there was one more strange coincidence: Richardson had a sister and a daughter, who lived with him in Boston, both named Keziah.[7]

Among Them (1746); Samuel Sewall, *The History of Woburn* (Boston: Wiggin and Luntt, 1868), pp. 202–319. Suffolk County Court Records (Boston), 68, 714. On the ministry and parish organization as locus of local conflict, see Christine Leigh Heyrman, *Commerce and Culture: The Maritime Communities of Colonial Massachusetts 1690–1750* (New York: W.W. Norton, 1984), pp. 182–208 and 273–303; Gregory Nobles, *Divisions Throughout the Whole: Politics and Society in Hampshire County, Massachusetts 1740–1775* (Cambridge: Cambridge University Press, 1983); and Laurel Thatcher Ulrich, *A Midwife's Tale: The Life of Martha Ballard, Based Upon Her Diary, 1785–1812* (New York: Alfred A. Knopf, 1990), pp. 103–133.

6 Public Record Office, hereafter PRO (London), T1/408, March 18, 1761. M. H. Smith, *The Writs of Assistance Case* (Berkeley: University of California Press, 1978), pp. 128–129.

7 Vinton, *Richardson Memorial*, pp. 208–209. Eugene Chalmers Fowle, *Descendants of George Fowle (1610/11–1682) of Charlestown, Massachusetts*, eds. Gary Boyd Roberts and Neil D. Thompson (Boston: New England Historic and Genealogical Society, 1990), pp. 35–37. Robert Treat Paine's minutes of the trial quotes testimony from Richardson's daughter, Keziah. John Adams, *Legal Papers of John Adams*, eds. L. Kinvin Wroth and Hiller B. Zobel, 3 vols. (Cambridge: Harvard University Press, 1965), 2:420.

When Bostonians turned to reinventing Richardson's biography, they enlisted this tale of adultery to serve their purposes. Richardson was blamed for fathering Henshaw's child. Perhaps because of his family connection, he was also charged by some, as Adams's comment suggests, with incest. In the words of his fictive verse confession: "A wretch of wretches prov'd with child/By me I know, at which I smil'd/To think the parson he must bare/The guilt of me, and I go clear." Shortly after winning the suit, Jackson died. His death was ascribed to the suffering experienced while defending his reputation. Richardson, in other words, was culpable not just of adultery, but of killing Jackson. Embellishing the invention of this criminal self, the verse confession levels the accusation: "And thus the worthy man of God/Unjustly felt the scourging rod/Which broke his heart, it prov'd his end/And for the whole blood I guilty stand." Establishing Richardson as twice guilty of another person's death had important legal implications. It legitimized Richardson's execution. Manslaughter could be pardoned with benefit of clergy for the first offense, but was a capital crime for the second. "The halter now is justly due/For I've killed no less than two."[8]

Slander of this kind was, of course, a set piece in eighteenth-century American politics. During the 1760s, for example, Lord Bute was accused of having an affair with George III's mother. Francis Bernard, Thomas Hutchinson, and Peter Oliver were the targets of merciless personal attacks. Not surprisingly, then, radical publicists leveled a battery of charges against other informers. John Malcom, a Boston informer who was tarred and feathered in November 1774, was called, like Richardson, an "old impudent and mischievous offender." He was accused of mistreating children and having "joined in the murders" of North Carolina Regulators.[9]

Yet Richardson's case was significant because of the way popular politics interjected itself into the judicial process. Richardson was being tried twice: once before magistrates and the other time in coffee houses and taverns where Bostonians debated his guilt. Rumor, fictive tales of fathering an illegitimate child, wild charges of murder, and sustained character assassination, all of which might have been dismissed as inadmissible evidence by an official court, was the very marrow of this street corner justice. Such accusations, tell us less about Richardson than about the

[8] Sewall, *Woburn*, pp. 319–325; Richardson, *Humble Confession*; Gordon Wood, "Conspiracy and the Paranoid Style: Causality and Deceit in the Eighteenth Century," *William & Mary Quarterly* 39 (1982): 401–444.
[9] *Boston Evening-Post*, April 23, 1770.

popular mood in Revolutionary Boston. Adultery was a striking motif to invoke. After all, Richardson was engaged in political infidelity by transferring his loyalty to the English.[10]

Criminal biography fit nicely with the inconsistencies of eighteenth-century criminal justice. Highly selective, this legal system tempered capital statutes with frequent pardons. One felon might be executed while another might be freed for the same crime. What justified punishment, then, was not simply the felony itself, but the character and persona of the felon. Richardson's fictive biographical narrative addressed this problem of discretion by framing the act of murder through his past as a "d–d villain."[11] Yet the genre of execution narratives failed to engage the social meaning of crime. These texts understood the criminal act – shirts stolen off a clothesline, counterfeiting, or murder – as united by the thread of a single individual's life history. The broader context was ignored. From the typical execution narrative, it cannot be known if the crime took place during a period of dearth, in the midst of a crime wave, or as part of a larger pattern of deviance. Both official law proceedings and execution narratives privileged a narrative centered on the individual felon. But in the case of Richardson, contemporary political events must be seen as important as the details of his private life. Intertextual readings did not only take place between one case and another, but also between a case and its context. It was the political narrative, though unspoken, that made this biographical tale transparent.

THE FORMS OF LAW

Well before the riot that led to Richardson's trial, Boston was seething with unrest. Promising to make the colonies pay for troops stationed in

---

[10] Another case tried before the Massachusetts Superior Court in 1763, *Rex v. Doaks*, demonstrates the limits placed upon admission of testimony of past character as evidence. Indicted for having a house of prostitution, the court refused to allow allegations of earlier sexual misdeeds. Josiah Quincy, *Reports Argued and Adjudged in the Superior Court of Judicature of the Province of Massachusetts Bay Between 1761 and 1772* (Boston: Little, Brown, and Company, 1865), pp. 90–91. On language as provocation, see Norman L. Rosenberg, *Protecting the Best Men: An Interpretive History of the Law of Libel* (Chapel Hill: University of North Carolina Press, 1986), pp. 12–56 and Richard Bauman, *Let Your Words Be Few: Symbolism of Speaking and Silence among Seventeenth-Century Quakers* (Cambridge: Cambridge University Press, 1983). Seduction and infidelity were common late-eighteenth-century literary themes: Susan Staves, "British Seduced Maidens," *Eighteenth-Century Studies* 14 (1980–81): 109–134; Jan Lewis, "The Republican Wife: Virtue and Seduction in the Early Republic," *William & Mary Quarterly* 45 (1988): 391–425 examines the political meaning of seduction.

[11] *Boston Gazette*, March 5, 1770.

America, Charles Townshend prompted Parliament to pass the Revenue Act of 1767. It levied import duties on lead, glass, paper, painter's colors, and tea. Seeking to stem smuggling, the Act also established an American customs commission to collect the taxes and strengthened the vice-admiralty courts. Colonial Americans were not pleased. James Otis called for resisting the act in "a legal ... way."[12] But finding themselves facing actions they thought illegal – Parliament usurping the right to impose colonial taxes, courts without juries, and improper search and seizure – Americans crafted their own codes for regulating trade. In effect, the nonimportation agreement was an extraofficial statute. Boston led the way by identifying a long list of English goods that should not be imported. As with official laws, there were sanctions: boycotts, public scorn, and extralegal crowd actions.

While contraband tea may be sold according to public opinion, Hutchinson complained, it is "a high crime to sell any from England."[13] Hutchinson's use of the phrase "high crime" was an admission of the ways that law had been turned upside down. While disobeying an act passed by Parliament, the nonimportation agreement, though lacking any official status, was seen by many colonials as law. A merchant importing contrary to the agreement, Theophilus Lillie ironically complained of crowd legislation without representation. Through the coercion of the nonimportation movement, he claimed that patriots chose "to make laws, and in the most effectual manner execute them upon me and others, to which laws, I am sure I never gave my consent either in person or by my representative."[14] Like England's attempt to halt smuggling, enforcement was difficult. By the fall of 1769, the merchants' nonimportation agreement had broadened as patriots attempted to have all Boston's citizens pledge not to consume those English products improperly imported.

Yet some merchants continued to violate the agreement. Drawing upon the eighteenth-century notion of shame as an integral part of punishment, they were punished through having their crimes publicized. Interestingly, the sanctions themselves took the form of official punishment. Boycott, like official fines, was a monetary penalty. By ostracizing merchants, patriots enforced, as the authorities did with transportation, a form of

---

[12] *Boston Post-Boy*, November 30, 1767. Arthur Meier Schlesinger, *The Colonial Merchants and the American Revolution 1763–1776* (New York: Frederick Ungar, 1957), pp. 91–155. Oliver M. Dickerson, *The Navigation Acts and the American Revolution* (Philadelphia: University of Pennsylvania Press, 1951), pp. 190–202.

[13] Hutchinson, letter to Hillsborough, April 27, 1770, 25 Massachusetts Archives (Boston), Schlesinger, *Colonial Merchants*, p. 179.

[14] *Massachusetts Gazette*, January 11, 1770.

social and economic exile. Handbills circulated to publicize the names of importers, and townspeople were urged to extend their boycott from simply the imported goods to the violators as well. Bostonians, in January 1770, voted to deny "not only all commercial dealings, but every act ... of common civility" from merchants who were especially flagrant violators. Four merchants – John Taylor, William Jackson, Nathaniel Rogers, and Theophilus Lillie – were singled out for special abuse. Schoolboys taunted them, their houses and shops were pelted with dirt, and potential customers suffered intimidation. Defaced shop signs were replaced with placards warning against buying from them. Three February Thursdays in a row, market day in Boston and a school holiday, crowds gathered at the merchants' homes.[15]

On the last of those Thursdays, February 22, a crowd collected at Lillie's home. A placard painted with the features of importers was erected pointing toward the house. According to one account of the event, Richardson, who lived nearby, became enraged by the sign. He urged others to knock it down with their wagons. Unable to convince anyone, he seized a cart and attempted to do so himself. Richardson and the crowd traded insults. Retreating to his home, he vowed to defend it with a seaman, George Wilmot, who appears to have had connections with the customs commission. Despite the danger, there was a theatrical, almost farcical, touch to the riot. Richardson and his wife repeatedly went into the street and menaced the schoolboys who had gathered. When the boys began throwing light rubbish, Richardson responded by pointing a gun out his door. The crowd, angered by this threat of violence, pelted the house with stones. Windows were broken. According to a sympathetic source, Richardson used his weapon only after being struck quite hard with a rock. He fired a volley of bullets, wounding two schoolboys. Eleven-year-old Christopher Snider, struck in the chest and pierced by almost a dozen bullets, would die later that night.[16]

---

[15] *Boston Gazette*, February 26, 1770; "At a Meeting of the Merchants of Traders at Faneuil Hall on the 23rd of January, 1770" [Broadside, 1770]. Thomas Hutchinson, *The History of the Colony and Province of Massachusetts-Bay*, ed. Lawrence Shaw Mayo, 3 vols. (Cambridge: Cambridge University Press, 1936), 3:193; Pauline Maier, *From Resistance to Revolution: Colonial Radicals and the Development of American Opposition to Britain 1765–1776* (New York: Alfred A. Knopf, 1972), pp. 114–130; Schlesinger, *Colonial Merchants*, pp. 156–183; Gary B. Nash, *The Urban Crucible: Social Change, Political Consciousness, and the Origins of the American Revolution* (Cambridge: Harvard University Press, 1979), pp. 352–360.

[16] Sparks Manuscripts, Houghton Library (Harvard University), New England Papers, March 16, 1770, 3:69; *Boston Evening-Post*, February 26, 1770; *Boston Gazette*, February 26, 1770, *Connecticut Journal and New-Haven Post-Boy*, March 9 and 16,

After the shooting, the mob seized Richardson and Wilmot. More people gathered as the bell at the New Brick meeting house was rung. The riot and shooting demonstrated that civil authority had broken down in Boston. What should be done with Richardson? "The first thought was to hang him up at once," Hutchinson claimed, "and a halter was brought and a sign post picked upon." Although Hutchinson had sent a sheriff to impose order, he was afraid to interfere. Patriot leaders were not. William Molineux rescued Richardson from hanging, and other Bostonians, acting like a sheriff or *posse comitatus*, captured him and brought the prisoner before Justice of the Peace John Ruddock. Richardson also understood this as the popular usurpation of police power. Denying the crowd's right to arrest him, Richardson threatened to resist. He demanded that he would only "resign himself to a proper officer."[17]

The justice of the peace consigned Richardson to constables, who escorted him to Faneuil Hall. They had to contend with "the mob endeavoring to put a rope around his neck and take him from the constables to execute him themselves."[18] At Faneuil Hall, Richardson was examined by a panel of judges – Richard Dana, Samuel Pemberton, and Edmund Quincy – and sent to prison for his own safety. Here, too, the public interjected itself in judicial proceedings. More than a thousand people, according to one newspaper's count, were present at the examination.[19] Popular justice and official justice were not distinct and separate spheres, as has sometimes been suggested, but intertwined. Peter Oliver, Tory chronicler of the early stages of the American Revolution, claimed that reliance upon the courts was simply a question of convenience: "As the term of the Supreme Court was very near, and they thought that the blood of the unhappy youth, which had been spilt would not be cold

1770; Hutchinson letter, February 23, 1770, 26 Massachusetts Archives, 446–447; John Boyle, "Boyle's Journal of Occurrences in Boston," *New England Historical and Genealogical Register* 84 (1930): 262; Dirk Hoerder, *Crowd Action in Revolutionary Massachusetts 1765–1780* (New York: Academic Press, 1977), pp. 219–223; Adams, *Legal Papers*, 2:396–400.

[17] Hutchinson to Hood, February 23, 1770, 26 *Massachusetts Archives*, 444, 445. Paine's Minutes, Adams, *Legal*, p. 417; Peter Oliver, *Origin and Progress of the American Rebellion* (1781), eds. Douglas Adair and John Schutz (Stanford: Stanford University Press, 1961), pp. 84–85; Hoerder, *Crowd Action*, p. 220. Hue and cry required a warrant by a justice of the peace except in cases where the felon might escape. See James Parker, *Conductor Generalis or the Duty and Authority of Justices of the Peace* (New York, 1788), pp. 222–227.

[18] Sparks Manuscripts, New England Papers, 3:69.

[19] *Boston Evening-Post*, February 20, 1770; *Virginia Gazette*, April 5, 1770; *Massachusetts Weekly Gazette and Boston Weekly Newsletter*, March 1, 1770.

before the court met; and they were pretty sure that they could procure a jury for conviction, so some of the leaders of the faction chose that he should be hanged by the forms of law, rather than suffer the disgrace of hangmen themselves."[20] Yet, as will be argued, the patriots and rioters chose to work with the system of official justice because they shared a common Anglo-American legal discourse. It was through this discourse that Bostonians, many of whom would have rejected the idea of lynching Richardson in the emotional aftermath of the shooting, would come through the course of the affair to demand his execution.

"When I came into town," wrote John Adams upon returning from the countryside, "I saw a vast collection of people near Liberty Tree – enquired and found the funeral of the child lately killed by Richardson." Adams was astounded by the number of people and carriages. "My eyes never beheld such a funeral. The funeral extended further than can be well imagined."[21] There were 500 school boys and 2,000 people. According to Hutchinson, not a sympathetic observer, the funeral was "perhaps the largest ever known in America."[22] Six youths supported the coffin from the Liberty Tree, where Snider's corpse was displayed, during the procession to the burial ground.

The funeral was grand political theater. An inscription in silver letters at the foot of the coffin read: "*Latet aguis in herba* – the serpent is lurking in the grass," a reference to Richardson and other political opponents. On the Liberty Tree a placard was hung with the threat that "thou shall take not satisfaction for the life of a murderer – he shall surely be put to death." While the Latin motto underscored the fact that the Liberty Tree, like the Tree of Life in the Garden of Eden, was surrounded by serpents, the placard borrowed its authority from an apodictic Hebrew scriptural code. The Bible provided a touch of official legality to what might be called law out-of-doors.[23]

Hutchinson expressed surprise at Snider's burial. "The boy that was killed was the son of a poor German. A grand funeral was, however, judged very proper for him."[24] The embattled lieutenant-governor failed

---

[20] Oliver, *Origin and Progress*, p. 85.

[21] John Adams, *Diary and Autobiography of John Adams*, ed. L. H. Butterfield, 3 vols. (Cambridge: Harvard University Press, 1961), 1: 348–349.

[22] Hutchinson letter, February 23, 1770, 26 Massachusetts Archives, 446–447. *Boston Gazette*, March 5, 1770.

[23] Rowe, *Letters and Diary*, p. 197; Sparks Manuscripts, New England Papers, 3: 69; *Virginia Gazette*, April 5, 1770; *Connecticut Journal and New-Haven Post-Boy*, 9–16 March 1770; *Boston Gazette*, March 5, 1770.

[24] Hutchinson, *Massachusetts-Bay*, 3:194.

to recognize how quickly traditional forms of status had been overturned. As broadsides and newspapers constantly repeated, Snider was the first colonial to die for the patriot cause. Phyllis Wheatley, Boston's black poetess, described his death, which would be overshadowed by those of the Boston Massacre less than two weeks later: "In the heavens eternal court it was decreed/How the first martyr for the cause should bleed." In fact, Snider was both a likely and unlikely revolutionary martyr. While unlike most martyrs, he did not suffer death for his convictions, his innocence was quite appealing. *Innocentia nusquam tuta*, read an inscription on his coffin, innocence itself is not safe. An eleven-year-old child, he was apparently merely a bystander at the riot. Snider was eulogized for his promise. He died with a copy of Wolfe's *Summit of Human Glory* in his pocket. In this regard, Snider was treated in similar fashion to Sammy Gore, a schoolboy whose fingers were lost through Richardson's gunfire and who was said to have shown talent as an artist. The motif for Snider's death was clear: a young martyr murdered by an old offender.[25]

As was the case with Richardson's criminal biography, the popular fictive imagination was again at work. It seized upon Protestant and Wilkite typologies of martyrdom to politicize Snider's death. Snider was repeatedly compared to Britain's Wilkite martyr William Allen: "The blood of young Allen may be cover'd in England," wrote a colonial radical, "but a thorough investigation will be made in America for that of young Snider."[26]

Such Wilkite imagery seemed especially resonant to colonial Americans. Like Snider, Allen was a bystander. He was shot only a year earlier during the St. George's Fields Massacre of 1769 when supporters of Wilkes were routed while they gathered to cheer their imprisoned leader. As the Richardson case remained unresolved, it must have appeared increasingly

[25] *Boston Gazette*, February 26, 1770; *Boston Evening Post*, February 26, 1770; *Virginia Gazette*, April 5, 1770. Phillis Wheatley, "On the Death of Mr. Snider Murder'd by Richardson (1770)," *The Poems of Phillis Wheatley*, ed. Julian D. Mason, Jr. (Chapel Hill: University of North Carolina Press, 1989), pp. 131–132. George Robert Twelve Hewes's memoir describes the riot and Snider's funeral (Benjamin Thackery, *Traits of the Tea Party, Being a Memoir of George R. T. Hewes* [New York: Harper and Brothers, 1835], pp. 88–95). See also Alfred Young's classic essay on Hewes: "George Robert Twelve Hewes (1742–1840): A Boston Shoemaker and the Memory of the American Revolution," *William & Mary Quarterly* 38 (1981): 561–623.

[26] Phillis Wheatley, "On the Death of Mr. Snider Murder'd by Richardson," in *The Poems of Phillis Wheatley*, ed. Julian D. Mason, Jr. (Chapel Hill: University of North Carolina Press, 1989), pp. 131–132; *Boston Gazette*, February 26, 1770; *Virginia Gazette*, 5 April 1770; American response to the St. George's Fields Massacre is described in Maier, *From Resistance to Revolution*, pp. 172–173.

similar to London's failure to punish the soldier who shot Allen. Even
Hutchinson recognized that Allen's funeral was a model for that of Snider.
Viewing the patriots as a cabal, he countered the Allen imagery by evoking another politicized funeral, Sir Edmundsbury Godrey's, which was
orchestrated by Shaftesbury in order to bolster paranoid fears of a popish plot.[27] What, then, did Snider's death symbolize? Was he an American
Wilkite martyr, an unfortunate casualty used, as Hutchinson suggested,
for political purposes, or – and this would be critical for any fair trial – a
simple case of manslaughter?

To answer this question, Bostonians drew upon another precedent from
the Anglo-American radical legal casebook: the case of John Porteous.
"The conduct of freemen in one age is frequently imitated in another,"
warned a Massachusetts newspaper. "Another Porteous may fall in this
country, and by an awful example … he that sheddeth man's blood by
man shall his blood be shed."[28] This appeal to Porteous's example was
telling. The Porteous affair began in 1736 with the hanging of a smug-
gler in Edinburgh. Showing their displeasure at the execution, spectators pelted the city guard with stones and dirt. Porteous, captain of the
guard, responded by opening fire. Six or seven people were killed and
more than twenty wounded. Although a jury found Porteous guilty of
murder and he was sentenced to death, his life was spared through a
royal reprieve. Angered, a mob stormed the prison, seized Porteous, and
hung him on the city gallows.[29] What happened in Edinburgh during the
1730s was relevant for Revolutionary Boston. The affair was set in the
context of a struggle between Scottish autonomy and the power of the
Crown. Richardson, like Porteous, killed a rioter and somehow eluded
justice. Interestingly, Boston radicals were mustering precedents for vigi-
lante action in the same way that law courts would draw upon earlier
cases. If Porteous could be executed by extralegal means for murder, why
not Richardson?

---

[27] Hutchinson, *Massachusetts-Bay*, 3:194.

[28] *Massachusetts Spy*, March 5, 1772. In Mercy Otis Warren's play *The Adulateur: A
Tragedy* (Boston, 1773), an attack on Hutchinson with classical motifs, Porteous appears
as a patriotic character who calls for revenge against Richardson.

[29] *Gentleman's Magazine*, 1736, pp. 230 and 1737, pp. 121 and 346–347; *Act of Council
against Throwing Stones &c. at the Execution of Criminals* (Edinburgh: 1737); T. B.
Howell, *A Complete Collection of State Trials* (London: T. C. Hansard, 1816–28), 34
vols. 17: 923–994; A. T. Dickinson and K. Logue, "The Porteous Riot: A Study of the
Breakdown of Law and Order in Edinburgh, 1736–1737," *Journal of the Scottish Labor
History Society* 10 (1976): 21–40. Adrian Randoll, Riotous Assemblies: Popular Protest
in Hanoverian England (Oxford: Oxford University Press, 2007), pp. 40–43.

TRIAL AS PERFORMATIVE DRAMA

On April 20 the Richardson trial began. Since no lawyer agreed to defend him, the court appointed Josiah Quincy as counsel. Samuel Quincy and Robert Treat Paine shared the role of prosecutor. Such a prominent role for counsel was unusual for colonial America. However, politicized trials were envisioned as performative drama. Full of appeals to emotion and public rhetoric, counsel was meant to do more than merely muster legal precedent. Both prosecutor and defense counsel would do their share of posturing.

Paine's roughly sketched minutes of the trial, read together with the public debate over the proceedings, provide a unique opportunity to explore the differences between popular and official definitions of criminal law.[30] How did the categories of official and unofficial justice differ? In what ways were Bostonians willing to construct their own codes? And how, ultimately, did the common people respond to the very different decision of the court? The major issue at stake was the definition of the crime – more precisely, the distinction between manslaughter and murder.

Such a distinction was one of the peculiarities of official English law. French law, for example, treated homicide as a single crime until the Napoleonic Code. "I don't know of a nation in the world," a Massachusetts grand jury was told in 1767, "that makes that distinction between murder and manslaughter which the English do." Following Biblical precedent, the earliest Massachusetts settlers failed to include manslaughter in its legal codes.[31] Even in England, it was only in the late sixteenth century that lawyers distinguished between murder, a capital crime for the first offense, and the less severely punished felony of manslaughter. The same crime, homicide, might be punished differently depending upon the circumstances. Not simply the commission of the act, but the murky and complex issue of intent also needed to be determined. Juries were entrusted with making subtle judgments about the emotional state of the felon at the brief, often confused, instant when the crime occurred.

---

[30] Robert Treat Paine, "Paine's Minutes of the Trial" and "Paine's Minutes of the Proceeding on the Motion for a New Trial," in Adams, *Legal Works*, II: 416–430. The manuscript is in the Massachusetts Historical Society, Robert Treat Paine Papers.

[31] Charge to the Grand Jury, March Term, 1767 in Quincy, *Reports*, pp. 232–237. The distinction between murder and manslaughter appears later in Massachusetts law; see the 1647 statute defining justifiable homicide in *The Charters and General Laws of the Colony and Province of Massachusetts Bay* (Boston: T. B. Wait, 1814), p. 150.

Underscoring this unusual need to weigh intent, Blackstone defines manslaughter as "the unlawful killing of another, without malice either express or implied, which may be either voluntary, upon sudden heat or involuntary ... it must be done without premeditation."[32] In Richardson's case, then, two issues needed to be determined. First, what was his intent at the time of the shooting? And, second, to what extent might Richardson's actions be justifiable homicide as defense of either his home or person?

Richardson's defense sought to show that he lacked any premeditated intent to kill Snider. In notes compiled while preparing for the trial, Josiah Quincy outlined the strategy for the defense: "To explain the nature of the crime of murder and the different kinds of homicide, as justifiable, excusable (as *se defendo*) and felonious: to show the distinction between felonious homicide of malice prepense, which is properly murder, and without such malice, which is manslaughter." Richardson, Quincy argued, acted without malice of forethought. The shooting took place in the heat of anger. The very fact that Snider was a bystander, struck by a stray bullet, shows that Richardson did not intend to kill him. Certainly, with patriot instigators present, Richardson must not have been aiming at an unknown schoolboy. "If A shoots at B, misses him and kills C," the defense admitted "it would have been murder." Yet if it was true both that Richardson fired out of sudden passion and the victim was not the intended one, then, according to precedent, the charge should be reduced to manslaughter.[33]

Official Anglo-American law understood malice aforethought as a specific and premeditated intention to harm another. At the level of popular judicial discourse, however, there was no doubt that malice was more broadly defined as describing an overall persona. As his fictive

---

[32] William Blackstone, *Commentaries on the Laws of England*, 4 vols., ed. Stanley N. Katz (Chicago: University of Chicago Press, 1979), 4:191; Thomas A. Green, "The Jury and the English Law of Homicide 1200–1600," *Michigan Law Review* 74 (1976): 413–499; J. M. Kaye, "The Early History of Murder and Manslaughter, *Law Quarterly Review* 83 (1967): 365–394 and 569–601.

[33] Adams, *Legal Papers*, pp. 411–416. The manuscripts of two judges at Richardson's trial show a firm grasp of the distinctions between murder and justifiable homicide. Trowbridge's papers contain notes entitled "Cases adjudged a Homicide," in Edmund Trowbridge, "Notes on Legal Actions and Extracts from Cases E–H," Dana Papers, Massachusetts Historical Society (Boston). In 1780, Cushing elaborated upon a manslaughter decision in a case where throwing stones led to the violent death of a child. William Cushing, *Indictment v. Daniels*, "Notes of Cases Decided in the Superior and Supreme Judicial Courts of Massachusetts 1772–1789," Manuscripts, Harvard Law Library (Cambridge).

biography suggests, Richardson was thought malicious by nature and habit. "Urged on by hell and malice unprovoked," claimed a 1773 drama about Richardson, "hurled through the crowd promiscuous death and slaughter." Witnesses at the trial echoed this perception. They portrayed an ill-tempered, vindictive man whose violent language betrayed his willingness to commit murder. Months before being faced with an anti-importation crowd, according to one witness, Richardson said "Let 'em come on me I'm ready, for I've guns loaded." During the course of the riot, he threatened to massacre the mob, adding "I'll make it too hot for you before night." Richardson showed no remorse about Snider's death. "Damn their blood," he was reported to have declared after the shooting, "I don't care what I've done." Richardson may not have intended to slay Snider, but, it was thought, he clearly wanted to kill someone in the crowd. How was it possible, Bostonians must have wondered, not to see malice behind Richardson's act?

Richardson was not an easy felon to defend. "Every newspaper was crowded with the most infamous and false libels against him in order to prejudice the minds of his jury." Faced with doubts about Richardson's character, his counsel argued for self-defense. Richardson "was in his house peaceably and there assaulted, by breaking his windows and throwing stones at him." "It is excusable homicide se defendendo," Quincy recorded in his trial notes, "... a man's house is his castle and he may defend it." The plea of self-defense had the advantage of subtly shifting the argument from Richardson's emotional state at the time of the act to solid facts, from the troubling persona of Richardson himself to his home. Yet the spatial configuration of the riot was also open to debate. What defined the boundaries between house and public space? Even in the midst of the riot, there was an engagement with the legal meaning of these boundaries. At one point, when Richardson ordered the rioters to disperse, they retorted "king's highway." The protesters were making a legal argument. Outside Richardson's house was, like any thoroughfare, public space where a demonstration may take place. Richardson did not agree. He threatened to make his own highway by firing his gun through the dense crowd.[34]

The dramaturgy of the confrontation took place at the liminal space between the private and public. As with most anti-importation protests, where houses were pelted with dirt, rioters resisted the temptation to

---

[34] Sparks Manuscripts, *New England Papers*, 3: 76, April 23, 1770; Adams *Legal Papers*, 2:411–425' Warren, *Adulateur*, pp. 10–11.

forcibly enter them. In this case, Richardson dashed out of his home to confront the crowd, but retreated when he felt threatened. This back and forth movement reflected the distinction between Richardson's home and the street. He "challenged them up to [the] door." The door as boundary repeatedly appeared in testimony at the trial. Richardson was reported to have said a day before the riot that violence would erupt if effigies were posted "before importers doors." Acknowledging the demarcation it signified, "boys got to the door, threw things." Nevertheless, this threshold remained a line that would not be crossed. Patriot agitators at the riot, according to the deposition of Richardson's daughter, "followed father up to the door and said come out you damn son of [a] bitch." Although the "front door [was] open, nobody had attempted to enter." Only Richardson's family would testify that the door had been broken open. But even they did not claim rioters had barged into their home.[35]

Such legal definitions of space were at the crux of Richardson's claim to self-defense. Quincy's notes for defending Richardson show a fascination with the threshold as boundary, asking "how far the attack upon the house was carried; whether and to what degree the windows were demolished before the firing, and whether the door was broken open, and any attempt made upon it; whether any actual attempt made to enter; or any evidence of such design from threatening words." Windows, like doors, were considered openings subject to being violated. For rioters, hurling stones through windows may not have breached borders between Richardson's home and the street. Those throwing, after all, remained outside. But the evidence of defense witnesses suggests that broken windows could also be seen as a kind of forced entry. One of Richardson's daughters described the destruction of the window until there was "no lead, no frame."[36]

Seeking to mitigate Richardson's crime, Hutchinson also attributed special significance to windows. "At length pelted and drove into his house ...," Hutchinson wrote, "and as he says windows broken and his person in danger he fixed upon the multitude and killed one lad and wounded another."[37] What was the legal model for this association of openings with violation? Rape and housebreaking share the same concern with

---

[35] Adams, *Legal Papers*, 2:416–420.
[36] Adams, *Legal Papers*, 2:411–421.
[37] Adams, *Legal Papers*, 2:411–421; Hutchinson letter, February 23, 1770, 26 *Massachusetts Archives*, 446–447.

defining the penetration of private space. Both demand actual entry/penetration for full prosecution. Bostonians who denied Richardson's claim to self-defense appear to have been concerned with such legal distinctions. A juror who found Richardson guilty of murder said he would have acquitted him "had the killing happened in the night instead of the day." This comment demonstrates a remarkable knowledge of Anglo-American law. It mimics the traditional English statute on housebreaking, which permitted the killing of a burglar in self-defense at night, but not during the daytime. The extraofficial call for finding Richardson guilty of murder, as well as the defense claim that his crime was simply manslaughter, was rooted in official Anglo-American legal doctrine.[38]

"The prisoner," Richardson's judges told jurors, "was attacked in his own house by a number of tumultuous people in that what he had done was his own defense." These instructions to the jury made clear the bench's interpretation of the law: It was justifiable homicide or, perhaps, manslaughter, not murder.[39] The Superior Court justices would later be accused of acting under the influence of politics. Yet their call for the jury to choose a verdict of manslaughter would have been standard for any similar case. In 1767, three years before Richardson was indicted, the Massachusetts Chief Justice's address to a grand jury dealt with the very issue of justifiable homicide in the course of a riot: If a man is attacked in his "own house, whether it be to treat him contemptuously for the diversion and sport of those who assault him," he will be guilty only of manslaughter with benefit of clergy. Manslaughter cases, however, followed a legal procedure that might make the court suspect. Today suspects are charged prior to the trial with the appropriate category of homicide. During the eighteenth century, however, the indictment of any homicide suspect, no matter how mitigating the circumstances, was always murder. It was the role of the jury to temper the murder charge and declare the crime to be simply manslaughter.[40]

The jury in the Richardson case declined to accept their customary tempering role. After a lengthy deliberation from eleven in the evening

---

[38] Oliver, *Origin and Progress*, p. 86. 23 Hen. VIII, c.1 (1531) and 1 Edw. VI, c.12 (1547). The distinction between housebreaking at night and during the daytime was eroded by later statutes. See Leon Radzinowicz, *A History of Criminal Law and its Administration from 1750: The Movement for Reform 1750–1833*, 4 vols. (New York: Macmillan Company, 1948), 1:41–49.

[39] Sparks Manuscripts, New England Papers, 3:76; Oliver, *Origin and Progress*, p. 86.

[40] Quincy, *Reports*, p. 263; J. M. Beattie, *Crime and the Courts in England 1660–1800* (Princeton: Princeton University Press, 1986), pp. 77–81.

until early the next morning, the jury returned its verdict on April 21: Richardson was guilty of murder. Wilmot was found not guilty. When the verdict was read, spectators clapped and cheered. Peter Oliver noted the inversion of traditional courtroom etiquette. "At acquittals there is often a huzza of joy in the hall of justice; but it is singular at a conviction. But now, the courtroom resounded with expressions of pleasure." The justices were faced with a dilemma. How should they respond to such a blatant disregard of the court's instructions?

Did the jurors, as Hutchinson asked, think "themselves better judges of the law than the court?" How could they "be obliged to give judgement upon a verdict which appeared to them directly against law?" It "was difficult, in the state of the town, to order the jury out a second time, or to refuse or delay sentence after the verdict was received."[41] In effect, two conflicting judgments had taken place: the mitigating decision of the justices based upon traditional categories of official law and a popular judgment – encapsulated by the jury's verdict – that defined Richardson's crime as murder.

Such competing legal authority evoked a major late-eighteenth-century legal debate. Were juries simply empowered to determine the facts of a case, or could they decide law? The medieval criminal trial jury functioned as a witness. It determined the circumstances of a crime and the credibility of testimony. By the mid-seventeenth century, however, the increasing discretionary powers of juries were met by the judiciary's attempt to curb them. *Bushell's Case* in 1670 established the principle that judges cannot coerce a jury to declare a predetermined verdict. Yet for the next century, the rights of juries remained ambiguous. While, on one hand, law was considered too complex for laypeople to decide, it was also thought that overturning their verdicts threatened to undermine the independence of the jury. In most cases, however, juries followed advice from the court. The few instances where bench and juries were at odds tended to be either homicide trials, where the question of intent posed special difficulties, or cases of seditious libel.

During the 1760s, this debate became increasingly relevant. A number of English seditious libel trials with strong political overtones made the question of jury autonomy a watchword for Wilkites and other radicals. In both *Rex v. Williams* (1764), which defended the publishing of Wilkes's *North Briton*, and a 1770 trial of the printers of the Junius letters, Wilkite

---

[41] Oliver, *Origin and Progress*, p. 86; Hutchinson letter, April 21, 1770, 26 Massachusetts Archives, 463; Hutchinson, *Massachusetts-Bay*, 3:206.

lawyers based their defense upon the right of juries to determine the law against instructions from the bench. Both cases were widely reported in the colonial press. Another case, *Smith v. Taylor* (1770), concerning a political brawl resulting in death, shared certain similarities with the Richardson trial. Despite the judge's determination that it was manslaughter, Wilkites sought a murder charge.[42]

John Adams linked attempts to undermine the power of juries in both England and America. At the very time that Richardson's fate was debated and Wilkites were creating a furor in London courtrooms, another Massachusetts trial brought to the fore the question of whether juries had the right to decide law. John Mein, the contentious antipatriot publisher of the *Boston Chronicle*, owed a sizable debt to Thomas Longman, a London merchant. For overtly political reasons, John Hancock initiated a lawsuit to recover the claim. The suit was a patriot ploy to harass Mein. Although the bench directed the jury to find for Mein, it chose to do just the opposite. *Longman v. Mein* (1770–1771) prompted the claim that eighteenth-century Massachusetts juries could determine questions of law. Writing in his diary at the time of the trial, Adams politicized the legal issue of the jury's role: "No wonder ... that attempts are made to deprive the freeholders of America ... of this troublesome power so dangerous to tyrants." For Adams and other American radicals, the jury

---

[42] John Brewer, "The Wilkites and the Law, 1763–74: A Study of Radical Notions of Governance," in *An Ungovernable People: The English and their Law in the Seventeenth and Eighteenth Centuries*, eds. John Brewer and John Styles (New Brunswick: Rutgers University Press, 1980), pp. 153–159 describes the jury's political role in English seditious libel cases. Beattie, *Crime and the Courts*, pp. 406–410; John M. Mitnick, "From Neighbor-Witness to Judge of Proofs: The Transformation of the English Civil Juror," *American Journal of Legal History* 32 (1988): 201–235. John Langbein and Thomas Green have provided the most thorough discussion of the changing role of the jury. See John H. Langbein, "Shaping the Eighteenth-Century Criminal Trial: The View from the Ryder Sources," *Chicago Law Review* 50 (1983): 1–136; Thomas A. Green, *Verdict According to Conscience: Perspectives on the English Criminal Jury 1200–1800* (Chicago: University of Chicago Press, 1985), pp. 267–317; Thomas A. Green, "A Retrospective on the Criminal Trial Jury, 1200–1800," in *Twelve Good Men and True: The Criminal Trial Jury in England, 1200–1800*, eds. J. S. Cockburn and Thomas A. Green (Princeton: Princeton University Press, 1988), pp. 358–400. The debate over the right of juries to determine law as well as fact inspired a number of polemic works in the 1760s and 1770s, most notably Joseph Towers, *An Enquiry into the Question whether Juries are, or are not Judges of Law as well as of Fact* (London, 1764), and Robert Morris, *A Letter to Sir Richard Aston ... and Some Thoughts on the Modern Doctrine of Libels* (London, 1770), and George Rous, *A Letter to the Jurors of Great Britain* (London, 1771). For the colonial response to this debate, see, for example, *Boston Gazette*, March 13, 1769 and February 4, 1771.

was invested with democratic authority. It was, in his words, "the voice of the people."[43]

Conflicts between judges and juries were not common. Adams estimated that in only one out of a thousand cases would the jury be at a loss about the law. But the question of a jury's right to determine law as well as fact revealed how eighteenth-century Americans had begun constructing a popular ideology of justice. It privileged the experiential or intuitive wisdom of juries over the casebook knowledge of judges. The juror was to be flexible, drawing upon their understanding of witnesses character and local knowledge to reach a decision "according to his own best understanding, judgement, and conscience." Underscoring the place of conscience in the jury's decision, Adams claimed that juries must not be coerced to submit a verdict against their will. The jury should not be made "a mere machine." This sort of legal epistemology meant a radical recasting of roles. Some colonial writers even doubted the right of judges to interpret the law: "The opinion of a judge is respectable if he be an honest man, but neither the opinion of a judge or any court of justice was intended to determine any issue." "They may advise" the jury, suggested an anonymous 1772 essay, "but it is the finding of the jury which is the determination and interpretation of the law."[44]

What Adams's comments suggest, then, was how differently juries might be perceived and how that perception might be altered by politics. At stake was not simply the legal role of juries, but its place in late-eighteenth-century political mythology. Two conflicting cultural representations identified juries with the common people. Adams thought of the jury as analogous to the legislature. It restrained the bench just as Parliament

---

[43] Adams, *Legal Papers*, 1:199–230. Adams, *Diary and Autobiography*, 2:3–5. Shanon C. Stimson, *The American Revolution in the Law: Anglo-American Jurisprudence before John Marshall* (Princeton: Princeton University Press, 1990), pp. 71–79. Based on considerable research, William Nelson, *Americanization of the Common Law: The Impact of Legal Change on Massachusetts Society 1760–1830* (Cambridge: Harvard University Press, 1975) argues that Massachusetts juries had the power to judge both law and fact, and that the exercise of that power remained virtually unchallenged. Nevertheless, as a question of legal authority, the power of juries was subject to debate. Those politicized cases where consensus between judge and jury did not exist demonstrated how little agreement there was on this issue. For research underscoring the ambiguity of the distinction between judging law and fact in the colonies prior to the mid-eighteenth century, see Bruce H. Mann, *Neighbors and Strangers: Law and Community in Early Connecticut* (Chapel Hill: University of North Carolina Press, 1987), pp. 74–81.

[44] *Massachusetts Spy*, May 9, 1771 and February 20, 1772; Adams, *Diary*, February 12, 1771, 2:2–5; William E. Nelson, "The Eighteenth-Century Background of John Marshall's Constitutional Jurisprudence," *Michigan Law Review* (1978): 893–960.

was meant to balance the power of the Crown. Yet if it was a scaled-down legislature for Adams, Peter Oliver viewed the jury at Richardson's trial as simply an extension of the mob. "A demonocracy," Oliver called it. He accused Boston selectmen of stacking juries so that only those with patriot political sympathies would participate. Richardson, according to Oliver, "fell into the hands of tigers, [jurors] whose tender mercies were cruelties." The jury foreman spoke with a "sullen pride of revenge."[45]

In their attempt to lessen Richardson's punishment, the justices followed a classic legal strategy: delay. They remanded him to prison, partly for his own safety. Richardson's defense counsel lodged a petition for a new trial, and the court, hoping to avoid another inflammatory legal battle, quietly consulted London about a pardon. The patriot press was quick to embrace Wilkite notions of the law. It argued that juries could judge not just fact, but law. "The notion of the jury's having no power to intermeddle with law is without foundation in law," protested an essay in the *Massachusetts Spy*, "it appears to me a perversion of justice and making a jury mere machines." "We see already the effect. A wretch, though by his country and a jury regularly sworn declared guilty of premeditated murder, yet lives exulting over the justice of his country."[46]

The debate about Richardson's fate was both within a legal discourse – using courtroom drama to argue about such questions as due process and the role of juries – and, at the same time, a direct challenge to legal authority. Richardson, Hutchinson declared, was found guilty "against the opinion of the court." Yet the passage quoted previously revealed a very different understanding of authority. It offers two alternative sources of judicial power: jury and, significantly, country. The question "who will judge?" was answered by investing not just the jury, but the common people with considerable legal authority.[47]

In *Rex v. Wemms*, Justice Edmund Trowbridge instructed the jury to rely only upon trial evidence, not upon "what you may have read or heard of the case out of court." But during the Richardson trial, the

[45] Oliver, *Origin and Progress*, pp. 85–86. On the relationship between the English jury and the people, see Douglas Hay, "The Class Composition of the Palladium of Liberty: Trial Jurors in the Eighteenth Century," in *Twelve Good Men: The Criminal Trial Jury in England 1200–1800*, eds. J. S. Cockburn and Thomas A. Green (Princeton: Princeton University Press, 1988), pp. 305–357, which sheds doubts upon the democratic pretensions of eighteenth-century juries. Property qualifications shaped the jury as a class institution. Of course, choosing a jury was no different in this regard than electing legislatures.

[46] *Massachusetts Spy*, May 9, 1771 and May 2, 1771.

[47] Hutchinson correspondence, *Massachusetts Archives* 26, 463, April 21, 1770.

borders between courtroom and street corner dissolved. Eighteenth-century courts were as much social constructions as architectural ones. More than anywhere else in colonial society, except churches, they demar-cated a special place ruled by its own rituals and authority. Perhaps this was because what took place in courtrooms was laden with the threat of sanctioned violence. Courts, after all, had the right to expropriate wealth, deny liberty, or even take away a person's life.

This awesome power, bounded by rules, was reflected in the architec-ture of the Superior Court chamber. It was, according to John Adams's evocative description, "as respectable an apartment as the House of Commons or the House of Lords in Great Britain, in proportion, or that in the State House in Philadelphia." The physical setting was dominated by the justices. "Round a great fire, were seated five judges ... arrayed in their new, fresh, rich robes of scarlet English broadcloth; in their large cambric bands, and immense judicial wigs." This dignity, "more solemn and pompous than that of the Roman Senate," underscored the well-staged distinctions between court ritual and extralegal crowd action.[48]

Instituted by Hutchinson in 1762, judicial robes were a novelty for Massachusetts Superior Court. Did such symbolic trappings demonstrate the court's hegemony or reflect the need to bolster waning power? A few years later, Hutchinson would elaborate upon the problem of sustaining judicial authority: "'Tis on the dignity and support of the executive courts that your own liberty depends. Let the respect of these courts be lost, let their dignity not be kept up ... and all order and government will soon be at an end. For what order can there be in a society where the courts which are to carry the laws in execution are treated with a contemptuous dis-respect?" Faced with rising discord, two years later, New York's Justices William Smith, Daniel Horsmanden, and Robert Livingston, also would require gowns to create "dignity, authority, solemnity, and decorum." But

---

[48] Trowbridge's Charge to the Jury, December 5, 1770 in Adams, *Legal Papers*, 3:282–302; John Adams to William Tudor, March 29, 1817, in *Works*, 10:244–245. The cultural significance of the courthouse in eighteenth-century America is best described in two works on Virginia: Rhys Isaac, *The Transformation of Virginia 1740–1790* (Chapel Hill: University of North Carolina, 1982), pp. 88–90 and A. G. Roeber, *Faithful Magistrates and Republican Lawyers: Creators of Virginia Legal Culture 1680–1810* (Chapel Hill: University of North Carolina Press, 1981), pp. 73–95. Other studies of the court as distinct space include Lawrence Rosen, *The Anthropology of Justice: Law as Culture in Islamic Society* (Cambridge: Cambridge University Press, 1989), pp. 1–19; Douglas Hay, "Property, Authority, and the Criminal Law," in *Albion's Fatal Tree: Crime and Society in Eighteenth-Century England*, eds. Douglas Hay et al. (New York: Pantheon Books, 1975), pp. 17–64.

robes do not make the judge. In a satirical play published in Boston, Justice Beau has to duck into his chambers to put on a robe before taking a deposition. "Be sure," says the vain justice, "to see my whig is combed and powdered." The use of robes may not have ensured deference. It did, however, reflect Hutchinson's hierarchical vision of justice.[49]

It was difficult to sustain such a hierarchy in the face of the vast number of spectators who gathered in the courtroom to witness the Richardson trial. "The authority of the courts," wrote Peter Oliver, "were now of little force. Forms were maintained without much power." Nowhere can this better be seen than during the instructions to the jury. From Justice Oliver came a statement assigning broader guilt to patriot leaders. He "charged the death of the boy upon the promoters of effigies and other exhibitions which had drawn the people together and caused unlawful tumultuous assemblies."[50] Such a statement from the bench meant that Oliver took advantage of the presence of another patriot crowd to "charge" them (the use of legal language is significant) with the crime. When the bench unanimously called upon the jury to reduce the crime to manslaughter, anger flared. "No manslaughter, but murder," Bostonians shouted at the departing jurors, "remember jury you are upon oath – blood requires blood." The crowd chose to deliver their own instructions to the jury. This charge, like the official one read from the bench, centered on the distinction between manslaughter and murder, and jurors' responsibility in framing a verdict. When the jury decided that Richardson was indeed guilty of murder, the spectators cheered. Richardson himself was whisked away to jail in order to prevent his being lynched. Prompted by what the defense considered intimidation of the jury, a motion for a new trial was quickly filed. This troubled case, clearly, would not set any official legal precedent. Nevertheless, it marked a watershed in the popular wresting away of judicial power. At almost every stage of the proceedings, Bostonians would declare judgments, craft fictive criminal

---

[49] Hutchinson, Charge to Grand Jury (1767) in Quincy, *Reports*, 245–246; Adams, *Diary*, 1: 54–58; *Trial of Atticus Before Justice Beau for a Rape* (Boston, 1771), p. 6; John M. Murrin "Anglicizing an American Colony: The Transformation of Provincial Massachusetts," (Ph.D. diss., Yale University, 1966), p. 238. On instituting judicial gowns in New York, see Manuscript of Moot Cases, 1770–1774, New-York Historical Society, 26 July 1774; Douglas Greenberg, *Crime and Law Enforcement in New York 1691–1776* (Ithaca: Cornell University Press, 1976), pp. 223–224.

[50] Hutchinson to Hillsborough, April 21, 1770, 26 *Massachusetts Archives*, 463. Unfortunately, a surviving diary from one of the justices sheds little light on the workings of the bench in this case. Benjamin Lynde, Jr., *Diaries of Benjamin Lynde and Benjamin Lynde, Jr.* (Boston: private printing, 1880), pp. 194–195.

narratives, decide questions of law, or demand the imposition of punishment. Even if they had not succeeded in having Richardson hanged, due
to their efforts, he would spend the next twenty-two months in prison
awaiting a pardon. Most importantly, the Richardson controversy was
the prelude to a broader challenge of English criminal law.[51]

A FELON'S PROGRESS

While Ebenezer Richardson languished in prison, Levi Ames pursued his
criminal career. Ames did not need anyone to invent past felonies for him.
From his earliest childhood, Ames led a life punctuated by crime. His first
thefts were small: a couple of eggs, a pocket knife, and some chalk. Yet he
quickly graduated to robbery as a profession. Like Richardson, Ames had
a verse broadside that justified his execution: "No goods were safe that
you could steal/How many doors you've open broke/And windows scal'd
and money took/Round houses you have all day been/To spy a place
to enter in." "Death and damnation," adds the poem called *The Speech
of Death to Levi Ames*, "is your due."[52] Such verse dying speeches, the
execution sermons preached by Boston ministers, and his long, rambling
execution narrative would leave no doubt that Ames – in ways that might
never apply to Richardson – was an old offender.

Born at Groton in 1752, Ames was only twenty-one years old when
sentenced to death. His father, Jacob Ames, died when he was age two.
This loss seems to have determined much of his early life. Finding herself
unable to discipline her child, Ames's mother contracted an apprenticeship agreement. Ames ran away from his master. This, he admitted, was
the beginning of his ruin. "For being indolent in temper and having no
honest ways of supporting myself, I robbed others of their property."
Richardson was emblematic of the kind of scoundrel who would do anything for his master. He was, in late-eighteenth-century idiom, a creature
of the customs commissioners – willing to lie, inform, or even murder
at their bidding. But Ames represented another *bête noire* of colonial
Americans: the masterless man. Without norms imposed by social superi-
ors, Ames was free to wander from town to town engaging in crime.[53]

---

[51] Oliver, *Origin and Progress*, p. 86 and Adams, *Legal Papers*, 2: 404–405 and 426–427.
[52] Ames, *The Speech of Death to Levi Ames* [Broadside, 1773].
[53] Levi Ames, *The Life, Last Words, and Dying Speech of Levi Ames* (Boston, 1773), p. 31.
   Boston Post-Boy, September 25, 1773. Although little work has been done on the connection between age and crime, Ames fits a pattern for youth offenders. See Natalie Zemon
   Davis, "The Reasons of Misrule: Youth Groups and Charivaris in Sixteenth-Century

Not surprisingly, then, Ames's execution narrative was constructed around the motif of motion. It was a sort of felon's progress, a grand larceny tour making its way across much of New England. Thefts were marked by where they took place: Waltham, Cambridge, Lexington, Boston, Marlborough, Watertown, Newburyport, or Worcester. Ames's crimes traversed three colonies: Connecticut, Rhode Island, and, especially, Massachusetts. After one arrest, he wandered like Cain with a mark. Ames's forehead was branded with a "B" for burglary. Ironically, Ames began his tale of theft at Richardson's hometown: Woburn. There he stole a gun from Josiah Richardson, probably a relative of Ebenezer. Quickly moving on, Ames stole twenty to thirty dollars at Plymouth, broke into a dry goods store at Groton where he took some cloth, and robbed two Waltham men of money and a hat.

Even such petty thefts were accompanied by the names of the victims. Ames's memory of his robberies was remarkable. "I stole," he acknowledged, "a pair of silver buckles and a pair of turned pumps out of a pair of saddle bags at Leason's tavern in Waltham; the buckles were marked I. D." Part of the purpose of the execution narrative was to inform victims of what happened to missing items. But Ames's ability to identify what was stolen, where, and from whom makes his narrative read like a crime blotter. The inventory of loot taken from a Lexington home, for example, included a tankard, twelve tea-spoons, a pepper-box, and two pairs of sugar tongs. Only rarely does he admit to a lapse in memory. "I have several times taken sundry articles off of lines, hedges, fences, bushes apple trees …," Ames confessed, "but I cannot recollect their owners."[54]

Ames's narrative provides a fascinating window into the life of a late-eighteenth-century petty criminal. Many of his robberies were

France," *Past and Present* 50 (1971): 41–75 and Steven R. Smith, "The London Apprentices as Seventeenth-Century Adolescents," *Past and Present* 61 (1973): 149–161. Demographic data like that of E. A. Wrigley and R. S. Schofield, *The Population History of England 1541–1971: A Reconstruction* (London: Edward Arnold, 1981) would establish if the colonies, as well as England, were experiencing a rapid rise in the number of adolescents during this period. On evolving attitudes toward minor offenders during this period, see Nancy H. Steenburg, "Changing Standards in the Criminal Law of Connecticut, 1650–1853," 41; *Connecticut History* (2002): 124–143. For an excellent examination of changing attitudes toward children, see Holly Brewer, *By Birth or Consent: Children, Law, and the Anglo-American Revolution in Authority* (Chapel Hill: University of North Carolina Press, 2007).

[54] Ames, *Life*, pp. 31–33. Minute Book of the Superior Court of Judicature, 1773–1774, 30–31, Massachusetts Archives (Boston).

opportunistic. He might find an unwatched basket of small coins at a baker's, an axe left carelessly in the back of a cart. When he took a horse, it was only in order to quickly slip out of town. It was a life marked by close escapes, sudden changes of dress – "I also stole ... two coats and jackets with which I dressed myself when I came to Boston" – or even of name. "I then went," Ames wrote, "by the name of Lawrence." Ames would sell his stolen goods to fences or peddle it himself. At times he must have missed a decent meal. While robbing a house at Marlborough, he searched for something to eat. Ames did not appear menacing. Shunning armed robbery, he limited himself to small-time pilfering and burglary. A number of his burglaries were committed on Sunday when there was less chance of encountering violent resistance.[55]

In his fictive verse confession, Richardson was portrayed as acknowledging terrible crimes: perjury, adultery, incest, and murder. The broadside poem justifying Ames's execution, however, could hardly summon anything worse than bad habits. Death, portrayed as a skeleton, demanded the right to take Ames: "In adding guilt you still went on/I doubly claim you for my own/How often you the Sabbath broke!/God's name in vain you often took!/A filthy drunkard you have been/And led your life with the unclean." Ames was not a heroic eighteenth-century criminal like Jack Shepherd or Jonathan Wild. No ballads would be written about Levi Ames. Often he was timid. If his execution narrative can be believed, Ames repaid certain of his victims. He refused to act as a fence for an associate because he "was afraid to do it." When another thief tried to lure him into robbing the governor's house, he declined. There were too many servants, and Ames would have to go armed. "This I absolutely refuse because I never thought of murdering any man in the midst of all my ... thieving." Unlike Richardson, no one would accuse Ames of murder.[56] With his execution narrative, Ames had crafted his own life's

---

[55] *Ibid.* For the social context of Ames's criminality, see Alan Kulikoff, "The Progress of Inequality in Revolutionary Boston," *William & Mary Quarterly* 28 (1971): 375–412; Douglas Lamar Jones, "The Strolling Poor: Transiency in Eighteenth-Century Massachusetts," *Journal of Social History* 8 (1975): 28–54; and Marcus Rediker, "Good Hands, Stout Hearts, and Fast Feet: The History and Culture of Working People in America," *Labour/Le travailleur* 10 (1982): 21–56. The literary theme of wandering has been explored in W. B. Carnochan, *Confinement and Flight: An Essay on English Literature of the Eighteenth Century* (Berkeley: University of California Press, 1977). Peter Linebaugh, *The London Hanged: Crime and Civil Society in the Eighteenth Century* (Cambridge: Cambridge University Press, 1991) explores the relationship between criminal narrative and working-class consciousness.

[56] Ames, *Speech of Death* [Broadside, 1773] and Ames, *Life*, pp. 32–33.

tale. Scholars have often envisioned such narratives as an instrument of the authorities for communicating a message of civil order. Yet, as I will argue in the next chapter, felons commonly seized upon the genre as a means to tell their own story. Ames was no exception. His narrative must be read like a pardon petition. In self-serving fashion, it emphasized his best moments: repaying stolen goods, his stance against violence, and Ames's claim to repentance. "Though I lived such a wicked life," Ames wrote, "it was not without some severe checks. For after I had stolen, I have been so distressed at times, as to be obliged to go back and throw the stolen goods at the door, or into the yard that the owners might have them again." Shortly before his last arrest, Ames claimed he felt the burden of his criminal life: "I passed the gallows on Boston Neck with some stolen goods under my arm when my conscience terribly smote me, and I thought I should surely die there, if I did not leave off this course of life." In contrast to Richardson, whose mock dying confession was fabricated *against* his being pardoned, Ames, who retained some control over his own narrative, reinvented his criminal self with the hope of a last-minute reprieve.[57]

Ames was sentenced to death for a crime not too different from others in his past: a simple burglary. It was planned with a confederate, Joseph Attwood, who Ames claimed he met for the first time in Boston toward the end of August 1773, shortly before attempting the burglary together. Here, again, was an example of Ames's selective memory. It appears that Ames and Attwood had broken into the house of a Lexington minister the previous spring.[58] Turning king's evidence against Ames, Attwood would later provide the testimony that would lead to Ames's capital conviction. Not surprisingly, then, Ames and Attwood had very different versions of their meeting. According to Attwood, Ames took him to dinner, plied him with wine, and told him that he had seen Martin Bicker return home from his auction house with a large sum of money. They walked from Market Square to the North End, and Ames tried to convince Attwood to join him in the theft. At the ship yard, the two slept a bit. Ames took a bottle from his pocket. After a few more drinks, Atwood succumbed to Ames's coaxing.[59]

[57] Ames, *Life*, pp. 34–35; Samuel Stillman, *Two Sermons ... Delivered the Lord's-Day Before the Execution of Levi Ames, who was Executed at Boston, Thursday October 21, 1773 for Burglary* (Boston: John Kneeland, 1773), pp. 63–66.
[58] Ames, *Life*, pp. 33–34; *Massachusetts Spy*, September 2, 1773.
[59] *Massachusetts Spy*, September 9, 1773.

Ames told a different story. "I was standing at a countryman's cart in the market at Boston, asking the price of a turkey; Attwood came up to me and we fell into conversation." Attwood and Ames walked up Beacon Hill. Attwood, Ames claimed, said he had no money, and Ames offered him dinner. Ames convinced Attwood to fence some stolen goods. Then, in Ames's version of the story, it was Attwood who first suggested robbing Bicker's house: "he told me he knew of [someone] ... who had a large sum of money by him, and if I would join him we would get it." Ames's description clearly attempts to shift the blame to Attwood. Tucked away in the midst of his execution narrative, it appears to be simply another straightforward tale of crime. But Ames was doing more than unburdening his conscience before he died. He had survived other convictions for burglary without suffering death. His narrative must be seen as an extraofficial species of testimony. A witness in his own defense, Ames followed the strategy of trying to create enough doubt about Attwood's evidence to prompt a pardon for himself.[60]

Such pleas stood squarely within traditional Anglo-American criminal law doctrine. Nowhere was this clearer than in the description of the crime itself. "Having come to Mr. Bicker's house," stated Ames, "we found a front chamber window open; we pulled off our shoes, and Joseph Attwood with my assistance climbed up to the window and entered the house, and opened the doors for me; we then went together to the desk which we broke open with the chisels." They stole forty pieces of silver, Spanish pieces of eight, and gold coins. Attwood's testimony was very different. He claimed that Ames supplied the instruments and climbed into a window while he waited outside and served merely as a lookout. Under the guise of making peace as he approached death, Ames pointedly underscored the fact that he insisted that Attwood had lied under oath. "I also forgive from my heart Joseph Attwood," Ames wrote in his narrative, "who swore on my trial that I entered the house of Mr. Bicker first, and let him in, when he knows in his conscience that he entered first and let me in."[61]

What Ames and Attwood disagreed about, of course, was the same issue as found in the Richardson case: the spatial configuration of the

---

[60] Ames, *Life*, p. 33. For other examples of Ames's earlier encounters with the criminal justice system, see Minute Book of the Superior Court of Judicature, 1773–1774, 30–31, Massachusetts Archives (Boston).

[61] Minute Book of the Superior Court of Judicature, 1773–1774, 118–119, Massachusetts Archives (Boston); Ames, *Life*, pp. 33–34; *Charters and General Laws*, pp. 406–407 and 668–669.

crime. Even as nonlawyers, they showed themselves aware of the legal definition of housebreaking. At issue was the actual entry into the house, which was a required element of the crime beyond the simple theft of goods. While Ames blamed Attwood for the first illegal entry, Attwood denied entering at all. The money was found on both of them when captured. Windows and doors once again proved significant as liminal structures. Although Ames pleaded not guilty, the court believed Attwood. On Friday, September 10, 1773, Ames was sentenced to death for burglary, with the execution set for October 14. Attwood, who was found guilty in part, would receive twenty stripes and pay triple damages and costs. Unable to pay, Attwood was placed at Bicker's disposal for ten years.[62]

Ames hoped for a pardon. The Sunday before the execution, a Baptist minister cautioned: "All prospects of living longer than the time appointed is cut off. I hope you will not flatter yourself with a longer time." Yet Ames, not unreasonably, relied upon the capriciousness of the eighteenth-century criminal justice system with its frequent reprieves. Like the execution narrative, his behavior must be seen as a sort of legal document – a performative, rather than written, petition for a pardon. Ames tried to be a model prisoner. He expressed appreciation toward the people of Boston, ministers, and the jail keeper. "Levi Ames," wrote a Boston diarist, "attends public worship every Sabbath and infinite pains is taken by the ministers of the town to enlighten his mind in the knowledge of divine truth." As was the case with many condemned felons, Ames's life assumed a typological significance. Overlaid upon the criminal self of the execution biography was a Protestant redemptive narrative.[63]

Ames cannily adopted the idiom of deference toward those who held the power to pardon. Claiming to be contrite, Ames tried the classic gambit of condemned felons: How could he face God's judgment without having the opportunity for a few more good deeds? "I feel I am lost," he told a minister. "I sometimes think that I am given over to destruction, and that there is no mercy for me. I am undone in soul and body. If I go to the place of execution as I am now, they must drag me like a bullock to the slaughter ... May I not have a little longer time than is now fixed?"

---

[62] Minute Book of the Superior Book of Judicature, 1773–1774, *Massachusetts Archives*, 118–119; *Boston Post-Boy*, September 13, 1773; *Boston Gazette*, September 13, 1773; *Massachusetts Spy*, September 16, 1773.

[63] Stillman, *Two Sermons ... Delivered the Lord's Day Before the Execution of Levi Ames, Who was Executed at Boston, Thursday October 21, 1773 for Burglary* (Boston: John Kneeland, 1773), pp. 23–24; Ames, *Life*, p. 36; John Boyle, "Boyle's Journal of Occurrences in Boston," *New England Historical and Genealogical Register* 84 (1930): 367.

Perhaps because of his penitent stance, perhaps because of the public outcry over the sentence of death, Ames was allowed a one-week reprieve.
Then, on October 21, with an exceptionally large number of spectators
present, Ames was hanged.[64]

THEFT AND MURDER

The execution of Levi Ames turned into something of a cottage industry
for Boston printers. During the course of the next month and a half,
a flurry of poems, broadsides, dying speeches, and execution narratives
and sermons would be published. What this collection of works reveals
is the diversity of tropes that might be applied to a single criminal life.
The execution sermons of ministers Samuel Stillman, Andrew Elliot, and
Samuel Mather, not surprisingly, drew upon Protestant motifs. According
to Stillman, Ames was Absalom, the beloved son who went astray. Eliot
described Christ on the cross with thieves. For Mather, God was a physi-
cian prepared to heal Ames on his deathbed. Ames was promised mercy
if he repented, judgment if he did not. "All heaven is purchas'd by His
cross/For such vile souls as thine," intoned an execution broadside full
of religious imagery, "You leave this earth, it is no loss/If you in heaven
may shine." Mixing Christian morals with civil authority, Stillman used
the execution sermon as a forum to denounce deism, excessive drinking,
gambling, and seducers who threaten the honor of women.

Ames was a bit more prosaic when he listed his own last warnings.
Parents and masters should discipline children. Beware, he cautioned,
against bad women, cursing, and drunkenness. Stepping beyond the con-
fines of Protestant execution sermon conventions, Ames offered some
practical advice: "To keep your doors and windows shut on evenings, and
secured well to prevent temptation. And by no means use small locks on
the outside, one of which I have twisted with ease when tempted to steal.
Also not to leave linen or clothes out at night." "Travelers," he added, "I
advise to secure their saddle bags, boots, etc., in the chambers where they
lodge."[65]

---

[64] Hewes, *Memoir*, p. 90; Stillman, *Two Sermons*, pp. 57–60; Rowe, *Diary*, p. 252; *Boston Gazette*, October 11, 1773 and October 28, 1773.

[65] Stillman, *Two Sermons*, especially pp. 49–51; Andrew Eliot, *Christ's Promise to the Penitent Thief, a Sermon Preached on the Lord's Day Before the Execution of Levi Ames, Who Suffered Death for Burglary, October 21, 1773* (Boston: John Boyles, 1773); Samuel Mather, *Christ Sent to Heal the Broken Hearted, a Sermon Preached at the Thursday Lecture in Boston on October 21st, 1773 when Levi Ames, a Young Man Under Sentence*

The number and variety of execution texts about Ames seem astonishing. After all, Ames was not very different from many other petty criminals who plagued the colonies during the 1760s and 1770s. He did not perform any spectacular escapes, lead a gang of felons, or even commit murder. Why, then, was Ames the subject of so many works? The answer, once again, leads back to Ebenezer Richardson and political agitation in Boston. Sentencing Ames to death for burglary contrasted with the failure to punish Richardson for the more serious crime of murder. Richardson remained in prison for almost two years. London had sent one pardon, but uneasy about the technical details of the form and perhaps fearing unrest, Hutchinson requested another. By spring 1772, the Newgate pardon finally came. On March 12, Richardson was secretly released from confinement.[66]

Just a few months later, an inflammatory broadside entitled *Theft and Murder* conjured up the sight of Ames hanging on the scaffold while Richardson went free: "Come ye spectators, and behold/And view a doleful scene today/My tender fainting heart grows cold/And I am fill'd with sore dismay … Behold a man condemn'd to die/For stealing his neighbor's goods/But murder doth for vengeance cry/But where's the avenger of the blood." *Theft and Murder* placed itself within the genre of execution poetics. Like many other examples of the genre, its frontispiece depicted the scene of execution. In stereotypic fashion, Ames was shown suspended from the gallows. Hovering above him stood a hangman on a ladder, while below a man on horseback appears to be issuing orders. Despite the cliché image, the message was radical: "'Tis a great crime to steal from men/And punishment deserves indeed/But murd'rers have released been/Who made our friends promiscuous bleed."

The broadside concerned Richardson as much as Ames. Drawing upon the popular culture genre of execution narratives, it read the two cases together to set forth an attack on the fairness of English law. It was not a full American critique of the English criminal justice

---

of Death for Burglary Was Present to Hear the Discourse (Boston: William M'Alphine, 1773); Ames, *A Solemn Farewell to Levi Ames, Being a Poem Written a Few Days Before His Execution for Burglary, October 21, 1773* [Broadside, 1773]. The Diary of Thomas Newell, *Proceedings of the Massachusetts Historical Society* 15 (1876–77): 343 mentions attendance at Eliot's execution sermon.

[66] 27 Massachusetts Archives (Boston), 210–211. PRO (London), "Domestic George III," IX: 84, 88 and "Domestic Entry Book, 1771–6," III:9 (September 4, 1771); Hutchinson to Hillsborough, May 15, 1771, PRO, CO 5, 768/198–200; *Massachusetts Spy*, March 12, 1772; Oliver, *Origin and Progress*, p. 87.

system – that would wait until the 1780s. Nor was the issue of class, which would become so important in the 1790s, yet raised in a truly conscious fashion. Nevertheless, Americans were clearly sensitive to the injustice of executing felons for crimes against property at the same time that homicide might be pardoned. "The life of man is more than gold/Or any other earthly good/But thieves are hang'd while murderers bold/Are freed."[67]

"Must thieves who take men's good away/Be put to death," asked the anonymous author of this broadside, "while fierce blood hounds/Who do their fellow creatures slay/Are sav'd from death? ... This cruel sounds." *Theft and Murder* demanded a pardon for Ames. A newspaper article signed by Brutus compared England's robbery of the colonies with Ames's small-scale pilfering. "He that riots on the plunder of his country deserves the gallows more than he that robs an individual."

Such patriot arguments would not go unanswered. Two other verse broadsides were printed defending capital punishment for property crimes. A burglar not only stole possessions, but peace of mind. *An Address to the Inhabitants of Boston* appealed to the fears of the city's hard-working citizens: "Industrious man o'ercome with sleep retires/Thinks to enjoy what he desires/The time that nature ordained for rest/When all the living may with sleep be blessed." Yet even as the working man rests, burglars like Ames are plotting their thefts. "Then at this hour/When all in sleep are lost/But crafty thieves who live at others cost" break into homes.[68] Life, too, was at risk during a nighttime burglary. "Thro' fear of death he [the householder] dares not descend/Lest that the night in blood and slaughter end." The political debate over the justice of English criminal law was couched in the vernacular form of execution literature.

In the Richardson affair, as well, Bostonians turned to the innovative use of vernacular legal culture. A judge had declared that Richardson committed justifiable homicide. Pardoned by the Crown, official legal process set him free. Richardson was, to borrow a phrase from Peter Oliver, found "guiltless in law." Yet a different verdict was issued by Boston's common people. Just as Richardson's name was linked during the trial with the term "informer," afterward he was inevitably referred

---

[67] *Theft and Murder, A Poem on the Execution of Levi Ames, Which Is to Be on Thursday, the 21st of October for Robbing the House of Mr. Martin Bicker, and Was Convicted of Burglary* [Broadside, 1773].

[68] Theft and Murder [Broadside, 1773]; *Boston Gazette*, October 25, 1773. Two works supporting Ames' execution are *An Address to the Inhabitants of Boston, Occasioned by the Execution of Levi Ames* [Broadside, 1773] and *Speech of Death* [Broadside, 1773].

to as a "murderer." An "infamous murderer," newspapers and broadsides called Richardson. "The guilty, guilty murderer walks abroad."[69]

American radicals demanded that Richardson be executed, or, at the least, there were hopes that he might be lynched. After the American Revolution, republicanism was identified with the rejection of capital punishment. But, ironically, during the 1770s, patriot writings urged death sentences for Richardson and those responsible for the Boston Massacre. "If that punishment is not inflicted," threatened one patriotic author, "innocent blood will cry from the ground – it will cry for vengeance to fall not only on the murderer wherever he is, but upon those, whoever they are, that divert the course of justice and cause murderers to go unpunished."[70]

Unable to hang Richardson in person, Bostonians at least chose to do so in their imagination. A broadside entitled *The Life and Humble Confession of Richardson* imitated the conventions of the capital felon's dying speech. Along the upper border was a typical woodcut illustration of the crime, depicting a street scene with Lillie's store clearly marked and the gathering crowd. A long, smoking rifle barrel extends from a second story window. It began with the formulaic prologue of the last confession: "Injured Boston now awake/While I a true confession make/Of my notorious sins and guilt/As well as the harmless blood I've spilt." In this fictive dying speech, Richardson admits to having been both an adulterer and an informer. Yet these are small crimes compared to murder. "But what's all that to this last crime/In sending Seider [Snider] out of time!/This cuts my heart, this frights me most/O help me, Lord, I see his ghost." From the last lines of the confession, it appears that the broadside was used with an effigy. Presumably, the effigy would be hanged with all the ritual and pageantry of official justice. "And now my injur'd friends/Since

---

[69] Oliver, *Origin and Progress*, p. 86. On Richardson's guilt, see, for example, *Massachusetts Spy*, May 2, 1771, March 12, 1772, and May 14, 1772; *Boston Gazette*, February 10, 1772; *A Monumental Inscription on the Fifth of March, Together with a few Lines on the Enlargement of Ebenezer Richardson* [Broadside, 1772].

[70] John Lathrop, *Innocent Blood Crying to God from the Streets of Boston. A Sermon Occasioned by the Horrid Murder on the 5th of March, 1770* (Boston: Edes and Gill, 1771), p. 12; David Brion Davis, "The Movement to Abolish Capital Punishment in America 1787–1861," in *From Homicide to Slavery: Studies in American Culture* (Oxford: Oxford University Press, 1986), pp. 17–40; Louis Masur, *Rites of Execution: Capital Punishment and the Transformation of American Culture 1776–1865* (Oxford: Oxford University Press, 1989), pp. 50–70. More generally, see Stuart Banner, *The Death Penalty in America* (Cambridge: Harvard University Press, 2003).

I can make you no amends," the Richardson figure urged, "Here is my body you may take."[71]

While the stuffed Richardson figure may have been executed, the real Richardson, upon receiving his pardon from London, was quickly spirited out of town. Here, too, Bostonians drew upon the forms of popular legal culture. They drafted a mock advertisement for him of the sort used for wanted criminals. "The infamous Ebenezer Richardson," its headline blazoned, "convicted of perjury & murder" was rumored to have fled to Philadelphia. "Richardson rioting in the spoils of his country, lurks about the wharves of this city, seeking an opportunity to distress the trade of Philadelphia and enslave America." Like any proper notice for an outlaw, it included a full description: "The above Richardson appears to be a man of 46 years of age is about five feet four or five inches high, pretty thick and broad across the shoulders, has a very ill countenance and down look, pits-burnt cut wig, and a blue surtout coat with metal buttons."[72]

No court reporter recorded Richardson's trial. Yet literary and artistic representations, including theater, prints, and poetry, meant that imagined proceedings were etched into popular memory. Street ritual and vernacular accounts forged a seamless representation. More than a year after the riot in front of Richardson's house, Paul Revere constructed a transparent painting, not of the scene itself, but of Snider's ghost in the same pose as when he was wounded. A couplet underneath read: Snider's "pale ghost fresh bleeding stands/And vengeance for his death demands." In some ways, the specter of the case was more important than either Richardson or Snider themselves. "Young Seider's [Snider's] blood from th' op'ning ground cries justice, justice – hear thee sound." The infamous murderer Richardson was released, went a demand for remembrance published in 1772, "tell this in Britain, publish it in Ireland, may America remember it forever."

These small pieces echoed any number of Biblical commonplaces. In them lies a code that can be deciphered when juxtaposed to their Biblical source. "Justice, justice," any literate colonial would know, referred to the passage in Deuteronomy that attacks bribing judges, a probable reference to the judicial salary dispute. The Biblical quote "justice, justice pursue" predicates living in the land of Israel upon following basic principles of justice. What this evokes, of course, is a Puritan historical

---

[71] *The Life and Humble Confession of Richardson, the Informer* [Broadside, 1770].
[72] *Humble Confession* [Broadside, 1770], *Boston Gazette*, November 1, 1773.

conceit: Massachusetts settlers are Israelites, America the promised land. "Tell this in Britain, publish it in Ireland" must be read as a text against David's eulogy of Saul and Jonathan, who were murdered by the Philistines. David demanded "Tell it not in Gath. Do not proclaim it in the streets of Ashkelon." Here the English take the pose of the enemies of Israel, the Philistines. But in this case, unlike the Biblical passage, the anonymous colonial polemicist wants the English/Philistines to admit their own crimes.

Finally, the most potent recurring Biblical trope was that of Cain and Abel. Cain and Abel were brothers, Richardson and Snider both countrymen. Snider's blood, like Abel's cries from the opening ground. The blood of Snider "crieth out for vengeance like the blood of righteous Abel." Richardson borrows Cain's visage, "a very ill countenance and down look." As with Cain, Richardson was not executed. Instead, he was marked as he wandered the earth in exile. "I believe," wrote a colonial, Richardson is "suffering Cain's punishment."[73]

Richardson and Ames were not the only ones tried on the streets of Boston. Having pardoned a murderer and chosen to execute a petty thief, the court was judged as well. Massachusetts Superior Court had been unpopular for much of the last decade. In 1761–1762, the court sanctioned writs of assistance, broadly defined search warrants employed by customs officers. It further alienated the population by supporting the Stamp Act and adjourning the court when faced with popular pressure. The people of Boston, Hutchinson wrote in 1765, "will oblige all judges to observe their orders or quit their places."[74] Alarmed by a court that actively buttressed English authority, the legislature curbed judicial salaries. Toward the end of the 1760s, the Crown adopted a strategy of trying to shift influence over the judiciary from the legislature to the executive. Judicial salaries were now paid by the royal authorities, and appointments to the bench were based largely upon political considerations. At the beginning of 1772, the resignation of two justices, John Cushing and Benjamin Lynde, created vacancies on the Superior Court. Peter Oliver was named chief justice, and Nathanial Ropes became an associate justice.

Both Oliver and Ropes were considered loyal supporters of the royal government. Oliver's brother, Andrew, was a stamp distributor. The same

[73] *Massachusetts Spy*, March 7, 1771 and March 12, 1772; *Virginia Gazette*, April 5, 1770; *Boston Gazette*, November 1, 1773; *Massachusetts Spy*, January 30, 1772.
[74] Hutchinson, 26 Massachusetts Archives, December 27, 1765.

year as his appointment to the court, Oliver participated in the unpopular investigation into the destruction of the *Gaspee*, a navy schooner assigned to stem smuggling in Narragansett Bay. Demonstrating his firm commitment to London, Ropes lost his council seat in 1769. Yet it was the issue of the judges' salaries that led to massive agitation against the Superior Court. Bostonians accused justices of being blinded by bribery and beholden to the Crown. "Base and mercenary wretches," wrote one newspaper, "fill the bench of justice, who will throw off all the restraint of law and give judgement according to the direction of their masters."[75]

As early as 1770, a placard was posted on the door of the town hall attacking the justices of the Superior Court. During the summer of 1773, barely a few months before Ames was hanged for burglary, the Massachusetts House of Assembly demanded that judges refuse the Crown grant or face impeachment. Boston mobs intimidated justices into signing a renunciation. Only Peter Oliver defied these threats. Impeachment proceedings were initiated, and there was a movement to boycott jury duty on a court that many considered no longer legitimate. Fearing that he might be attacked, Oliver absented himself from the bench. Without Oliver, the court failed to fulfill its duties.[76]

Such popular disaffection with the judiciary, then, must be seen as the context for the debate over the contrasting fates of Richardson and Ames. The presiding judge for both trials was Peter Oliver. Not surprisingly, Bostonians echoed the tone of the judicial salary dispute and argued that the outcome of Richardson's trial was determined by politics. "Political motives," it was suggested, "influenced a delay in judgement and execution of this criminal." Quincy warned that if "political views" should ever shape the decisions of judges, "who have the lives, liberty and property of us all in their power, society is worse than a state of nature."

---

[75] *Boston Gazette*, August 31, 1772.

[76] *Massachusetts Spy*, December 13–17, 1770; *Boston Evening-Post*, July 5, 1773; House of Representatives Impeachment of Peter Oliver, February 12, 1774, Miscellaneous Bound Manuscripts 1765–1776, Massachusetts Historical Society; "Refusal of Certain Gentlemen to Serve as Grand Jurors," (August 30, 1774) in Hezekiah Niles, *Principles and Acts of the American Revolution* (Baltimore, 1822), p. 319; Smith, *The Writs of Assistance Case*, pp. 202–230; Barbara Aronstein Black, "Massachusetts and the Judges: Judicial Independence in Perspective," *Law and History Review* 3 (1985): 101–162; John D. Cushing, "The Judiciary and Public Opinion in Revolutionary Massachusetts," in *Law and Authority in Colonial America*, ed. George A. Billings (Barre, Mass.: Barre Publishers, 1965), pp. 168–186; Peter Edmund Russell, "His Majesty's Judges: The Superior Court of Massachusetts, 1750–1774," (Ph.D. diss., University of Michigan, 1980), pp. 95–149.

Mercy Otis Warren's satiric drama on the Hutchinson administration, *The Adulateur*, again raised the notion of political corruption as the basis for any pending pardon of Richardson: "You know who fills that sacred bench ... mere creatures of the tyrant [Hutchinson]. Depend upon it, they'll vilely wrest the law, and save the villain [Richardson] – yes depend upon it." The term "wrest" clearly alludes both to its meaning as altering interpretation and to the image of seizing the law – away from the people? – and taking possession of it by force. "Should he be brought before that bribed tribunal, they'll plead his case, and save the murderer's life." Following the classic literary inversion of the justice as criminal, Warren adds "I've seen such crimes by ermined wretches as would have shock'd a century."[77]

More than any other legal proceedings, criminal justice should be the least affected by politics. The protection of citizens from criminals, after all, was considered by eighteenth-century legal theorists as fundamental for every society. Yet according to contemporaries, precisely because Richardson's case was criminal, it established the right of the people to judge the legal system. "When a breach of criminal law is made, it is the public who are injured by the infraction ... shall the injured not call for redress?" Criminal law was public law. By pardoning a murderer, the court sanctioned the greatest of felonies. The Superior Court, declared a town meeting at Sandwich, has been "rendered dependent on those who rob and murder us." Law would lose its legitimacy if people "perceive the destruction of their fellow citizens is treated as a slight thing and blood, innocent blood, crimsoning their city."[78]

As with his trial, Richardson's confinement and pardon prompted legal issues that overflowed from the courtroom to the popular press. Was it right, for example, that Richardson should be held in prison so long without being either executed or released as innocent? What law justified this breach of habeas corpus? Many Bostonians, of course, wanted Richardson hanged, not freed. But Richardson's extended confinement, a legal netherworld, provoked questions about the role of prisons. Prior to the rise of penitentiaries in the 1780s, their use as an instrument of punishment remained controversial. One newspaper article adopted the traditional stance toward prisons as simply way stations and chided the

---

[77] *Boston Gazette*, February 10, 1772; Warren, *Adulateur*, pp. 11–13 and 30.
[78] Sandwich, Massachusetts, town meeting, March 17, 1773, reported in the *Massachusetts Spy*, March 18, 1773; *Boston Gazette*, February 10, 1772; *Massachusetts Spy*, March 5, 1772.

criminal justice system for letting Richardson languish in jail: "A jail was never intended for punishment, but only to hold the debtor till he fulfilled his voluntary contracts; the suspected till his offence could be conveniently ascertained; and the convicted till speedy justice could be executed." The administration of justice, it warned, retains its integrity by being swift and without hesitation. Imprisoning Richardson only to await a pardon shows a "secret cunning," and such conduct in justices is "base, odious, and execrable."[79]

"Ebenezer Richardson remains alive," complained one Bostonian, "to insult and defy the avengers of blood to obtain of him the least satisfactions. And this unaccountable political phenomenon is solved only by the extension of the ancient notion of clergy."[80] The New England colonies had long been troubled by the idea of benefit of clergy. It seemed obscure, an arbitrary form of pardon, and overly Catholic. Benefit of clergy traced its origins from the right of clerics to the separate jurisdiction of ecclesiastical courts. As the use of separate courts shifted to the practice of trying clergymen in the same court as laymen, clerics were provided with a special privilege, benefit of clergy, which protected them from capital punishment. The classic test for identifying a cleric was the ability to read. By the fourteenth century, benefit of clergy was extended to anyone demonstrating minimal literacy. Ultimately, it came to be used as a general form of pardon that provided a way for courts to temper the many capital statutes found in English criminal codes. "An unreasonable exemption of popish ecclesiastics," Blackstone claimed, was gradually transformed "into a merciful mitigation of the general law with respect to capital punishment."[81]

Patriot lawyers increasingly considered benefit of clergy a remnant of canon and feudal law. England imposed the doctrine in Massachusetts in 1686 during the much-hated anglicizing governorship of Edmund Andros. After the American Revolution, Massachusetts law would quickly move to dismantle benefit of clergy as, in the words of the 1785 repealing act, "originally founded in superstition and injustice."[82] A verse broadside,

---

[79] *Boston Gazette*, February 10, 1772.

[80] *Boston Gazette*, April 1, 1771.

[81] Blackstone, *Commentaries*, IV: 358–364; Beattie, *Crime and the Courts*, pp. 141–148; George W. Dalzell, *Benefit of Clergy in America and Related Matters* (Winston-Salem: John F. Blair, 1955), pp. 169–181; Arthur Lyon Cross, "Benefit of Clergy in American Criminal Law," *Massachusetts Historical Society Proceedings* 61 (1928): 154–181.

[82] "An Act Taking Away the Benefit of Clergy," March 11, 1785; "*The General Laws of Massachusetts from the Adoption of the Constitution to February 1822*," 2 vols. Boston: Wells & Lilly, 1823, 1: 183–184.

punning on written lines and Justice Ropes, mocked Richardson's pardon by benefit of clergy: "Oh! Wretched man! The monster of the times/You were not hung by 'reason of old lines'/Old lines thrown by/'twas then we were in hopes/That you would soon be hung with new made ropes."

In contrast, Ames did not have recourse to benefit of clergy. Just a few years before Ames was convicted, in 1770, a new Massachusetts statute, which was enacted in the midst of a crime wave to replace a more mild 1715 law, removed burglary as a clergyable offence. Bostonians must have marveled that a murderer could be pardoned with benefit of clergy while such a loophole was recently closed to a burglar like Ames.[83]

There was yet another contradiction between the fates of Richardson and Ames that would have troubled Bostonians. According to the English Murder Act of 1752, murderers, not any other felons, would suffer dissection "to add some further terror and peculiar mark of infamy ... to the punishment of death." The act was, in fact, intended to distinguish lesser capital crimes such as burglary from murder. No statutory basis yet existed for dissection as a form of punishment in the colonies – that innovation would come with a flurry of laws in the late 1780s and early 1790s, but colonial Americans were well aware of its punitive role. In the streets of Boston, Richardson was judged guilty of murder. He nevertheless escaped not simply the gallows, but the surgeons as well. Yet Ames, though simply convicted of housebreaking, was threatened by dissection.

Eighteenth-century Anglo-Americans feared the surgeons. Not just at London's Tyburn, where the common people frequently rioted to retrieve the bodies of hanged criminals, but also in America dissection was seen as a worse fate than the gallows. During a 1771 riot at Worcester, an angry crowd rescued the corpse of a hanged felon from dissection. Ames, too, appeared to share that fear. Probably one reason for the special relationship formed between Ames and the minister who cared for him as a condemned prisoner, Reverend Samuel Stillman, was that Ames hoped Stillman would protect him from the surgeons.

Three parties contended for Ames's body after the execution: established doctors, including James Lloyd and John Clarke, under the direction

---

[83] *On the Enlargement of Ebenezer Richardson Convicted of Murder* [Broadside, 1772]; "An Act for Preventing and Punishing Burglary, and for repealing of an act entitled, An Act Against Burglary," 10 Geo. III (1770) and 1 Geo. I (1715) in *Charter and General Laws*, pp. 406 and 668–669; *Boston Gazette*, July 9, 1770; and *Massachusetts Spy*, 21 October 1771. "Old lines" refers to the literacy test as the basis for granhing benefit of clergy. The reference to "new made ropes" is a pun on Justice Nathaniel Ropes, who was recently appointed to the Superior Court.

of Dr. John Jefferies; a coterie of young medical students at Harvard; and a rescue party employed by Stillman. Hutchinson, in fact, was ready to order the corpse handed over to Jefferies when Stillman intervened. Much to the disappointment of the competing anatomists, Stillman secretly buried Ames at Dorcester Point. Nevertheless, Bostonians must have been struck by the irony of how different were the fates of Richardson and Ames. Hutchinson was willing to sanction Ames's dismemberment.[84]

What lessons, then, do we learn from these two remarkable cases? It seems clear that the street, as much as the courtroom, was the locus of legal discourse. The debate over the justice of Richardson's pardon and Ames's hanging could be found in newspapers, political broadsides, and such productions of vernacular legal culture as execution sermons, dying speeches, and the mock executions of effigies. Popular culture mediated between politics and official law. Eighteenth-century Bostonians demonstrated their ability to grasp complex legal doctrine: criminal intent, distinctions between murder and manslaughter, the role of juries in judging fact and law, the weighing of appropriate punishment for theft, and the place of incarceration or dissection as an instrument of punishment.

More strikingly, the transformation of these cases shows how adept colonial radicals were at manipulating legal symbols. Marxist historians have claimed that rebellion is antinomian, a rejection of the rule of laws. But just the opposite occurred in Revolutionary Boston. The common people made themselves part of legal discourse. Precisely because legal process, and especially criminal law, was invested with a newfound political meaning, Americans would be able to construct a different understanding of punishment in the late 1770s and 1780s.

Nothing better illustrates the popular appropriation of punishment in these cases than two small advertisements appearing in colonial papers. Barely a few lines each, these notices appear insignificant. But they demonstrate how radically the topography of justice had shifted. Levi Ames's confessions, one advertisement read, are "available in the shop across from the courthouse." Separated only by a street, the printing press – with

---

[84] "An Act for the Better Preventing the Horrid Crime of Murder" (25 Geo. II, c. 37, 1752); Peter Linebaugh, "The Tyburn Riot Against the Surgeons," in *Albion's Fatal Tree: Crime and Society in Eighteenth-Century England*, ed. Douglas Hay (New York: Pantheon Press, 1975), pp. 65–118; Steven Wilf, "Anatomy and Punishment in Late Eighteenth-Century New York," *Journal of Social History* 22 (1989): 507–530; Albert Mathews, "Early Autopsies and Anatomical Lectures," *Publications of the Colonial Society of Massachusetts, Transactions* (1916–1917): 273–290.

its vernacular execution narratives – and the courthouse marked alternative seats of legal authority. Similarly, a mock advertisement identified Richardson as a wanted man. It called on Philadelphians to "produce him tarred and feathered at the coffee house, there to expiate his sins against his country by a public recantation." This notice embodied what must be understood as a demand for Richardson's retrial. But there were significant differences. The purpose of the new trial would be retribution. Punishment would proceed his appearance, and Richardson would not be allowed to escape unchastised. This time the public confession would be crafted by Richardson himself, not fabricated as a piece of popular culture. Imagining justice had created a new legal public sphere for judging, where the coffee house replaced the courthouse as the place of law.[85]

[85] *Boston Gazette*, October 25, 1770 and November 1, 1773.

2

"The Language of Law Is a Vulgar Tongue"

It would have been frightening to meet Isaac Frasier. At least that was the impression from the wanted notice printed after he broke out of a New Haven jail in the summer of 1768. He was of middling stature with black hair and a face pitted from smallpox. Dressed in a brown coat, check shirt, and a pair of homespun breeches, Frasier's appearance showed signs of wear from a life on the run.[1] Although only twenty-eight years old, his front teeth were already missing. What really made Frasier look so terrifying, however, were the markings imposed by others: both ears cropped and the branding two times on his forehead with the letter "B." If, as Alexis de Toqueville claimed, "the language of law is a vulgar tongue," it was even more common when engraved upon the body.[2]

These markings were part of an official iconography that made felons the bearer of their own criminal record. In Frasier's case, they were inflicted after being caught for a series of crimes throughout Connecticut from breaking into stores, his specialty, to stealing linen. He was finally tried in New Haven and punished with whipping and the mutilated ears of a petty criminal. The "B" on his forehead stood for burglary. The next year, Connecticut would consider expanding its system of mnemonic tattoos by adding an "H" for horse stealing and, two years later, a "C" for counterfeiting. Both ears mutilated meant two convictions. Felons had little control over such signs other than to hide them.

---

[1] "The language of law is ... in some measure a vulgar tongue," Alexis de Toqueville, *Democracy in America*, eds. Francis Bowen and Henry Reeve, 2 vols. (Cambridge: Sever and Francis, 1862), 1: 357–358.
[2] *The Connecticut Journal and New-Haven Post Boy*, July 27, 1768, August 5, 1768, and August 12, 1768.

Executed in 1773, John Wall Lovely kept his cropped ears hidden beneath a cap. A spectator at the hanging "had the curiosity to take off his cap and saw ... that he was cropped." The scars discovered on the back of a felon whipped for theft in 1762 conveyed that this particular stranger had a history of recidivism. At a time when records were scanty and techniques of identification rudimentary, it was convenient to transform the body into a legal record. Frasier's visage was a narrative of sorts. It told of his involvement with the colonial criminal justice system.[3]

Such a symbolic narrative was very much from the point of view of the legal system itself. Colonial law transformed the body into the locus of punishment and its recorded memory. But what about crimes where the guilty felon did not suffer retribution? Perhaps the felon never encountered the legal system, was found not guilty, or was simply warned out of town? Frasier's bodily markings were many fewer than his crimes. More significantly, such markings failed to relate other details of the criminal biography. Why, for example, did Frasier turn to crime? What was his upbringing like? Did he have accomplices, and what other felonies were simply never discovered? Against the official narrative etched into his flesh, another, more inward, extraofficial one would have to be written that emerged from Frasier's own memory. It was a first-person narrative quite simply because autobiography made the narrative more compelling – both as evidence and as a story.

This chapter is about how through such storytelling offenders created narrative strategies contradicting official legal determinations and, ultimately, how the realm of popular politics appropriated vernacular legal culture for its own purposes. The criminal process has often been seen as a boundary-tending device. But crucial to both individual offender and political uses of legal storytelling, however, is the idea that the law's

---

[3] Connecticut Archives, First Series, Connecticut State Library (Hartford), 5:412 and 3:156 and 158; *Massachusetts Gazette*, April 22, 1773; *Virginia Gazette*, April 29, 1773; *Boston Gazette and Country Journal*, March 15, 1762. For criminal procedure in Connecticut, see *The Superior Court Diary of Samuel Johnson 1772–1773*, ed. John T. Farrell (Washington: American Historical Association, 1942), pp. xi–lxv. Other states had similar systems. See, for example, Vermont's "An Act for the Punishment of Diverse Capital and Other Felonies" (1787) where those found guilty of manslaughter would be branded with the letter "M." Anyone with such a mark would be denied the right of serving as a witness in court. *Revised Laws of the State of Vermont* (Windsor: Hough and Spooner, 1784). A number of works of literary criticism have explored the role of the body as text: Elaine Scarry, *The Body in Pain: The Making and Unmaking of the World* (Oxford: Oxford University Press, 1985); Francis Bacon, *The Tremulous Private Body: Essays on Subjection* (London: Methuen, 1984); and Peter Brooks, *Body Work: Objects of Desire in Modern Narrative* (Cambridge: Harvard University Press, 1993).

boundaries might ultimately be redrawn to encompass texts and contexts beyond the instant cases.

INTERPRETATIONS OF VERNACULAR LEGAL CULTURE

Narratives composed by condemned criminals were part of what might be called vernacular legal culture. Autobiographical execution narratives followed a set pattern. They began with early upbringing and parentage, detailing the temptations of petty thievery as a child, and often ended with the psychological changes undergone as the date of execution drew closer. Rachel Wall, executed in 1789 for highway robbery, describes the genre succinctly: "Without doubt the ever-curious public ... will be anxious to know every particular circumstance of the life and character of a person in my unhappy situation, but in particular those relative to my birth and parentage." The unifying thread of the narrative was the question of character. How can we explain the emergence of a criminal persona? How could someone begin life as an innocent child and end up swinging on the gallows? Execution narratives and a related vernacular literature did not emerge from official courtroom sources, like court reporting or the judge's addresses to grand juries, but from an extraofficial tradition of relating the crimes and punishment of felons to the public at large.[4] Included among the ephemera of vernacular legal culture were various popular literary genres, such as hanging ballads, last words and dying confessions, and the biographical form of execution narratives, as well as mock executions and rough music – shaming by communities of those who violate their norms, and iconographic representations of retribution.

Such a variety of forms suggests three important points. First, it underscores the dialogic character of vernacular legal culture. Official legal codes spoke in authoritative, often univocal, fashion. While rules crafted by legislative and judicial elites depended upon sanctions, vernacular legal culture sometimes had to rely upon persuasion as much as compulsion and therefore employed a range of storytelling and ritual strategies. One fragment of vernacular legal culture, secondly, often addresses another. The hanging ballad might respond to an autobiographical execution narrative, which might speak to an execution sermon as well. But ultimately, all these forms "speak" to the public. This creates a web of intertextuality. Although at the core of this web often lies official legal culture, the

[4] *Life, Last Words, and Dying Confession of Rachel Wall* [Broadside, 1789]. On Rachel Wall, see Alan Rogers, *Murder and the Death Penalty in Massachusetts* (Boston: University of Massachusetts Press, 2008), pp. 5–52.

understanding of its meaning varies. What must be stressed, then, is that any piece of vernacular legal culture needs to be deciphered in relation to other pieces of legal culture, both official and vernacular.

Vernacular legal culture, thirdly, shifted the perceived definition of law from nomos – a body of rules and regulations – to narrative. Law becomes a social fact embedded in a context of racial and economic distinctions, local settings, and individual lives. By emphasizing the experiential rather than the normative, these narratives create their own terms for choosing and weighing evidence. Facts are considered accurate not because they meet some kind of legal evidentiary standard, but because they are convincing within social contexts. No other eighteenth-century documents, it will be suggested, better demonstrate the literary strategies of the common people. More importantly, no other text empowers this storytelling capacity, the molding, fabricating, and privileging of narrative like vernacular legal culture.[5]

Narrative is a form of social transaction: It requires both authorship and readership, construction and deconstruction. Not surprisingly, then, vernacular legal culture almost by definition had political consequences. Official law was a bounded canon whose watchword for construction was exclusion. It might be made and unmade only by legislators and judges. Vernacular legal culture, on the other hand, was open to participation by a broad range of society. This openness created a unique accessible forum for discourse about legal process – a forum that, as will be seen at the end of the chapter, was available as a vehicle for popular political rhetoric as well.[6]

Calling these cultural fragments vernacular rather than another term highlights the importance of the speech act itself rather than authorship. The classic distinction between elite and popular culture, such as E. P. Thompson's rarified categories of patrician and plebe, suggests two separate spheres of cultural production or, at the very least, consumption predicated upon class. But vernacular legal culture bridged such divisions. It was produced and consumed by a variety of classes, dependent upon both oral and print cultural conventions. An execution narrative,

---

[5] Official legal culture provides for forms akin in settings where there is either more informal dispute resolution, as described by Lawrence Rosen, or where there is broad discretion in post-conviction pardoning. Lawrence Rosen, *Law as Culture: An Invitation* (Princeton: Princeton University Press, 2008); Natalie Zemon Davis, *Fiction in the Archives: Pardon Tales and Their Tellers in Sixteenth-Century France* (Stanford: Stanford University Press, 1990).

[6] Barbara Herrnstein-Smith, "Narrative Versions, Narrative Theories," *Critical Inquiry* 7 (Autumn 1980): 213–236.

as shown in the next chapter, might be written by both an ex-slave and a future Yale law professor working in partnership, and read by a readership every bit as diverse. What makes vernacular legal culture vernacular or perhaps even "popular" is not its association with social position but its distinct production and consumption outside of the courtroom.[7]

Vernacular legal cultural artifacts are oral expressions, iconography, or texts about the legal process constructed through language other than that of official law, and meant for the consumption of the public at large. According to this definition, then, the execution sermon would be vernacular legal culture, though not, of course, vernacular religious culture, since these sermons were crafted by Protestant ministers acting within their official capacity. Although in London a chaplain was appointed to minister to condemned felons, this task fell upon local ministers in the colonies. As a result, the colonial execution sermon was more notably directed to the immediate social context. The execution sermon genre emerged remarkably early, with the oldest American example printed in 1674, the first year of publishing at Boston. Not surprisingly, Cotton Mather was a prolific contributor. Establishing the execution sermon as an independent literary genre, Puritan ministers crafted a language of Protestant penitence that strongly influenced vernacular legal discourse. Nevertheless, the colonial execution sermon as a vehicle for religious moralism was later adopted by Anglicans and Methodists as well. Some of the most prominent ministers in America delivered execution sermons, including Nathan Strong and Richard Dana. Listeners or readers of printed sermons were drawn from a broad cross-section of the population.

---

[7] The literature on popular culture is vast. Neither of the two classic works for English and French historians, Peter Burke, *Popular Culture in Early Modern Europe* (New York: New York University Press, 1978) and Robert Muchembled, *Culture Populaire et Culture des Elites dans La France Moderne* (Paris: Flammarion, 1978), provide an adequate definition or theoretical framework. Stuart Clark, "French Historians and Early Modern Popular Culture," *Past and Present* 100 (1983): 62–99; Suzanne Desan, "Crowds, Community, and Ritual in the Work of E. P. Thompson and Natalie Zemon Davis," in *The New Cultural History*, ed. Lynn Hunt (Berkeley: University of California Press, 1989), pp. 47–72; E. P. Thompson, "Patrician Society, Plebeian Culture," *Journal of Social History* 7 (1974): 382–405. Rather than seeing print and oral culture as oppositional, I would argue that vernacular legal culture embraced oral traditions of tales in a print form. The role of ballads, which might well have been read aloud, and the fact that dying speeches are the print embodiment of oral performative rhetoric, demonstrates the intermeshing of these two forms of cultural production. Print culture probably served to sustain earlier oral narrative conventions. See Natalie Zemon Davis, "Printing and the People," *Society and Culture in Early Modern France* (Stanford: Stanford University Press, 1975), pp. 189–226 and Po Chia-Hsia, *The Myth of Ritual Murder* (New Haven: Yale University Press, 1988) on the ways print culture can be appropriated.

Execution sermons generally began with a proof text. "Deliver me from blood guiltiness, O God!," quoted from David's plea after the death of Uriah, was the choice for the last sermon to an African American found guilty of murder. One of Samuel Stillman's sermons for Levi Ames in 1773 began with the passage "a foolish son is a grief to his father."[8] The life of the felon was intended to illustrate a biblical text, which in turn, illustrated some greater theological truth. But from the point of view of listeners intrigued by a felon's biography, the life may have been the core narrative and the biblical proof text the illustration. These representations of criminal life nevertheless appropriated the moral religious language of Protestant penitence and, at times, even borrowed legal language.

For the most part, however, the centrality of selfhood in shaping its literary style was much more akin to contemporary fiction. After the first third of the eighteenth century, autobiographical and biographical narratives replaced execution sermons as the leading form of vernacular legal discourse. It seems likely that this genre was transmitted in part by the waves of felons transported to the colonies. The number of convicts rapidly increased in the 1730s just as the American execution narrative came into its own. What this indicates is a shift from a vernacular voice dominated by legal and nonlegal elites to an increasingly prominent role for the felon himself. By the end of the eighteenth century, I will show, increasingly autonomous felons will leave a firm imprint of authorial control upon the production of their biographies.[9]

[8] Byles Mather, *The Prayer and Plea of David, to Be Delivered from Blood-Guiltiness ... Before the Execution of a Young Negro Servant for Poisoning an Infant* (Boston: Samuel Kneeland, 1751); Samuel Stillman, *Two Sermons ... Delivered Before the Execution of Levi Ames* (Boston: John Kneeland, 1773).

[9] A. Roger Ekirch, *Bound for America: The Transportation of British Convicts to the Colonies 1718–1775* (Oxford: Oxford University Press, 1987), pp. 70–96. Daniel A. Cohen, *Pillars of Salt, Monuments of Grace: New England Crime Literature and the Origins of American Popular Culture 1674–1860* (Oxford: Oxford University Press, 1993), pp. 13–14; Marmaduke Johnson, *The Cry of Sodom Enquired Into* (Cambridge, 1674). On execution sermons, see Ronald A. Bosco, "Lectures at the Pillory: The Early American Execution Sermon," *American Quarterly* 30 (1978): 156–176 and Wayne C. Minnick, "The New England Execution Sermon, 1639–1800," *Speech Monographs* 35 (1968): 77–89. The best work on New England sermon traditions is Harry S. Stout, *The New England Soul: Preaching and Religious Culture in Colonial New England* (Oxford: Oxford University Press, 1986). On execution narratives, Lawrence W. Towner, "True Confessions and Dying Warnings in Colonial New England," in *Sibley's Heir: A Volume in Memory of Clifford Kenyon Shipton* (Boston: Colonial Society of Massachusetts, 1982), pp. 523–540. The question of transmission in both colonial history as a whole and colonial legal history has focused upon the diffusion of regional English legal norms to distinct parts of the colonies. Little work, however, has been done upon the transmission of class- and gender-defined legal traditions. A notable exception is Alfred

Little is known about the authorship of vernacular legal genres other than the execution sermon. Hanging ballads may have been scribbled by the colonial equivalent of Grub Street writers. Produced as a broadside on a single sheet, these verses were most likely distributed at the execution itself. Johnson Green, hanged for burglary in 1786, asked another prisoner at Worcester to write a poem to append to his confession.[10] Execution narratives written as first-person autobiographies pose an even greater problem of authorship. For the few narratives that can be clearly attributed, authors include both well-educated local elites and petty criminals. The use of a first-person narrator, of course, bolstered claims for authenticity. Samuel Stoddard's 1762 narrative was said to be written in his own hand, whereas others reproduced the signature marks of felons. John Ryer's narrative, the printer claimed, "can be proved to have dropped from his own lips." Nevertheless, ministers and jailers appear to have exerted a great deal of influence upon the production of narratives. Illiterate, Charles O'Donnell related his tale to a minister.[11]

If claims to be popular literature cannot be based upon authorship, might the consumption of execution narratives be considered popular? But here, again, difficulties arise. From the available evidence it seems that all levels of society consumed execution narratives. Narratives were advertised in newspapers, meant largely for more established individuals,

Young's far-ranging essay, "English Plebeian Culture and Eighteenth-Century American Radicalism," in *The Origins of Anglo-American Radicalism*, eds. Margaret and James Jacobs (London: Allen and Unwin, 1989), pp. 185–212. For English vernacular legal culture, see J. A. Sharpe, "'Last Dying Speeches': Religion, Ideology and Public Execution in Seventeenth-Century England," *Past and Present* 107 (1985): 144–167; Peter Linebaugh, "The Ordinary of Newgate and His *Account*," in *Crime in England 1550–1800*, ed. J. S. Cockburn, pp. 246–269; Peter Linebaugh, *The London Hanged: Crime and Civil Society in the Eighteenth Century* (Cambridge: Cambridge University Press), pp. 7–41; Lincoln B. Faller, *Turned to Account: The Forms and Functions of Criminal Biography in Late Seventeenth and Early Eighteenth-Century England* (Cambridge: Cambridge University Press, 1987); Randall McGowen, "'He Beareth Not the Sword in Vain': Religion and the Criminal Law in Eighteenth-Century England," *Eighteenth-Century Studies* 21 (1987/88): 192–211.

10 *The Life and Confession of Johnson Green* (Worcester, 1786). Hanging ballads and execution verse was a common genre in England. For American examples of these broadsides, see *A Poem, On the Execution of William Shaw* (Hartford, 1771); *A Solemn Farewell to Levi Ames* (Boston, 1773); Robert Young, *The Dying Criminal: Poem By Robert Young on His Own Execution* (Worcester, 1779).

11 *A Narrative of the Unhappy Life and Miserable End of Samuel Stoddard* (Philadelphia, 1762); *Narrative of the Life and Dying Speech of John Ryer, Who Was Executed at White-Plains, ...October 2nd, 1793* (Danbury, 1793); *The Life and Confession of Charles O'Donnell* (Lancaster, 1798).

but others were apparently hawked as inexpensive broadsides in the streets. Frasier's minister appended a summary of the autobiographical narrative to his execution sermon, uniting a rather sophisticated religious and moral discourse with rather blunt descriptions of Frasier's crimes. Since some vernacular legal forms were reflected in both print and oral culture, such as execution sermons and hanging ballads, literacy was not a prerequisite for access to extraofficial legal knowledge.

Nevertheless, literacy rates in parts of early America were high enough to suggest the possibility that execution narratives penetrated all levels of society. In New England, male literacy rates were 85 percent by 1785. Suffolk and Middlesex counties in Massachusetts approached 90 percent male literacy in 1790. Female literacy lagged significantly behind that of males. In 1790, the female literacy rate in New England hovered around 50 percent. Nevertheless, it is possible that men read broadsides or narratives and shared them with wives and daughters. Much of the information contained in such narratives must have become the common currency of gossip and thus available to both men and women who themselves did not purchase a printed text.[12] The price of a narrative was minimal. Valentine Duckett's 1774 narrative cost a mere six pence, for example, while that of Whiting Sweeting, executed at Albany in 1791 for murder, cost nine pence. Both of these were well within the reach of working-class individuals.

As a widely circulating commodity like any other, printed narratives made knowledge of the workings of the legal process broadly available. But linking such knowledge to the marketplace may have shaped the

---

[12] Kenneth A. Lockridge, *Literacy in Colonial New England: An Enquiry into the Social Context of Literacy in the Early Modern West* (New York: W. W. Norton, 1974), pp. 3–71; Alan Tully, "Literacy Levels and Educational Development in Rural Pennsylvania, 1729–1775"; *Pennsylvania Magazine of History and Biography* (1973), pp. 301–312; E. Jennifer Monaghan, "Literacy Instruction and Gender in Colonial New England," *American Quarterly* 40 (1988): 18–41; David D. Hall, *Worlds of Wonder, Days of Judgement: Popular Religious Belief in Early New England* (New York: Alfred A. Knopf, 1989), pp. 21–70; Richard D. Brown, *Knowledge Is Power: The Diffusion of Information in Early America 1700–1865* (Oxford: Oxford University Press, 1989), pp. 110–131. For a comparative understanding of the cultural impact of print culture, see Elizabeth Eisenstein, *The Printing Press as an Agent of Change: Communications and Cultural Transformations in Early Modern Europe* (Cambridge: Cambridge University Press, 1979) and Harvey J. Graff. *The Legacies of Literacy: Continuities and Contradictions in Western Culture and Society* (Bloomington: Indiana University Press, 1987). See also Irene Quenzler Brown and Richard D. Brown, *The Hanging of Ephraim Wheeler: A Story of Rape, Incest and Justice in Early America* (Cambridge: Harvard University Press, 2003), esp. pp. 257–290, on how the print culture of crime creates an aftermath in local memory.

voyeuristic style of the narratives. Other kinds of legal knowledge in the late eighteenth century were made public as statutory obligations. Connecticut, for example, mandated by law that town constables should read aloud the statutes passed in the latest legislative assembly. Each new law was also to be written in a designated book by each town. But reading bills aloud was regulated by the state, while the marketplace – influenced by individual choices, curiosity, and a desire for a compelling tale – shaped the construction of execution narratives.[13]

The shopworn dichotomy of elite and popular, then, does not seem suitable for vernacular legal culture. Instead, the linguistic paradigm may be more apt: Such texts were vernacular in precisely the way that English as a vernacular language transformed the Anglo-American legal process. Latin was, of course, the traditional stem language of English law. Popular agitation during the English Civil War led to a 1650 act that required legal procedures to be in English. Nevertheless, English language legal discourse, often full of phrases derived from Latin, remained quite opaque to the average reader. Even a work like *Conductor Generalis*, meant to make legal procedure accessible to lay readership, was forced to include a glossary of legal terms. Touching all levels of society, legal process was inclusive in its reach. Anyone as debtor or creditor, victim or felon, might find him- or herself in court. But the language of law was exclusive: deferential toward authority, enigmatic for the uninitiated, and distinguished by a formalist syntax and vocabulary that required either a sophisticated education or a hired professional to decode it.[14]

During the eighteenth century, a new political language emerged in the press and writings of radical publicists like Tom Paine. It made politics accessible in a way that earlier opposition writings did not. A similar kind of process was taking place at the same time with legal texts. The rise of vernacular legal culture, like the previous shift from Latin to English, was a watershed in the making of a political challenge toward legal conventions. Through both the widespread dissemination of criminal tales and

---

[13] *Connecticut Courant*, November 7, 1791; *Acts and Laws of His Majesty's Colony of Connecticut in New England* (New London, 1715), 106; Cornelia Hughes Dayton, *Women Before the Bar: Gender, Law, and Society in Connecticut, 1639–1789* (Chapel Hill: University of North Carolina Press, 1995), pp. 11–14.

[14] Donald Veall, *The Popular Movement for Law Reform, 1640–1660* (Oxford: Oxford University Press, 1970), pp. 190–193. On the relationship between language, learning, and class in the colonies, see Rhys Isaac, "Books and the Social Authority of Learning: The Case of Mid-Eighteenth-Century Virginia," in William L. Joyce, David Hall, et al. *Printing and Society in Early America* (Worcester: American Antiquarian Society, 1983), pp. 228–249.

their transparent language, legal process was open in a way that it had never been previously. The implications were radical. Readers could now judge the quality of evidence, the character of the felon and nature of the crime, and indeed the very fairness of the criminal justice system itself. Most scholars have seen execution narratives as a means of "spreading official ideas about crime and punishment, and the whole nature of authority and disorder, down to the lower orders." But were these official claims to authority truly communicated? Or were the common people themselves, both the felons who contributed to their authorship and readers, able to transform this literature to reflect their own notions about justice? As will be shown, the hegemony of elites has been much exaggerated. Vernacular legal culture may have arisen as an instrument of order or even as a vulgar bibliothéque bleu meant to titillate and amuse a curious public. But it increasingly evolved into a robust cultural vehicle for challenging official law.[15]

This chapter traces how late-eighteenth-century Americans reinscribed criminal narratives with personal and political meaning. Criminal narratives were appropriated in two ways. They were employed strategically

---

[15] Sharpe, "Last Dying Speeches," p. 162. Louis Masur, J. A. Sharpe, Daniel Cohen, and David Rothman have all stressed the significance of execution literature for imposing civil authority. Louis P. Masur, *Rites of Execution: Capital Punishment and the Transformation of American Culture, 1776–1865* (Princeton: Princeton University Press, 1989), pp. 25–49 and David J. Rothman, *The Discovery of the Asylum: Social Order and Disorder in the New Republic* (Boston: Little, Brown and Company, 1971), pp. 16–18. Addressing the question of social control, Cohen ("A Fellowship of Thieves: Property Criminals in Eighteenth-Century Massachusetts, *Journal of Social History* [1988]: 65–92), contests David Flaherty's contention that provincial Massachusetts successfully contained criminal activity. But, of course, the use of execution narratives as a source for statistical information about criminal activity misses the richness of the source. What is intriguing about the narratives are the literary strategies, compelling self-inventions, and rare glimpse into popular culture that they provide. The approach in this chapter is much closer to that of Natalie Zemon Davis, *Fiction in the Archives: Pardon Tales and Their Tellers in Sixteenth-Century France* (Stanford: Stanford University Press, 1987). My understanding of the political importance of transparent language has been much influenced by Olivia Smith, *The Politics of Language, 1791–1819* (Oxford: Oxford University Press, 1984). The significance of language in the cultural construction of Revolutionary America is explored in literary criticism: David Simpson, *The Politics of American English 1776–1850* (Oxford: Oxford University Press, 1986); Robert Lawson-Peebles, *Landscape and Written Expression in Revolutionary America: The World Turned Upside Down* (Cambridge: Cambridge University Press, 1988); Michael P. Kramer, *Imagining Language in America: From the Revolution to the Civil War* (Princeton: Princeton University Press, 1992); and Thomas Gustafson, *Representative Words: Politics, Literature, and the American Language 1776–1865* (Cambridge: Cambridge University Press, 1993). Gustafson's work, especially, suggests the anxiety Americans felt about the plasticity of language.

by felons who crafted narratives to accommodate their own purposes. Instead of transmitting subordination to official law, they often demonstrated a notable insistence upon their own autonomy. After the American Revolution, felons increasingly dominated the production and literary strategies of the execution narratives so as to contribute even more markedly to the decline of deference. It was, secondly, appropriated as part of popular politics. American patriots drew upon the idiom of the scaffold: effigies and mock execution rituals, scaffold iconography, and their own versions of politicized execution narratives and confessions.

The period from the 1760s through the 1790s is remarkable for the large-scale proliferation of fictive criminal narratives, street rituals such as mock executions, and scaffold iconography centering on the punishment of felons. Mock executions and execution narratives were legal forms of popular culture that readily lent themselves to use for mass communication. No late-eighteenth-century cluster of symbols played a more prominent role than that of punishment. Yet the evocation of legal imagery reflected more than simply a vehicle for expression. What will be suggested is that the appropriation of traditional forms of legal culture out-of-doors – criminal narratives and effigies – invested the common people with an extraordinary law-like power to judge and to create narratives about the process of judging.

HIDDEN TRANSCRIPTS AND THE ART OF CRIMINAL SELF-INVENTION

What literary strategies were employed to embed other messages within the traditional execution narrative? Return, for a moment, to Frasier's storytelling. "I, Isaac Frasier," began his execution narrative, "being condemned to die and expecting to soon leave this world, am desirous to inform my fellow men of my execrable wickedness in housebreaking and stealing, hoping my example and untimely end may be a means to deter others from the like heinous iniquities." Frasier explains the purpose of the narrative: part confession, part means of discouraging others from following a criminal life.

Historians, too, have summarized these tales as simply an appeal to civil authority. But was that all? The narrative clearly had other purposes for both Frasier and readers. For Frasier, its functions were legal – the final act of witnessing and perhaps a species of pardon petition – and personal: a last testament and an opportunity to craft an autobiography of a self that was so often objectified by others. Beyond curiosity, for readers, the narrative provided a glimpse of both a criminal life and a judicial process that might be otherwise hidden from view. The execution narrative, then, was simultaneously private and public. It was voyeuristic precisely because it broke down these conventional spheres.

Frasier began with his birth. Prompted by imminent death, execution narratives had the advantage of a neatly defined endpoint. Why not introduce a biography with an equally obvious beginning? But this commonplace decision was also fueled by the need to show how the criminal self was shaped by influences and especially parents. Frasier's case is typical. His father died during the expedition to Louisburg when he was only five years old. "My mother, though poor ... always had the character of an honest person among her neighbors, and she took pains to inculcate a principle of honesty to me." When Frasier took some corn from a neighbor, she severely punished him. But at eight years, Frasier was bound to a shoemaker. As in so many execution narratives, this tale resurrects the classic image of the brutal master. Allotted little food, he was forced by hunger to satisfy his needs. Moreover, his master's wife taught him to steal snuff for her and countenanced other petty thefts.[16]

Following a biographical literary tradition, Frasier's tale showed movement away from his birthplace. But the shift toward distance reflected both actual and moral topography. Becoming increasingly independent, he abandoned his master for military service at the beginning of the Seven Years' War and, finally, escaping after the remainder of his indenture had been sold to a privateer. He enlisted in the military again in 1760, but deserted. By the middle of the 1760s, Frasier was wandering through Connecticut supported by makeshift jobs and small thefts. His journey took him to Newtown, New Canaan, Goshen, Sharon, Litchfield, and Fairfield. In New Canaan he formed a romantic attachment. But after being caught for stealing sheep in order to set up a household, the woman refused any further connection. As with the apprenticeship, Frasier's loss of social connections (perhaps of a nurturing figure like his mother?) led to a series of crimes.

Frasier was caught in Litchfield and Fairfield, but escaped both times. At New Haven, he again turned to robbery. This time he was whipped, his ears cropped, and the letter "B" branded on his forehead. "Branded with the letter B," went a rhyming broadside printed at the time of his

---

[16] Isaac Frasier, *A Brief Account of the Life and Abominable Thefts of the Notorious Isaac Frasier, Who was Executed at Fairfield, September 7th 1768, Penned from his Own Mouth and Signed by Him, A Few Days Before his Execution* (New Haven, 1768).

execution, "that everyone can plainly see." Now Frasier was truly an outcast. Fleeing to Massachusetts, he continued his thefts and escapes, breaking out of the Cambridge and Worcester jails. As with Levi Ames, many of his thefts were opportunistic: linen, watches, pelts, stockings, and cheese. After having made off with a gun to use for robbing furs, he found it much too heavy to carry. He then stole a horse.

Returning to Connecticut in 1768, Frasier was again imprisoned. Desperate, he set fire to the Fairfield jail and was almost burnt to death. The newly constructed jail, built at great expense, was destroyed, while the courthouse and the jailer's lodgings were badly damaged. Such behavior appears not to have helped his case. Two weeks later, Frasier was found guilty on two counts, burglary and arson, and sentenced to death. Frasier was remarkable for his escapes. As has been shown, the theme of flight in popular culture was highly evocative. It represented the ability to slip away from confining social structures such as rigid patronage networks or labor dependency. Frasier was a master of escape, a less celebrated American version of Britain's Jack Sheppard. He had already broken out of at least four Connecticut and Massachusetts jails. Confirming his reputation as an escape artist, he would find a way to flee yet one more time. After the burning of the Fairfield prison, Frasier was remanded to New Haven. There, handed a knife and a small saw, he slipped out of jail and made his way to Massachusetts. The night after his escape he robbed three shops in Middletown. Within a month, Frasier traveled 500 miles and committed five or six more burglaries. Captured in Worcester, he was returned to New Haven and bound with heavy chains. A nightly guard was ordered. On September 7, Frasier was hanged.[17]

Frasier left behind an execution narrative that was said to be from his own mouth and signed with his hand. As with his cropped ears, branding, and the scars from lashes, these body parts – mouth and hand – were intended as a display of civil and religious authority and order. Indeed, at first glance, the narrative seems to be a conformist text with more than

[17] Isaac Frasier, *A Brief Account*. Connecticut Archives, "Crimes and Misdemeanors," 6:25; *A Poem, Wrote Upon the Execution of a Man, Who [Was] Whipt, Cropt, and Branded at Fairfield for Burglary, the First Day of March in the Year 1769* [Broadside, 1769]; *The Connecticut Journal and New-Haven Post-Boy*, 26 August and September 9, 1768. See Peter Linebaugh's excellent discussion of Jack Shepherd and the art of escape in *The London Hanged: Crime and Civil Society in the Eighteenth Century* (Cambridge: Cambridge University Press, 1992), pp. 7–41 and W. B. Cochran, *Confinement and Flight: An Essay on English Literature of the Eighteenth Century* (Berkeley: University of California Press, 1977).

its share of heavy-handed didacticism. It began with a confession and concluded with gratitude toward local authorities. "I acknowledge the lenity of my judges in allowing me so long a space after condemnation," wrote a seemingly submissive Frasier, "and the kindness of the ministers." But the remainder of the narrative suggests that Frasier the escape artist slipped through these formulaic clauses.

As a genre, the execution narrative promised full disclosure.[18] Yet Frasier's silence haunts this seemingly transparent text. He chose to remain silent about his accomplices. Who provided the saw and helped him break out of New Haven prison? They were, stated an evasive Frasier, "from a person whose name I am under solemn obligation to conceal." He also refused to name the woman he married under an alias in 1767, most likely to spare her from abuse. It is significant, too, that his mother's residence was not divulged. He may have sought to shield her as well. Perhaps he did not know whether she was living in Rhode Island or dead, or perhaps this was yet another example of Frasier's disingenuousness.

The conventions of the execution narrative allow us to see where Frasier has departed from them. Like Levi Ames, he lists what had been stolen. But he also takes the opportunity to disavow certain crimes: Frasier claims not to be guilty of stealing £3 from a Newton man. His confession is marked by subordination, feigning ignorance, and accommodation. This is not surprising. No other status, besides slavery or conscription, made a late-eighteenth-century American so dependent upon the will of the local authorities. Frasier needed their help to obtain a pardon or simply an extension before the execution. At times this deference appears a bit hard to believe. "I found what I have never experienced before," claimed Frasier referring to the half-dozen thefts that took place after breaking out of New Haven's jail, "a guilty conscience." He clearly wished to attribute some change to the ministers who counseled him.

But Frasier's testament must also be read for its silences. Arthur, an African-American burglar who would be hanged the same year at Worcester for rape, confessed in his execution narrative to having committed a number of robberies with "the late celebrated Isaac Frasier" during his flight to Massachusetts. Based largely on the immediate needs of two prisoners on the run, their robberies had the quality of a shopping list. They stole a goose, then a kettle for boiling it. At Marlbrough,

---

[18] Confessions are always suspect texts, however, whose trustworthiness might be greeted with skepticism. See Peter Brooks, *Troubling Confessions: Speaking Guilt in Law and Literature* (Chicago: University of Chicago Press, 2000), pp. 8–34.

Frasier and Arthur robbed a shoemaker's shop for shoes and a distillery for cider brandy. Other robberies included a barbershop, and various essential eighteenth-century commodities, including bread, meat, and rum. If Arthur's narrative was accurate, and there is no reason to assume that it was not, Frasier could have mentioned these items. Such inclusion would have followed the conventions at the beginning of the narrative. But it would also have undercut his claims to pangs of conscience. Frasier, not surprisingly, chose silence.[19]

Frasier also showed a less deferential side: his insistence upon pleading not guilty, resorting to arson against the prison, and the indifference with which – according to witnesses – he treated his sentence. Interestingly, none of these facts was found in his printed confession. Nor did Frasier include another critical detail. His last conviction contained a warning that the next offense would be punished with death. To understand the execution narrative as a public document, it is necessary to peel off the layered conventions and read what James Scott has called the hidden transcript, the use of language that often modifies and contradicts the behavior of subordinate classes in the face of public power. Perhaps, then, there is reason to be skeptical of Frasier's seeming deference.[20]

Like most eighteenth-century trials, Frasier's lasted for only a few hours. In reality, however, another trial of sorts took place during the four months from sentencing to execution. This period was allotted for repentance and to petition for a pardon. Its paradoxical nature was exemplified by Thomas Goss, a Connecticut felon convicted of murder in 1778, who immediately after being found guilty arranged with a lawyer for a clemency appeal and a minister for an execution sermon – just in case the reprieve was not granted.[21] Ministers met frequently with the condemned. With Frasier's minimal religious education, there was a great

---

[19] *The Life, and Dying Speech of Arthur, a Negro Man, who was Executed at Worcester* [Broadside, 1768].

[20] James C. Scott, *Weapons of the Weak: Everyday Forms of Peasant Resistance* (New Haven: Yale University Press, 1985) and *Domination and the Arts of Resistance: Hidden Transcripts* (New Haven: Yale University Press, 1990) both distinguish between the deference of public discourse by subordinate classes and what is often embedded in it. I am not suggesting that execution narratives reflect a hidden transcript of social rebellion. Instead, what is significant is the way that the plasticity of vernacular legal culture allowed it to be used as a vehicle for a variety of messages, including the self-interest of felons, authoritative calls for social order, and, as will be seen later in this chapter, revolutionary politics. For another work on altered languages of deference, see Smadar Lavie, *The Poetics of Military Occupation: Mzeina Allegories of Bedouin Identity Under Israeli and Egyptian Rule* (Berkeley: University of California Press, 1990).

[21] *Connecticut Journal*, November 23, 1785.

deal of work to do. The practice in England, where the hanging generally followed rather quickly after a conviction, was different from the practice in the colonies of providing an extended period for the spiritual welfare of felons.

During the period between conviction and the hanging, frayed bonds between the criminal and society were often repaired. The felon had a number of practical reasons for choosing deference, such as care while in prison or providing for a family after his or her death. "Now as a dying man," stated a criminal convicted of raping and murdering a fourteen-year-old girl, "I recommend to the charity of my Christian neighbors my distressed wife ... whom I leave with two small children destitute ... and she big with child."[22] Moreover, since the criminal justice system was akin to a lottery, it was realistic to expect a pardon to come. This was an important period for a felon. If he or she could demonstrate sincere contrition or perhaps, like Frasier, attempt an escape, there was a fair chance of not facing the gallows. Not the crime itself, but the biographical narrative was most important for a pardon plea. The execution narrative included, though belatedly, the general public in this act of judging. Did Frasier deserve to go free? Was there the possibility of change or was he incorrigible? This meant judging the criminal justice system as well: Did the state unfairly put a person to death?

It would have been possible to miss the legal significance of Frasier's biography without another document: his pardon petition. Frasier pleaded for a pardon on the grounds that he was the first person ever to be executed in Connecticut for a third offense of burglary. A 1735 statute for burglary created a hierarchy of punishments. For the first offense, the felon was flogged with fifteen stripes, branded with the letter "B," and had "one of his ears nailed to the post and cut off." The second offense meant the loss of the other ear and twenty-five stripes, and, finally, for the third offense the punishment was death. Frasier's past history of two offenses, in a very real sense his criminal biography, led to a capital sentence. What Frasier understood was that he was not to be executed for the act of robbing a Fairfield store, but for being "the notorious Isaac Frasier." At stake, then, was the question of identity: Who was Isaac Frasier?

Vernacular legal texts must be read against each other. The issue posed by Frasier's pardon petition, the unusual capital conviction for a third burglary offense, was answered by the execution sermon delivered by Noah Hobart shortly before Frasier's execution. It sought to legitimize

---

[22] *The Last Words and Dying Speech of Edmund Fortis* (Exeter, 1795).

this judgment. Hobart admitted that only one crime, murder, clearly elicited capital punishment. Nevertheless, there was a type of person who through being "over-much wicked" deserved death. By doing wrong over time despite warnings and even when threatened with death, Frasier proved himself to be worthy of death as a reprobate. "His crimes have been frequently repeated and carried to an astonishing excess. He has persisted in them under warnings and reproofs.... He has been a remarkable instance of impertinence."[23]

Yet the discourse about Frasier's punishment could not be contained to a conventional forum such as the execution narrative, his pardon petition, or an execution sermon. As with Levi Ames, this capital conviction for a property crime provoked a public debate. An essay in New Haven's newspaper published after the trial doubted whether a community has a right to punish theft with death. This time, however, the critique used in the Ames affair against the English was turned against the legal system of the colonies themselves.

While a murderer might be executed out of self-preservation, life in other cases is inalienable. This essay put the authorities on the defensive. Hobart's sermon also must be seen as a response to such a critique of the criminal law. He believed that a right of self-preservation extended to society as a whole. If people "cannot rest safely in their beds, but must be in continual danger of having their houses broken open ...," Hobart preached, "the happiness of society is at an end" and it becomes a state of nature. "Human laws consider crimes in a political view."

Hobart's reference to politics was significant. As has been suggested, politicized notions of justice often depended upon instrumentalism. What Hobart was doing, of course, was shifting the question from the justice of assigning death to a particular crime to the need for social order. Both Frasier's autobiography and Hobart's sermon demonstrated that the sentence was open to debate. But were the terms of the debate the same? Frasier personalized his tale; Hobart placed it in a broader impersonal social context. The choice of voice, first person or third person, was

---

[23] Frasier pardon petition, "Crimes and Misdemeanors," 5:261, Connecticut Archives; "An Act in Addition to the Law Entitled an Act Against Theft and Burglary" (1735) in *The Public Records of the State of Connecticut*, ed. Charles J. Hoadley, 15 vols. (Hartford: Lockwood and Brainard, 1850–1890), 7:561; Richard Gaskins, "Changes in the Criminal Law in Eighteenth-Century Connecticut," *American Journal of Legal History* 25 (1981): 309–342. Just two days before Frasier was executed, the court at New Haven warned a repeat offender found guilty of housebreaking that he might suffer death next time (*Connecticut Courant*, September 12, 1768).

critical. Vernacular legal culture was multivocal. Within it the voice of authority intermingled with the voice of the felon himself.[24]

LEGAL STORYTELLING AS SUBVERSIVE ACT

During the first half of the eighteenth century, execution narratives were written largely to bolster civil authority. Criminals were portrayed as repentant. Drawing upon the Protestant language of fall and redemption, these tales rarely strayed from formulaic tropes that showed the felon submitting to a just law. "I must take the sole blame to myself of the dreadful and distressful situation I am brought into," wrote a burglar sentenced to death at Worcester in 1770, "I would be far from reflecting the least blame upon the court or jury." Yet by the mid-1760s, criminal narratives increasingly expressed discontent with the judicial apparatus, sometimes even measured hostility. Perhaps this change emerged from the broader assault against authority that was part of resistance against England. If English law, as the Levi Ames affair showed, might be criticized, why not the American legal process as well? Felons like Frasier appropriated vernacular legal culture to shape narratives for their own purposes.[25]

Denial, dissimulation, feigning indifference, countertestimonies, shifting blame, and defiance were by the second half of the eighteenth century as common literary postures for execution narratives as submission. Sometimes the felon simply wanted to set the record straight. "The stories that have been propagated round the country that I confessed" to previously murdering a man, claimed a New Hampshire man found guilty of murder, "are devoid of foundation." Moses Paul, an African American executed in New Haven for murder, said that despite rumors, he was innocent of killing another man, a sailor in the West Indies. "Having been questioned about a great robbery that was committed near Brunswick," stated Valentine Duckett, who was executed in 1774, "as a dying man I declare that I had neither act nor part of it, nor even knew any of the men."[26]

---

[24] Hobart, *Excessive Wickedness*, pp. 6–13; *The Connecticut Journal and New-Haven Post-Boy*, July 8, 1768 and the response October 14 and 21, 1768.

[25] William Linsey. *The Dying Speech and Confession of William Linsey* (Boston, 1770). On self-fabrication as a literary genre, see John Eakin, *Fictions in Autobiography: Studies in the Art of Self-Invention* (Princeton: Princeton University Press, 1985); Marie-Paul Laden, *Self-Imitation in the Eighteenth-Century Novel* (Princeton: Princeton University Press, 1987); and Stephen Greenblatt, *Renaissance Self-Fashioning: From More to Shakespeare* (Chicago: University of Chicago Press, 1980).

[26] *The Last Words, and Dying Speech of Elisha Thomas* (Boston, 1788); *A Short Account of the Life of Moses Paul* (New Haven, 1772); *The Life, Last Words, and Dying Speech of Valentine Duckett* [Broadside, 1774].

Others fabricated excuses for their lives: cruel stepparents, the lack of a proper moral upbringing, unhappy marriages. A counterfeiter executed in 1770 explained his crime this way: "I gave myself over to an uneasy and restless mind, with an undue desire of gaining riches; which disposition pushed on by the enemy of my soul has been the means of my downfall." Reversals of fortune led him to think of any way to become rich. "We might all live a gentleman's life," he told a confederate. Such a temptation may have been easily understood by contemporaries. Family economies were precarious in the eighteenth century and well-heeled leisure scarce. While appealing to common emotions, criminals sought to assert authorial control over their own life histories.[27]

Confessions were counternarratives. As an act of self-fabrication, they stood independent of official legal texts. Recognizing that the oral circulation of tales often comprised a narrative itself, some confessions were prompted as a counternarrative against gossip as much as any sort of official record. Felons tell of false accusations with a sense of injury. "I have lived a hard life by being obliged to keep to the woods, have suffered much hunger nakedness, cold and fears of being detected and brought to justice – have often been accused of stealing when I was not," wrote Johnson Green, who was executed in 1786 for burglary. Green admitted to thefts but denied highway robbery, just as Levi Ames agreed to robbery while claiming he foreswore violence. In similar fashion, Herman Rosencrantz, hanged in 1770 at Philadelphia for counterfeiting, admitted to making false money but rejected the accusation of having aided horse thieves. "The command in my heart," he claimed, "was always thou shalt not steal." A man executed in 1776 at Newport for sedition denied robbery or theft.[28]

But the legal meaning embedded in the narratives should be stressed. This meaning might be broadly said to assume two forms: narrative as confession and narrative as pardon petition. John Langbein has shown that self-incrimination was at the heart of the eighteenth-century Anglo-American criminal trial. Such a system showed judicial economy. Trials were remarkably short and to the point. Instead of long, drawn-out battles over evidentiary questions or points of law, the felon was supposed to simply confess. Confession might take place in court with an oath or,

---

[27] For examples of this, see the use of such appeals in the accounts of Joseph Mountain and John Young described at length in Chapters Four. and Six.

[28] *The Life and Confession of Johnson Green* [Broadside, 1786]; *The Life and Confession of Hermann Rosencrantz* (Philadelphia, 1770); *The Last Speech and Dying Words of Thomas Hickey* [Broadside, 1776].

in unusual circumstances, even through some thaumaturgic act, like the one that occurred in Bergen County in 1767. There, a murder suspect, an African American, was forced to touch the dead man's face with his hands. He was charged when blood rushed out of the corpse's nostrils. The centrality of confession to vernacular legal culture mirrored its central position in the criminal trial. Felons were *supposed to* engage in self-incrimination partly because in the early modern period there were limits to forensic evidence and partly because confession legitimized the punishment. Publishing a confessional execution narrative was a public means of justifying a capital conviction.[29]

Public confession made better known to all what was previously concealed. "Whatever you do in tone dark," warned a counterfeiter sentenced to death in 1770, "shall be set on the house top in a short time." About the 1790 murder in bed of a sea captain, it was said that "although the deed was done under the darkness of the night, yet it is now made public and manifest of day." "There ought to be a public confession," according to a 1792 execution sermon, "where the offence is of a public nature." Often the felon appealed directly to the public. Batsheva Spooner, convicted in 1778 for planning the murder of her husband with hired accomplices, petitioned for a stay of execution on the grounds of pregnancy. A jury of matrons denied her petition twice. Spooner "at her own desire that the public might be satisfied" requested that her belly be opened after the hanging. She was found to be carrying a male child of five months. Claiming insanity, Thomas Goss appealed directly to the public. During the trial, Charles O'Donnell denied the facts surrounding the strangling of his own son to death. But he fully confessed through the medium of the execution narrative.[30]

---

[29] *New-York Journal or General Advertiser*, October 1, 1767 and October 29, 1767. On the nineteenth-century origins of the privilege against self-incrimination, see Alan G. Gless, "Self-Incrimination Privilege Development in the Nineteenth-Century Federal Courts: Questions of Procedure, Privilege, Production, Immunity, and Compulsion," 45 *American Journal of Legal History* (2001): 391–467.

[30] *The Last Speech, Confession, and Dying Words of John Smith* (New Haven, 1773). *Norwich Packet and Country Journal*, July 2, 1790; Matthew Merriman, *Sermons Preached to Joshua Abbot at York, September 3, 1792* (Newburyport, 1792); *The Rev. Maccarthy's Account of the Behavior of Mrs. Spooner after her Commitment and Condemnation for Being an Accessary in the Murder of Her Husband* (1778); *Massachusetts Spy*, December 8, 1785; *The Life and Confession of Charles O'Donnell Executed at Morgantown, June 19, 1797 for the Wilful Murder of his Son* (Lancaster, 1798); Debrah Navas, *Murdered By His Wife: The Absorbing Tale of Crime and Punishment in Late Eighteenth-Century Massachusetts* (Amherst: University of Massachusetts Press, 1999).

In many cases, narratives also reflected hope for a pardon or reprieve. One purpose of this storytelling was to mobilize local elites. Often the minister would play a critical role in acquiring a pardon. Ezra Stiles, for example, wrote a petition to the Rhode Island legislature on behalf of a young African-American woman who murdered her illegitimate child. Unable to find any other mitigating circumstances, Stiles argued that her mental powers were weak, and clemency was granted. The significance of religious connections, of course, depended upon whether a religious sect held political power. A member of a Pennsylvania gang pretended to be a Quaker. But the Society of Friends soon discovered that he had no connection to the sect and that "his present pretensions ... were with a view rather of being saved in this world than in the next." Sometimes, however, a felon was able to convert in order to win the support of a minister. William Welch, for example, converted from Catholicism to Protestantism in his prison cell.[31]

There were advantages to being well connected. The coachman of Governor William Franklin of New Jersey was granted a reprieve at the gallows as he was about to be hanged for the rape of a fifteen-year-old girl. But even in such cases the storytelling craft served to recast details of the crime in a more favorable light. The coachman's pardon was "upon the recommendation of the Chief Justice and sundry inhabitants of the city who were of the opinion that some circumstances appeared to be in his favor." As defense counsel became more common toward the end of the century, lawyers joined in the creation of pardon tales.[32] Richard Doane was sentenced to death for the death of a fellow artisan committed while intoxicated. Doane believed that he should have been tried for manslaughter, not murder. He was assigned a member of the Connecticut Assembly, Gideon Granger, Jr., as his counsel. Granger delivered an impassioned speech to his fellow representatives in a failed attempt to win a pardon.[33]

[31] Rhode Island Archives (Providence), Petitions 12:67 (May 9, 1767), Letters 7:86; *An Account of the Robberies Committed by John Morrison* (Philadelphia, 1751); William Welch, *The Last Speech and Dying Words* [Broadside, 1754]. On religious pluralism in revolutionary America, see Patricia U. Bonomi, *Under the Cope of Heaven: Religion, Society, and Politics in Colonial America* (Oxford: Oxford University Press, 1986), pp. 131–217 and Jon Butler, *Awash in a Sea of Faith: Christianizing the American People* (Cambridge: Harvard University Press, 1990), pp. 164–193.

[32] On the use of counsel, see James D. Rice, "The Criminal Trial Before and After the Lawyers: Authority, Law, and Culture in Maryland Jury Trials 1681–1837," 40 *American Journal of Legal History* (1996): 455–475.

[33] *Pennsylvania Gazette*, December 15, 1763; Connecticut Archives, Crimes and Misdemeanors, 2nd series. IV: 78–84 (1797).

Asking for a pardon was an art. It was bad form for autobiographical execution narratives to hint too broadly that this was their purpose. Better to appear repentant, show willingness to die for the wrongs committed, and petition for a bit more time to put one's spiritual house in order. Remaining alive meant still being able to tell your tale and, perhaps, continuing to lobby for a pardon. Born in Chester County of a respectable family, Elizabeth Wilson blamed her fall on the sin of fornication. She had three illegitimate children. According to her tale, Wilson asked the father for child support. Instead he forced her to strip the babies in a deserted field, leaving them to die. In 1785, Wilson was convicted of infanticide. Persisting in claiming her innocence, she gathered public support. The execution was prolonged out of hope for a last-minute pardon. Wilson's brother raced back from Philadelphia bearing a stay of execution. But he arrived nearly half an hour too late.[34]

It is possible to untangle the excuses, apologies, and pretexts of legal storytelling in clemency petitions and execution narratives in order to understand what makes a good legal story. Sometimes pardons were based upon lingering doubts about evidence. A Pennsylvania woman was convicted of infanticide, for example, but there was no proof other than the fact that the child was illegitimate. Other pardon requests were based upon the suitability of the individual as an object of mercy. Sentenced to execution for bestiality, an eighty-four-year-old Litchfield, Connecticut, man petitioned that he had little time left to live anyway. By the end of the century, pardon petitions increasingly reflected broader political and social concerns. Barrach Martin, an African American, was sentenced to be hanged for the common slave crime of arson. His excuse is intriguing: "having been deprived by his birth in Africa of education or if educated was only taught perhaps that revenge was a virtue."[35]

As an escape artist, Isaac Frasier still dreamed of flight. According to witnesses, he remained unconcerned about his death sentence as he hatched new plans for escape. How must the linguistic subordination of the execution narrative be seen against schemes or even attempts to escape? Take, for example, the 1773 case of John Wall Lovey. In exchange for favorable consideration, Lovey named his fellow counterfeiters. But hopes for a pardon never materialized. Lovey's dying speech seems an

---

[34] *A Faithful Narrative of Elizabeth Wilson who was Executed at Chester, January 3d 1786* (Philadelphia, 1786).

[35] Pennsylvania Colonial Records, VIII, 336 (May 24, 1754); Connecticut Archives, Crimes and Misdemeanors, 2nd series II: 87–89 (1799); *The Universal Asylum and Columbian Magazine* (1790): 74.

exemplar of contrition: "I forgive … my prosecutors and die in peace with all men, praying God to pardon my sin and be merciful to my soul. Amen." Yet, in fact, his end was less than peaceful. Lovey was angry at what he considered the betrayal of the examining justices. Somehow breaking free from his irons and barring the cell, Lovey set fire to the Albany jail. He threatened to light a bottle filled with gunpowder if the sheriff came any closer.[36]

When finally the sheriff launched an assault against him, Lovey lit a match to the bottle. It failed to catch fire. Lovey was clearly following simultaneously two strategies of escape – storytelling and flight. Through pardon petitions and a contrite execution narrative, he elaborated upon a deferential presentation of the self while he may have been planning a physical flight from his confinement. After his thwarted escape attempt, Lovey was brought to the gallows. He returned, oddly, to a subordinate posture. Lovey sung psalms and, according to one observer, "seemed to die penitent." A critical question nevertheless remained: Who provided the gunpowder for Lovey? He apparently had confederates or friends still at large.[37]

Another counterfeiter, Owen Sullivan, showed a similar mixture of cockiness, assent, petitioning, and dreams of flight. Sullivan had a way with words. When sentenced at Boston to have his ears cropped and branded for counterfeiting, Sullivan "being a man of good address found means to prejudice the population in his favor" so that the punishment was inflicted in such a way as to be barely visible. The cropping most likely entailed the removal of just a small part of the ear lobe and the brand of "C" placed near his hairline. After being punished in Massachusetts, Sullivan shifted the base of his counterfeiting operation to Rhode Island, where he was arrested. But Sullivan broke out of the Providence jail with some ease. The sheriff of Providence almost lost his job over the matter, and, according to Sullivan's execution narrative, Sullivan quietly returned to the prison. He broke out of jail again. Caught, returned to jail, and confined with strong irons, he somehow escaped one more time. Finally, in New York he was captured and sentenced to death.[38]

---

[36] *New-York Gazette or the Weekly Post-Boy*, 12 April 1773; John Wall Lovey, *The Last Speech, Confession, and Dying Words … Executed the 2d of April, 1773* [Broadside, 1773].

[37] *New-York Gazette or Weekly Post-Boy*, April 12, 1773; *Massachusetts Gazette*, May 6, 1773.

[38] *Connecticut Gazette*, March 25, 1756; *Boston Evening Post*, 9 October 1752; *A Short Account of the Life of John*****, Alias Owen Syllaven, Alias John Livingston, Alias*

Sullivan's autobiographical narrative follows the form dictated by convention. Yet one tale in the narrative is especially noteworthy. Conflict with his parents had reached the point where he was confined in a room with a diet of bread and water for a considerable time: "Then I seemed to humble myself till I again obtained my liberty, and after that I was ten times worse than I was before." Not too long afterwards, he ran away from home. That psychological model of confinement, subordination, and flight sets the pattern that would emerge in his criminal prosecution. The dying confession suggested that Sullivan was conforming to his role in the traditional execution ritual. He admitted that he deserved the gallows, set himself as a warning to others, and said that his accomplices should "burn and destroy all the money, plates, and accoutrements that they have by them that they may not die on a tree as I do."

Yet there were limits to his compliance. He shed doubt on capital punishment's legitimacy by not naming his confederates because he did not want to "be guilty [as he termed it] of shedding their blood." Nor would he identify the bills printed. "You must find that out," he responded to questioning, "by your own learning." It would be easy to parcel out these different representations of Sullivan among different genres of vernacular legal culture. The Sullivan seen through the autobiographical execution narrative was certainly more accommodating than the Sullivan portrayed by newspaper reports. But more to the point, it seems, is that Sullivan himself drew upon a repertoire of responses to the capital sentence. Sullivan sought mercy by admitting that his sentence was just. Nevertheless, he protected his confederates despite pressure from the authorities to reveal their names.

It appears that Sullivan was hoping his old confederates would come to his rescue. Unable to find a hangman, the execution had to be delayed. Members of his gang might very well have frightened away the executioner. The hanging was postponed yet another day because the gallows were cut down. Apparently still hoping to be rescued, Sullivan approached the gallows smirking. "I cannot help smiling," he said, "'tis the nature of the beast." But Sullivan grew frightened as death approached, crying out, "Don't pull the rope so tight."[39]

John Brown ... Found Guilty ... For Counterfeiting (New York, 1756); Kenneth Scott, *Counterfeiting in Colonial America* (Oxford: Oxford University Press), p. 188; and *Counterfeiting in Colonial New York* (New York: The American Numismatic Society, 1953), pp. 91–93.

[39] *New-York Gazette or Weekly Post-Boy*, May 10, 1756 and May 17, 1756; *New York Mercury*, May 17, 1756; *A Short Account of the Life of Owen Sullivan*.

Literary strategies of storytelling were one facet of an arsenal of strategies drawn upon by those caught in the web of the criminal judicial process. Owen Sullivan appealed simultaneously to the authorities and to old confederates still at liberty. Herman Rosencrantz, who was sentenced to death for counterfeiting in 1770, on the other hand, fully named his associates and relied solely upon the mercy of the state. What was striking about the last days of felons was how so often offenders moved to repair the patronage relationships that were frayed during their lives. These offenders, generally masterless men who had run away from parents or masters, led transient lives. Yet as condemned prisoners, they were forced to come to terms with local elites.

Pardons were only one possible reward for cooperation. Executions were frequently delayed at the request of ministers. Physical conditions, food and warmth, remained at the discretion of jailors. A 1738 execution sermon for a New London woman convicted of infanticide put this equation quite baldly: "If they [condemned felons] should prove stubborn and hard hearted, these good offices will indeed be done with so much less good will. But when they appear truly sensible of their faults and humble under them, we may minister to them with readiness and delight. We must feed them when they are hungry, clothe them when they are naked, see that they be not exposed to the cold, and not suffer them to want anything that is their convenience." The minister closed by adding that "besides the public allowance there is room for private charities to be exercised." Finally, treatment and support of those left behind, aging parents, children, and widows, often depended upon the generosity of the populace. "And now as a dying man, I recommend to the charity of Christian neighbors my distressed wife whom I leave with two small children destitute," stated a man convicted of the rape and murder of a fourteen-year-old girl, "and she big with child."[40]

Not surprisingly, execution narratives raised traditional evidentiary questions. Women accused of infanticide claimed that their child was stillborn or pointed toward the father's role in the death. Counterfeiters made distinctions between the reproduction and circulation of specie. Rapists raised the critical evidentiary question of the woman's consent.

[40] *The Life and Confession of Herman Rosencrantz, Executed in the City of Philadelphia on the 5th Day of May, 1770 for Counterfeiting* (Philadelphia, 1770); Edmund Fortis, *The Last Words and Dying Speech of Edmund Fortis, A Negro Man who ... was Executed ... on the 25th Day of September 1794 for a Rape and Murder* (Exeter, 1795); Eliphalet Adams, *A Sermon Preached on the Occasion of the Execution of Katherine Garret ... for the Murder of her Spurious Child on May 3rd 1738* (New London, 1738).

Bryan Sheehan, who was executed for rape in 1772, for example, claimed that the sexual relations were consensual. According to the victim, however, Sheehan's repeated propositions were rejected. He came to her while she was in bed with two children, put his hand over her mouth, and raped her. The redactor of the execution narrative included both tales perhaps so the reader could make his or her own weighing of the evidence. Consent was often difficult to ascertain. But blood found on Sheehan's hand supported the woman's claim that she was assaulted against her will.[41]

Peculiar to infanticide was that the burden of proof rested upon the woman. The Stuart Bastard Neonaticide Act of 1624 determined that any woman concealing the death of an illegitimate child shall suffer death as in the case of murder. This was a woman's crime, and women responded by arguing either that their child was a live birth or that the father of the child was responsible for its death. A twenty-seven-year-old woman hanged for infanticide at Boston stated that she did not believe at the time that the child was alive, "tho' I confess it's probable there was life." Elizabeth Wilson said a man forced her at gunpoint to strip the twins she had left in a field to die. Alice Clifton, an African-American slave executed in 1787, took both tacks. She claimed the child was born dead. Although the child was not fully grown, however, its throat was found cut. In a remarkable example of the broad diffusion of eighteenth-century secular thought, Clifton blamed the father. Another black servant, he convinced her that "she had nothing to fear for there was no heaven or hell, no God or devil – that he knew better ... [because he] had travelled in Europe." The issue with murder was malice aforethought. It was denied, for example, in the case of a murder that followed a drinking bout aboard ship: "I solemnly declare that I had no enmity against Captain Drowne, nor do I know how it happened, unless it was done [in the midst of] the scuffle getting me out of doors."[42]

---

[41] *An Account of the Life of Bryan Sheehan* [broadside] (Portsmouth, 1772). On rape prosecution, see Barbara S. Lindemann, "'To Ravish and Carnally Know': Rape in Eighteenth-Century Massachusetts"; *Signs: Journal of Women in Culture and Society* 10 (1984): 63–82 and the case of Joseph Mountain in Chapter Three.

[42] *The Declaration, Dying Warning, and Advice of Rebekah Chamblit* [Broadside, 1733]; *The Trial of Alice Clifton* (Philadelphia, 1787). 21 James I, c. 27 (1624). On infanticide, see Peter C. Hoffer and N. E. H. Hull, *Murdering Mothers: Infanticide in England and New England, 1558–1803* (New York: New York University Press, 1981); Cynthia S. Jordan, *Second Stories: The Politics of Language, Form, and Gender in Early American Fictions* (Chapel Hill: University of North Carolina Press, 1989); *The Last Words, and Dying Speech of Elisha Thomas, Who was Executed at Dover on the 3d June, 1788 for the Murder of Captain Peter Drowne* [Broadside, 1788].

Who, then, is the "I" of the execution narrative? Does the reader believe the unqualified submission to a capital sentence, hidden transcripts, or words of defiance? The major problem facing this confessional genre was one of sincerity and authenticity. In a sense, as biography, the execution narrative was essentially fictive – fictive not simply when the facts were imagined, as in Ebenezer Richardson's case, but even when they conformed more closely to reality. Narrative strategies shaped the life into a text. What makes for a captivating tale, a paradigmatic image repentance, or, as has been argued, the designs of the criminal as author, exercised an overwhelming influence over the biography. The problem, of course, was that the more compelling the narrative, the more artificial it appeared.

To counteract the image of artifice, the criminal narrative relies upon two literary techniques. The first is the careful presentation of facts in a seemingly objective narrative voice. Packing the narrative full of elaborate detail, some of it quite irrelevant, invested it with the texture of authenticity. Lists of crimes and full descriptions of the felon's early upbringing served this function. Feelings about the crimes, secondly, were almost always linked to external change: rejection by parents, the bad influence of companions, capture and sentencing, or the awesome period experienced by a felon awaiting death. Eighteenth-century readers were expected to believe in sudden pangs of conscience but only if they took place in the appropriate context.[43]

The traditional role of the condemned felon was threefold: to warn others, to grant forgiveness, and to confess what crimes still remained hidden. But criminals turned these narrative conventions in unexpected directions. The usual warnings delivered before a hanging included such commonplace admonitions as not to break the Sabbath, to steal, or to become involved with lewd women. John Ryer, however, convicted for murdering a sheriff who came to arrest him for debt, chose a different warning. A sheriff, he warned, should not "crowd up" a person when taking him prisoner. If he should die in the attempt, Ryer added, there was no one to blame. Another murderer executed in Albany during the last decade of the eighteenth century believed that some of the testimony against him was false. His last warning was against perjury. "Let a dying man earnestly exhort all witnesses in the future not to forget the oaths

---

[43] For a broad-based understanding of the literary construction of evidence, see Alexander Welsh, *Strong Representations: Narrative and Circumstantial Evidence in England* (Baltimore: Johns Hopkins University Press, 1992); Barbara J. Shapiro, *Beyond Reasonable Doubt and Probable Cause: Historical Perspectives on the Anglo-American Law of Evidence* (Berkeley: University of California Press, 1991).

they take." Last warnings were appropriated to reflect the felon's agenda. The burglar Thomas Mount warned of crooked fences.

What about the role of granting forgiveness? "God forbid my heart should retain malice," said John Shearman, executed for burglary at Newport in 1764 as he was about to die. Nevertheless, he "cannot help expressing my desire that the man and wife by whose means I was apprehended in Boston may consider what a heinous nature their sins are." "I forgive Daniel Lewis who swore falsely against me," wrote a New York counterfeiter sentenced to death in 1773, "excepting what I did in the woods, also my prosecutors." The capital sentence was meant as a form of conflict resolution: The victim, friends and family of the victim, and society itself were supposed to abandon anger and vengeance with the capital sentence. In turn, the felon needed to affirm the justice of the capital sentence. The execution narrative must be understood in an anthropological sense as a ritual of reconciliation. By the middle of the eighteenth century, convicted felons were increasingly unwilling to offer forgiveness without caveats. It was difficult to both settle scores and appear magnanimous. A felon executed in New Hampshire for murder added "the witnesses' own conscience will best determine whether from prejudice they did not in some parts of their testimony injure me."[44]

There was, finally, the task of confessing crimes not included in the indictment. Sometimes these confessions were quite detailed. "As for the dollar that was swore against me was true," declared John Smith, executed for counterfeiting in 1773. Not surprisingly, however, denial became increasingly common among late eighteenth-century felons. The execution narrative often included a kind of countertestimony meant to shed doubt on witnesses at the trial, or simply made disclaimers. Executed at Philadelphia for murder in 1765, Henry Halbert admitted to "all manner of vice – drinking, whoring, cursing, swearing, breaking the Sabbath, and keeping all manner of debauched company." But he denied stealing money from his master and was angry at the court's insistence that he repay it. Sentenced to death for robbery in 1789, Rachel Wall cleared the name of a crippled woman at the Boston Alms-House who suffered

---

[44] *Narrative of the Life and Dying Speech of John Ryer* (Danbury, 1793); *The Narrative of Whiting Sweeting* (Exeter, 1791); *The Confession of Thomas Mount* (Newport, 1791); *The Last Words and Dying Speech of John Shearman* [Broadside, 1764]; *The Last Speech, Confession and Dying Words of John Wall Lovey* [Broadside, 1773]; *The Last Words and Dying Speech of Elisha Thomas* [Broadside, 1788]; Nicholas Tavuchis, *Mea Culpa: A Sociology of Apology and Reconciliation* (Stanford: Stanford University Press, 1991).

lashes for robbery. But, Wall insisted, she was not guilty of the theft for which she herself was sentenced to death.[45]

Some felons used the narrative as a vehicle to critique the very law that held them accountable. Executed for counterfeiting at Albany in 1773, John Parker distinguished between making and passing false currency: "I never considered that it was criminal for a mechanic to finish any piece of work that he is employed to execute, whatever mischievous purposes the instrument he makes is applied to, after the artist delivers it out of his hands." Parker compared engraving the plates to a gunsmith. Is a gunsmith culpable if a musket he forges is used for murder? Owen Sullivan intimated that inflicting a capital sentence for a property crime was to be guilty of shedding blood. Sentenced to death for murder in 1791, Whiting Sweeting took the opportunity of his execution narrative to state his differences with God's law. In his dying speech he critiqued at great length the doctrine of election.[46]

Strategies of legal storytelling underwent a marked transformation after the American Revolution. Felons increasingly exercised authorial control over autobiographical and biographical execution narratives. Formulaic language was pushed aside by a newfound sense of the contending voices that swirled around the criminal law. Compare for a moment two texts. Published in 1791, both works underscore the depth of this change. The first text is Thomas Mount's *Confession* and the second a guidebook for ministers caring for felons awaiting death. Linking these two works is the fact that William Smith, the author of the guidebook and minister at Trinity Church in Newport, was also the editor of Mount's narrative.

The beginning of Mount's narrative follows closely the formulaic presentation of a life of crime. Although born in 1764 at Middletown, New Jersey, Mount was raised in New York. At the age of eleven he ran away from home. After serving briefly in the army, according to the narrative, he defected at Valley Forge from the American troops and joined the British. It was then that he began to steal. In order to avoid detection, he changed sides again – this time returning to the American troops. Mount includes a lengthy list of crimes. Tried for theft when informed upon by a receiver

[45] *The Last Speech, Confession, and Dying Words of John Smity* (Albany, 1773); *The Last Speech and Confession of Henry Halbert* (Philadelphia, 1765); *Life, Last Words, and Dying Confession of Rachel Wall* [Broadside, 1789].

[46] *A Journal of the Life and Travels of Joseph-Bill Packer* (Albany, 1773); *Massachusetts Gazette*, April 29, 1773; *The Narrative of Whiting Sweeting who was Executed at Albany, the 26th of August, 1791* (Albany, 1791).

of stolen goods, he escaped from jail. Pretending to be a sailor, he committed crimes up the coast – New York, New Haven, Milford, Hartford, Norwich, Dedham – and down it: Baltimore, Annapolis, Wilmington, and Alexandria, Virginia. Mount remembers his crimes with surprising clarity. A protean protagonist, he changed from one eighteenth-century wandering figure to another. Soldier, sailor, and even fortune teller were among his guises. It is that shifting quality which hints at the criminal self. Any man can tell a thief, Mount claims: He asks too many questions, often steals glances behind his back, and shows signs of nervousness. The thief remains silent about himself.

Nevertheless, the best method to distinguish a thief from an honest man is through his complex relationship to language. Although Mount confesses to murdering a confederate who might inform upon his gang, Mount turned informer himself. He named thieves, receivers, and those who supplied the tools for breaking into houses and out of jails. Breaking the silence, Mount provides the reader with a linguistic entrée to the cultural milieu of late eighteenth-century criminals: "At my desire, the language and songs of the American Flash Company are published to inform the world at large of how wicked that company is and how necessary it is to root them up like so many thorns and briers." The *Confession* includes a lexicon of the Flash gang's vocabulary. Shoes are called crabs, a jacket is a jarvix. A prig is a thief, a gambler a sharb. Rum is called suck. Cat means a lewd woman. And the sun is rather poetically renamed Phoebus.

Execution narratives are, for the most part, about *individual* felons. But here it is the gang – with all its rituals, language, and songs – that becomes central. No longer simply an exemplar of penitence, Mount, like his minister, writes a guidebook. Taking us down a steep descent to the criminal underworld, Mount becomes an informer of sorts. But he demands that we follow him, not the other way around: learn *his* canting language, abandoning formulaic subordination for a glimpse of what was feared the most – an English-style gang of highwaymen. With Mount's *Confession*, the criminal appropriation of the execution narrative had reached a new watershed. It invites us through language to join a fellowship of thieves.[47]

---

[47] *Confession of Thomas Mount, Who Was Executed at Little-Rest in the State of Rhode-Island on Friday the 27th of May 1791 for Burglary* (Newport, 1791). Mount's lexicon shares many commonalities with the language of contemporary English canting dictionaries. See, for example, Francis Grose, *A Classical Dictionary of the Vulgar Tongue* (London: S. Hooper, 1785).

Mount included a compendium of Flash gang company songs:

> Who said I'll have your body hung
> Before tomorrow night
> I said, ye gallows rogue
> Haul in your bridle reins
> Or else a leaden bullet
> Shall pierce your bloody brains

Mount and his fellow thieves used gallows imagery as a central element of their criminal subculture. But, as has been suggested, executions also exercised a powerful influence over the Protestant imagination. The hanging represented a liminal moment, suspended between earth and heaven. Few stand knowingly so close to death, so full of evil, and with such a clear opportunity to repent. William Smith notes with surprise at the beginning of his guide, *The Convict's Visitor*, that there is not one devotional tract "professedly written for unfortunate victims of justice." He rushed his own book from the press in order to present it to Thomas Mount and another prisoner before their executions.

Unlike Mount's narrative, which Smith edited, his manual is a rather wooden affair. Much of it consists of responsive readings between the minister and the condemned:

MINISTER: O Lord, turn them from darkness to light.
CONDEMNED: And from the power of Satan unto God.
MINISTER: From the blindness of mind, hardness of heart, and contempt of Thy word and commandments.
CONDEMNED: Good Lord deliver us.
MINISTER: Increase their faith in the divine promises – alarm their minds with a view of thy terrors – and help them to take their station at the foot of the savior's cross that the blood of Jesus may save them from the angel of death.

After the formulaic confession comes a formulaic absolution. The minister recites part of the Lord's Prayer and calls for mercy, and the felon – for his or her part – simply adds amen. No moment is left without set linguistic paces. Smith's guide is stuffed full of prayers, exhortations, and meditations. Five private meditations were to be said shortly before the execution. A last confession to be delivered before the execution of a murderer included blank spaces where the name of the victim was to be inserted. Names of the murdered individual's kin might also be added at the appropriate junctures.

Such a prescriptive text underscores the breakdown of traditional forms of execution rituals at a time when felons could no longer be counted upon to adhere to convention. Undoubtedly, Smith was seeking to reassert a language of subordination that had been shunted aside by assertive felons. "God bless the United States of America with all their rulers, officers, judges, and counselors, and all their people" went a formulaic prayer for the day of execution, "and the Lord increase them a thousand fold." Smith prescribed a dramatic enactment of submission that paralleled linguistic subordination. Convicts were instructed to kneel and prostrate themselves before a minister. Such transparent mechanical prose was meant to leave little room for the felon's voice.[48]

Yet did it work? Mount was supposed to recite Smith's formulae. But Smith, too, as the editor of Mount's *Confession*, became the instrument through which Mount articulated his own imaginative readings of a criminal life. "I must complain to the public of the receivers of fences as well call them in the Flash Language," wrote Mount, "They cheat us confoundedly." "We never receive from them more than a tenth part of the value." Mount's complaint reflected the economic realities of petty crime rather than shopworn pieties. Receivers instigated fights among thieves while betraying them by sleeping with their whores. And fences often bargained while wielding the threat of informing. "In one word, a thief or a highway man is a pitiable criminal; he risks his life every adventure he engages in, and all the recompense he gets for his pains is the treachery of his whores and comrades."

Such an earthy description is clearly a play for sympathy. But it is more. Mount justifies his own treachery by naming that of confederates. The *Confession* evoked a world of confidence men where one huckster is bested by another. It is a picaresque portrait of competing interests and ambitions. Perhaps this is what takes place within vernacular legal culture itself. One voice jostles with another: Criminal and victim, religious and civic moralism, legal language and vernacular forms become interwoven in provocative ways. Language and trickery, Mount reminds us, are never far apart.

POLITICIZING VERNACULAR LEGAL CULTURE

In the early eighteenth century, an intriguing law was passed in Massachusetts criminalizing the publication of a mock sermon or the

---

[48] William Smith, *The Convict's Visitor: Or, Penitential Offices in the Ancient Way of Liturgy, Consisting of Prayers, Lessons, and Meditations with Suitable Devotions Before and at the Time of Execution* (Newport, 1791).

imitation of preaching. Anyone convicted would be forced to stand in the pillory with a placard in capital letters affixed over his head that would detail the crime. To mock – or at least to mock clerical authority – was illegal in Massachusetts. But the punishment itself had a touch of mockery about it. No lashes would be delivered in the pillory. Instead, the public would be invited to mock the author of the parodies.[49]

Embedded in the notion of mock punishment were the two meanings of mockery: both imitation and derision. The authorities themselves linked mockery and punishment, especially through employing mock executions as a sanction. The most common form of official mock execution was sitting at the gallows with a rope around the neck. Often this punishment was inflicted for moral crimes, such as adultery in Vermont, sodomy in Rhode Island, or dueling in Massachusetts. In Massachusetts, a woman was sentenced to sit one hour upon the gallows with a rope around her neck for having an adulterous affair with an African American while her husband was in the army. Another Massachusetts court ordered the same punishment for a father found guilty of manslaughter for his daughter's death.

Mock executions were intended to alter the behavior of the felon through a close brush with capital punishment. While a young burglar was granted a pardon by the Pennsylvania authorities, they waited until he was on the gallows to receive it in order "to leave a more lasting impression." Partly, the mock execution served to embody one aspect of the punishment found in the public hanging: shame. It is not surprising, then, that a mock execution was sometimes followed by a mock execution narrative.

John and Anne Richardson, an especially notorious couple who confined their bastard child in a small room without food, were sentenced to the scaffold for one hour. A broadside expressed collective anger at their cruelty to the child. "Behold how well the pliant halter suits," it rhymed, "these hardened monsters and unnatural brutes." Sentenced to sit upon the gallows for bestiality in 1773, John Sennet was most likely the object of public ridicule. Further mockery took place in a set of vernacular verses published at the same time: "See the knave exposed to public view/And for his wickedness receive his due/While all the crowd behold him with disdain/And laugh to see him thus expos'd to shame."[50]

---

[49] *Massachusetts Statutes*, "An Act Against Impertinence, Immorality and Profaneness, and for the Reformation of Manners (1712)," pp. 395–399.

[50] *Revised Laws of the State of Vermont*, "An Act Against Adultery, Polygamy, and Fornication (1787)"; *Rhode Island Statutes*, "An Act to Reform the Penal Laws

The boundaries between mockery and official justice were not clearly drawn. Court-directed retribution often included a role for popular participation. What made the pillory such a potent punishment was not the immobility, but shame and being subject to crowd anger. Three Massachusetts counterfeiters were sentenced to stand one hour in the pillory, to have one of their ears cropped, and to twenty lashes. Without the shaming, this seems a stiff enough sentence. Yet a hanging verse about the case shows how potent an additional weapon popular retribution could be:

> What multitudes do them surround
> Many as bad can be found
> And to increase their sad disgrace
> Throw rotten eggs into their face
> And pelt them sore with dirt and stones
> Nay, if they could, would break their bones
> Their malice to such heights arise
> Who knows by they'll put out their eyes

Not all crowds, of course, were as threatening. Nevertheless, the fact is that punishment was a public affair. The differences between official and extraofficial retribution often became blurred.[51]

Compare two cases from Connecticut, one official, the other extraofficial. Andrew Peters, a horse thief, was sentenced by a court to ride a wooden horse. The punishment was clearly aimed at the felon's bottom. But Peters stuffed a blanket into his breeches. "As others may not have the same wise sagacity [as the sheriff who discovered Peters' ruse]," read a report of the event, "it seems necessary to caution all sheriffs who may have the command of this new species of cavalry to observe the breeches of their recruits and see that they are of no more than legal size and thickness that ... the law against horse-stealing may not be defeated." What this satirist found humorous, of course, was the way an overtly legal

(1798)"; "An Act Against Dueling (1789)"; *The Perpetual Laws of the Commonwealth of Massachusetts From the Commencement of the Constitution* (Boston: Adams and Nourse, 1789); *Pennsylvania Colonial Records*, 4:224, June 23, 1737; *Pennsylvania Mercury*, December 16, 1785; [Boston] *Independent Chronicle*, April 27, 1786; *Inhuman Cruelty: Or Villainy Detected, Being a True Relation of the Most Unheard-of, Cruel and Barbarous Intended Murder of a Bastard Child Belonging to John and Anne Richardson* [Broadside, 1773]; *A Dialogue Between Elizabeth Smith and John Sennet, Who were Convicted Before His Majesty's Superior Court* (Boston, 1773). For work of criminology arguing for the effectiveness of shame as a punishment, see John Braithwaite, *Crime, Shame, and Reintegration* (Cambridge: Cambridge University Press, 1989).
51 *A Few Lines on Magnus Mode, Richard Hodges, and J. Newington Clark, Who are Sentenced to Stand One Hour in the Pillory* (Boston, 1767).

implementation of the punishment marked by rules contrasted with its almost extralegal character. In 1768 at Lebanon, Connecticut, another horse-riding punishment was inflicted. This time the person involved was John Allen, who was accused of abusing his wife. Seventeen male citizens of the town forced him to ride a white horse because he had been "guilty of great miscarriages and abuses towards his own wife." The punishment was carried out in the "streets where the offense was most notorious."[52]

Both Connecticut punishments were remarkably similar. But the horse thief experienced sanctions at the hands of the sheriff, while the extraofficial crowd who responded to domestic violence suffered a fine for breach of peace. Such official and extraofficial forms of rough justice were politicized during the street protests of the 1760s and early 1770s. In 1774 at Manchester, Virginia, for example, Lord North was tried in abstentia before a court of the Sons of Liberty "on suspicion of his having betrayed his trust and endeavored to enslave his majesty's subjects in America." After what was declared an impartial trial, his effigy was sentenced to ride an ass through the streets led by a deformed African American whose body was tarred and feathered and his face painted. The African-American figure represented the dangers of slavery. But, as with the popular punishment of riding the stang for abusing a wife, North's effigy was forced to ride through the streets in order to demonstrate another type of domestic violence inflicted by a mother country upon its daughter.[53]

Emerging from popular traditions, other types of rough justice contained similarities to official justice. Alfred Young has convincingly argued that tarring and feathering owes a debt to official sanctions. Tarring and feathering had its origins in the practices of sailors. It was used, Young shows, not by crowds directed by patriot leaders, but by working-class mobs. Nevertheless, the iconographic depiction of tarring and feathering in the print "The Bostonians Paying the Excise Man" (1774) underscores the contribution of the execution ritual. The customs officer has a noose around his neck, while another noose, threatening the next possible punishment, hangs upon the branches of the tree behind him.

The skimmington, too, drew upon official forms. At Attleborough in the fall of 1764, a mob of some twenty to thirty men surrounded Jonathan Shepardson to punish him for poor treatment of his family.

---

52 *Pennsylvania Journal and Weekly Advertiser*, January 28, 1786; Connecticut Archives (second series), 4:152 (May 1768). See also, for example, the case of Moses Parker, who was sentenced to sit on a wooden horse as a punishment for horse theft (*Connecticut Journal*, January 5, 1785).
53 *Virginia Gazette*, August 25, 1774.

Echoing official public punishments like the execution ritual and pillory, the skimmington, a kind of charivari, involved parading the victim through the town. Then, as with the official punishment of lashes, he would be stripped below the waist and his bottom flogged. In this instance, Shepardson resisted and stabbed to death one of his assailants. The notion of popular courts and popular punishment meant that rough justice replicated some kind of legal norms. A piece that may have been simply satiric assumed that even African Americans appropriated official legal culture. In New Hampshire, the article claimed, African Americans tried one of their own before a court, choosing a sheriff to inflict the punishment: thirteen stripes for each state, adding one for all African Americans.[54]

As suggested previously, permeable boundaries between official and extraofficial punishment existed because court-directed sanctions included public participation. Eighteenth-century legal process was what literary critic Mikhail Bakhtin called dialogic. As much a part of the punishment as the stocks or scaffold, the crowd created its own discourse (sometimes supportive, sometimes censoring) about the official sanction. Not simply the crowd present, but the common people as a whole were critical in sustaining this dialogic imagination. Common people were the instruments through which vernacular legal culture was reproduced. Two types of cultural reproduction took place: oral reproduction – gossip, tale bearing, voyeuristic stories transmitting information about the executions as an event, and even debates about the justice of the sentence itself – and print culture. Print culture extended the reach of nonprint legal ritual and oral tales far beyond the local community. But literary or iconographic representation of punishment was a form of punishment itself. It was inflicted as a shaming device. In some cases, it augmented; in others, it substituted for actual sanctions.

Take, for example, the 1762 case of counterfeiter Seth Hudson. "How do you do," Seth Hudson was asked, "after your imaginary picture punishment?" This question referred to an engraving made by Nathanial Hurd

---

[54] *Boston Evening Post*, October 29, 1765; *Newport Mercury*, November 8, 1764; *Pennsylvania Mercury*, March 25, 1788; Alfred Young's "English Plebeian Culture and Eighteenth-Century American Radicalism," in *The Origins of Anglo-American Radicalism*, eds. Margaret C. and James R. Jacobs, (London: Allen & Unwin, 1984), pp. 185–212; Bryan Palmer, "Discordant Music: Charivari and Whitecapping in North America," *Labour/Le travailleur* 1 (1978): 5–62. On English popular punishments, see E. P. Thompson, "'Rough Music': Le charivari anglais," *Annales: Economies, sociétés, civilisations* 27 (1982): 285–312; Martin Ingram, "Ridings, Rough Music, and the 'Reform of Popular Culture' in Early Modern England," *Past and Present* 105 (1984): 79–113.

that depicted Hudson on a pillory high above the surrounding crowd. Hudson, a counterfeiter with social pretensions and dreams of wealth, was mocked for achieving an "elevated station." Lying upon the raised platform was a series of round objects, most likely eggs. A passing devil flying through the air exclaimed "this is the man for me." It is striking that imagination and depiction might be considered instruments of punishment. But for a counterfeiter, such a sanction was fitting. As a counterfeiter, Hudson had forged names on treasury notes. Now an engraver would craft a counterfeit likeness. Moreover, his own confession and speech from the pillory were falsely attributed. Two counterfeit confessions and a satiric dialogue would be published about the case. Focusing upon the popular role in Hudson's punishment, these artifacts of vernacular legal literature serve as a reminder of the ways that representation stood at the intersection of official and extraofficial punishment.[55]

In the fall of 1761, Hudson was arrested with his confederate Joshua Howe for counterfeiting. Howe was convicted and sentenced to the pillory, twenty lashes, a fine of £20, and twenty years hard labor. Not anxious to face an equally stiff sentence, Hudson broke jail. Soon recaptured, Hudson's trial was said to be the most well attended Boston had ever seen. It was relocated from the courthouse to a meetinghouse. In addition to two years imprisonment and a £100 fine, Hudson was sentenced to four hours in the pillory. This was the official punishment. Its extraofficial aspect – as Hudson's fictive confession so nicely phrased it – was to be "tried by the mob."

What was this punishment? Rotten eggs would be thrown at Hudson while at the pillory. "I wish all kinds of eggs were in the bottom of the sea! And all sellers and purchasers of eggs," claimed Hudson in a fictive speech, "in the same place! I wish all hens were dead, all ducks barren, all turkeys impotent! I wish that every goose was bury'd, all eggs burnt, and all fowl beheaded." Perhaps this fictive beheading reflected transference. Could this have been what Bostonians imagined was a just fate for counterfeiters themselves? New England had limited sanctions against counterfeiting, while mid-Atlantic colonies such as New York imposed death. Hudson's speech was a fantasy about sanctions: castration, death, and beheading. But the desire to inflict punishment was displaced from felons to ducks in this satiric piece.[56]

55 *A Serious-Comical Dialogue Between the Famous Dr. Seth Hudson and the noted Joshua How, Who Were Lately Tried in Boston and Convicted of Counterfeiting* (Boston, 1762); p. 25.
56 *Boston Gazette and Country Journal*, October 12, 1761, February 8, 1762, March 1, 1762. H-DS-N's *Speech from the Pillory* [Broadside, 1762].

Not everyone felt that the mob should be so tough on Hudson. A mock verse confession included an admission of his crimes and a plea for mercy. It attacked those "whose marble hearts disdain to feel," demanding that Bostonians first judge themselves rather than others. Why was Hudson the object of such antipathy? Perhaps the answer lies in the colonial debates about currency that were then at a fever pitch. After 1760, English success in the North American theater of the Seven Years' War led to slowing of the flow of specie into the port cities. Capital grew short, and paper instruments of exchange became more common. Counterfeiters, of course, were not the main cause of colonial currency problems, but they made an easy target. Less willing to be vindictive, officials commuted Hudson's prison sentence to a short stint in the navy. But Hudson's "picture punishment" demonstrates the power of representation to crystallize crowd action and, in light of the currency crisis, perhaps contribute as well to a sense of political rage.[57]

During the 1760s, 1770s, and beyond, vernacular legal literary texts such as dying speeches and hanging ballads were marshaled for political purposes. The "picture punishment," retribution by representation, reflected the inability to actually bring political opponents to justice. As in the case of Ebenezer Richardson, mock justice was modeled on official legal process. The proliferation of effigies in the 1760s and early 1770s is well known. Their origin has been traced to Boston's Pope's Day. Adapted from Guy Fawkes Day in England, commemorating the 1605 Gunpowder Plot of Catholics against the reigning Protestant monarchy, it took place as well on November 5. During the 1740s and 1750s, Pope's Day assumed a set ritual pattern. Working men from the north and south ends of town paraded carts carrying effigies of the devil, the pope, and sometimes the Stuart pretender. The effigies were burnt at the conclusion of the day. By the mid-1760s political figures such as Grenville and Bute were added. Pope's Day was appropriated for political purposes in much the same way as official legal process. In 1764 at Newport, for example, two large popes carried around the city were accompanied by effigies of Thomas Hutchinson and Lord North. That evening a fictive pamphlet by Lord Dartmouth in "justification of popery" was, along with the effigies, committed to the flames.[58]

[57] *The Humble Confession of that Notorious Cheat, Doctor Seth Hudson* (Boston, 1762); Kenneth Scott, *Counterfeiting in Colonial America* (New York: Oxford University Press, 1957), pp. 222–24.

[58] *Boston Gazette and Country Journal,* November 11, 1765; *Newport Mercury,* November 7, 1774; *Boston Gazette,* June 27, 1774; Shaw, *American Patriots and the Rituals of Revolution,* pp. 5–25; Alfred Young, "Pope's Day, Tar and Feathers, and Cornet Joyce,

Yet what must be stressed and what has often been less explored is the *legal* meaning of effigies. The power to judge and to impose capital sentences – even mock capital sentences – was a fundamental act of sovereignty. It is ironic that the rapid proliferation and politicization of effigies should have its origins in the Stamp Act Crisis of 1764–1766. Parliament required stamps to be affixed to all legal documents. While access to official justice meant submitting to the Stamp Act, mock executions created an extraofficial "court" out-of-doors, where stamps had a very different meaning: They were stamped upon as punishment. In the case of a 1765 effigy representing the anti-Christ from the *Book of Revelation*, the stamp was transformed into the mark of the beast. Instead of proof of legal documents, stamps became signs of criminal shame, like the telltale scars left by lashes or cropped ears on a common felon. Such shared political and legal iconography marked the boundaries of law's cultural and political empire as surely as codes set the authority of official law. Mockery had its own jurisdiction.[59]

Late eighteenth-century criminal sanctions were often expressed as local justice. Highly participatory with effigies displaying their symbolic narratives, mock executions shared the immediacy of localism. Yet a common symbolic language was forged which suggested that colonial Americans as a whole appropriated the sovereign powers of political and legal judging. Real flesh-and-blood felons might be hanged only once, but mock executions repeatedly reproduced the same representational figures. Lord North and Bute might be condemned to death in a string of communities across the eastern seaboard. Appointed Connecticut's stamp distributor, Jared Ingersoll was hanged in effigy in New London, Lebanon, Windham, and Norwich. What this means, of course, is that the ritual of politicized mock executions was local but at the same time bolstered the making of a new vernacular legal culture that extended across colonial America.

Jun.: From Ritual to Rebellion in Boston, 1745–1775"; *Bulletin of the Society for the Study of Labour History* 27 (1973): 27–59.

[59] *Boston Gazette*, 19 August 1765; Ruth Bloch, *Visionary Republic: Millennial Themes in American Thought, 1756–1800* (Cambridge: Cambridge University Press, 1985), pp. 54–56 discusses eschatological associations with the Beast of Revelation. I take issue here with Peter Shaw's claim that "an orgy of symbolic destruction was necessary to the establishment of popular sovereignty." What I am suggesting is that the appropriation of the right to levy capital punishment, the execution of the effigy itself, was an act with sovereign meaning. Peter Shaw, *American Patriots and the Rituals of Revolution* (Cambridge: Harvard University Press, 1981), p. 15.

Effigies were executed with *vernacular* due process. A 1765 description of the hanging of Ingersoll's effigy, for example, emphasized the following of legal forms:

> He made his appearance at the bar of the said court in the person of his virtual representative and was denied none of those just rights of Englishmen, being allowed the sacred privileges of a trial by his peers, etc. After a full hearing, he was sentenced to be taken from the tribunal of justice, placed in a cart, with a halter about his neck, carried in a procession through the streets of the town to expose him to just ignominy and contempt, and then to be drawn to the place of execution, and hanged by the neck till dead.

This mock trial and mock execution were notable in two ways. First was the implicit critique of English justice. Virtual representation signifying an effigy was, of course, a pun on Parliament's claim to virtual representation. While jury trials were seen as threatened by English vice-admiralty courts, this right was ensured in the extraofficial justice launched by the Stamp Act protesters. Americans claimed the sovereign right to judge because, it was felt that they could judge with the utmost concern for law and due process.[60]

Secondly, due process of punishment paralleled the due process of courtroom trial. Trials had their forms: presence of the accused, trial by peers, and even the formulaic sentencing of "hanged by the neck till dead." But so did the spectacle of executions themselves. Hangings frequently took place on the town gallows. An effigy of George Grenville, for example, was hanged at the gallows on the neck where pirates were executed. Effigies were carried on carts in processions much as real felons, hanged upon gallows remarkably similar to actual ones, and buried with a great deal of pomp. Often the common executioner was employed. In 1765, newspapers marked with stamps were burnt in Boston by the usual executioner to "show as much abhorrence as possible." At Fairfield, Connecticut, in the same year protesters erected their own gallows but used the town hangman.[61]

In August 1765, Bostonians followed a familiar ritual after the mock execution of the effigy of Andrew Oliver, designated Massachusetts distributor of stamps. His figure was carted to a bonfire and burnt. Committing an effigy to the flames, of course, had its psychological and political purposes.

---

[60] *Pennsylvania Journal*, September 19, 1765; Morgan, *Stamp Act Crisis*, pp. 280–300.
[61] Belknap Papers [Harvard University], III: 116; *Boston Gazette and Country Journal*, November 4, 1765; *New York Mercury*, December 16, 1765.

It was a ritualistic destruction. Spectators greeted the burning of the straw image with cheers. Not only was fire all-consuming, but it evoked popular images of the ultimate punishment, the flames of Hell.

Moreover, it often allowed two processions through town: the first to the gallows and the second to the bonfire. In this case, the hanging took place before Oliver's house and the bonfire took place at the traditional place for burning effigies, Fort Hill. A legal tradition was also embedded in this particular form of disposing of the effigy. One crime in English law was punished with posthumous burning, petit treason, where the body of the convicted felon would first be hanged and then committed to the flames. Petit treason was defined as the murder of a husband by a wife, a master by a servant, or an ecclesiastical superior by an inferior. All these cases were thought analogous to high treason not simply because they overturned essential hierarchies, but also because they violated a relational bond. Almost all the victims were women who murdered their spouses. Here there was an inversion of sorts. The superior female, Britannia, sought to destroy her offspring, the colonies.[62]

In other ways, effigies were punished according to the dictates of Anglo-American legal traditions. Some figures, after being cut down by the populace, were dismembered. A 1765 pair of Boston effigies were torn apart limb by limb and thrown up in the air. Men were drawn and quartered for high treason while women were burned in the same fashion as for petit treason. An anecdote attributed to Boston's Sons of Liberty suggests how readily punishment imagery for treason came to mind: "That as hanging, drawing, and quartering are the punishments inflicted by law in cases of high treason we are determined at each others' houses to hang the tea kettles, draw the tea, and quarter the toast." Imagining other kinds of crimes, such as theft, led to other kinds of punishment. The citizens of Charleston in 1770 sentenced the effigy of a woman violating the embargo on English goods to the pillory. In Talbott County, Maryland, an effigy was hanged in chains following the English tradition of punishment for a highway robber. Like executed highwaymen, the figure was to remain on display "*in terrorem.*" The effigy of George Mercer, named stamp distributor in Virginia, suffered whipping, pillorying, and cropping as well as hanging. These were, of course, common punishments for felons.[63]

---

[62] Shaw, *Rituals of Revolution*, p.11; *Pennsylvania Journal*, August 29, 1765.

[63] 23 Edward III (1352); Withington, *Toward a More Perfect Union*, pp. 144–184; *Boston Gazette*, November 11, 1765; *London Chronicle*, March 31, 1774; *Virginia Gazette*, July 26, 1770; *Maryland Gazette*, September 12, 1765.

Or examine, for example, the mock punishment meted out to the effigy of James Otis. According to the English Murder Act of 1752, executed murderers would also be sentenced to dissection as "some further terror and peculiar mark of infamy [added] ... to the punishment of death." No American code mandated dissection as a punishment prior to a New York Act of 1789. Nevertheless, American opponents of Otis, called in a satiric piece "Hector Wildfire," envisioned his dissection in just such a fashion. The surgeons found a distended belly filled with air, a gall bladder full of a liquid that immediately corroded the dissecting instrument, and lungs so full of tainted air that it is a wonder that the surgeons were not poisoned. Dissection presented a striking image. It exposed the inner workings of the authentic criminal self – and in that sense the surgeon and the author of criminal biographies were much alike. Through this mock description, Otis was transformed into a poisonous creature, a serpent of sorts. His tongue, not surprisingly, was forked. Portraying Otis as hardhearted and small-minded, the anatomists were said to have found only a tiny and very hard heart along with a skull of uncommon thickness whose contents could barely fill a teacup. What must be seen as remarkable here is that by imitating a purely English statute, this satire demonstrates its roots in a broad-based popular transatlantic legal imagination. Not only in the case of punitive dissection, but also Thomas Mount's English-style canting language and the maritime punishment of tarring and feathering, demonstrated the way vernacular legal cultural forms crossed legal jurisdictions.[64]

Effigies of Lord North, Thomas Hutchinson, British Solicitor General Alexander Wedderburn, and the devil suffered a mock execution at New York City at 1774. They were carried through the streets and burnt at the coffeehouse door. The mention of the coffeehouse tells us something about the way culture – and legal culture in particular – replicated itself in late-eighteenth-century America. In the Ebenezer Richardson case, as we have seen, American radicals transformed the coffeehouse into a courthouse. Here it served as the forum of public debate. Gossip was at the center of vernacular legal culture. It is possible to imagine the discussions

---

[64] *Boston Evening Post*, March 7, 1763. See also the mock execution of William Cobbett: *The Last Confession of Peter Porcupine with an Account of his Dissection* (Philadelphia, 1797). On Cobbett's new form of belligerent journalism, see Marcus Daniel, *Scandal and Civility: Journalism and the Birth of American Democracy* (New York: Oxford University Press, 2009), pp, 187–230. Dissection as punishment is described in Steven Wilf, "Anatomy and Punishment in Late Eighteenth-Century New York," *Journal of Social History* (1989): 507–530 and Chapter Five.

about the trial and execution of these figures that took place. Perhaps, like at many other patriot events, there were even toasts. As argued previously, spectacles of punishment and oral transmission were closely tied together.[65]

Straw-stuffed images, effigies were meant to be "virtual representatives." Like Frasier, whose cropped ears recorded vital information about his life, effigies, too, signified the individuals they represented. When New Yorkers hanged a figure of Lieutenant Governor Caldwaller Colden, they broke into his carriage house and took his coach to use for carting the effigy through town. During a 1765 Stamp Act protest in Boston, two effigies hanged were dressed in "gentleman's breeches." As has been well noted, boots representing Lord Bute often accompanied the effigies. In Colden's case, there was a boot and a drum "supposed to allude to some former circumstances of his life" when he was a drummer in the Pretender's army. This Richardson-like symbolic narrative of earlier crimes, perhaps, would not have been decipherable without the aid of a paper affixed to his chest.[66]

Placards established a written text for the effigy ritual. The effigies "were decorated with suitable emblems, devices, and inscriptions." The corpses of hanged effigies were not covered with a sheet, went a newspaper report from 1765, except the sheet of paper which bore the inscription. Placards were attached to felons suffering such official mock punishments as the stocks or sitting in the scaffold. These signs described the nature of the crime or included a simple confession. Pinned to the coat of one figure hanged in Boston, for example, was a bit of threatening gallows poetry: "My mother always thought me wild/The gallows is thy portion child ... But if some brethren I could name/Who shar'd the crime, should share the shame/This glorious tree tho' big and tall/Indeed would never hold 'em all." The effigy of Andrew Oliver underscored the significance of print vernacular legal culture. Out of a boot representing Lord Bute peeped a devil. As a placard attached to the effigy explained: "The devil has me outwitted/And instead of stamping others, I've hang'd myself." The devil, we are told, was the printer's devil. In a sense, the press assumed an impish role, urging political action. Print culture made vernacular legal forms a commonplace of political ritual in

---

the 1760s and 1770s through mock hanging ballads, dying confessions, and execution narratives.[67]

Effigies would be lifeless, dumb objects without placards affixed or mock narratives. A dying confession was handed "to the criminals for their perusal just before the execution," went one mock complaint about the silence of stuffed straw figures, "but they continuing silent, would not read a single word of it ... as a punishment on their contemptuous taciturnity it was affixed before their faces to the gallows." This, of course, was an echo of common law peine forte et dure where offenders who stood mute and refused to plead might face extra punishment, including solitary confinement and crushing the naked body to death. As has been seen, flesh-and-blood felons often appropriated vernacular legal culture for their own purposes. In the case of mock executions, however, when effigies remain mute it is a collective politicized authorial voice that dominates the criminal confession.

The effigy of the designated stamp distributor for Maryland, Zechariah Hood, for example, was said to have been taken to the whipping post and received lashes so well inflicted that "he was incapable of speaking anymore." Such anthropomorphic imagery lies at the ironic heart of the mock execution. In some ways the question for the political patrons of the mock execution was precisely how well to fashion the criminal self. Should there be a narrative of birth and parentage? Should a confession describe its crimes in detail? And should the effigy truly repent its deeds? In Hood's case, the effigy seemed visceral and somewhat inert. It was described as vomiting – losing straw – its "countenance never once changed until he was burning." Perhaps this reflects the frustration of Hood having fled to New York and taken refuge in Fort George. Without Hood himself, Maryland citizens had nothing but a representational figure in his place. Not surprisingly, then, the silence of the stuffed figure was substituted with a political voice that claimed to have heard faint murmurings about penitence. If Hood became the classic petty criminal figure expressing a reluctant touch of regret, protestors assumed the role as the boisterous execution crowd. The Sons of Liberty would not hear of mercy. They cried, we are told, "hang him, burn him."[68]

---

[67] *Virginia Gazette*, July 7, 1774; *Boston Post-Boy and Advertiser*, July 26, 1765; *Boston Gazette and Country Journal*, August 19, 1765.

[68] *New York Gazette*, November 21, 1765; *Virginia Gazette*, August 29, 1771; Withington, *Toward a More Perfect Union*, pp. 172–180; Morgan, *Stamp Act Crisis*, p. 199.

The architects of Hood's mock execution drew upon vernacular legal culture to fabricate a fictive past and confession similar to those of common felons:

I was indulged too much in my younger years by my tutors. I never was instructed in the true and virtuous principles of religion ... such as to fear my God and love my neighbors. Nor did I ever regard honor, honesty, or liberty, but I said 'What's my country to me, I'll get money'. ...I once more acknowledge my villainy to my country. Nor have I any consolation in my last moments to afford myself, as having always when in my power, defrauded king, the proprietor, and my countrymen.

Many of the familiar tropes are there: a spoiled childhood, poor religious instruction, and greed. Yet what is the purpose of bringing them to bear in Hood's case? Do they not in some way serve as pretexts or excuses? Perhaps the confession was simply meant to mirror as closely as possible the formulaic structure of the last confession. Or, perhaps, it is meant to shift the blame back to English political mentors.[69]

Other politicized fictive confessions drew upon vernacular legal culture as its model. In *The Last Speech, Confession, and Dying Words of Francis Bernard*, the former governor of Massachusetts confessed at his mock execution to robbery. Ascending to the governorship through patronage, he found it a rich source of profits. Most striking is the way that the confession sets apart official law – with its rogues like Bernard – and the extraofficial legal structures represented by mock executions: "I found the trick, quibble, and demurs ... of the law exactly coincided with the baseness of my heart." More than one kind of inversion is taking place here. A high government is turned topsy-turvy into a robber. But a verse broadside modeled on the genre of the hanging ballad, entitled "On the Departure of an Infamous B-R – T," goes one step further. Returning to England after his failed governorship, Bernard was recast as a transported felon: "But like a robber, be exil'd from home/[find] what best become a thievish wretch/A Tyburn salutation from Ketch." America turns the legal world upside down by transporting felons back to England, and to Tyburn, instead of the other way around.[70]

Refusing to abide by the nonimportation agreement, Boston merchant Nathanial Rogers fled to New York City. The Sons of Liberty continued

---

[69] *New-York Gazette*, November 21, 1765.
[70] *Massachusetts Spy*, October 15, 1772; *On the Departure of an Infamous B-R – T* [Broadside, 1769].

to harass him there. After a mock execution, the effigy of Rogers was committed to the flames. A letter warned him to leave town within twenty-four hours. Yet Rogers's fictive dying speech extended the threat to include "people among yourselves as culpable as me." "I acknowledge the justice of my sentence," the confession concludes, "and sincerely wish that all that are guilty of the crime for which I suffer may be ninety-two degrees more severely punished than me." As with the storytelling of flesh-and-blood felons, it is important to read between the lines. The dying speech followed the convention of describing the criminal's parents. In this case, however, the kinship was meant to be humorous: "My father was one of Oliver Cromwell's descendants and my mother was only forty-five generations removed from the witch of Endor" – or, perhaps, not so humorous. Both figures were implicated in acts of regicide.[71]

Common formulae of vernacular legal culture, then, were appropriated for political purposes. The Protestant penitential theme was altered almost beyond recognition. Protestant Francis Bernard said in his dying speech that he died in the Catholic faith. In his 1775 mock confession, General Thomas Gage was seen in a dialogue with a friar. Gage is told that he will be made clean with a few dozen masses and small pains in purgatory. The confession is cut short when his confessor insists upon supper. Gage's mock confession is especially interesting because it inscribes in legal imagery what had already been imagined in rhetoric. John Cleveland, minister at Ipswich, called Gage "a robber, a murderer, a usurper but a wicked rebel ... who will be consigned to Hell."[72]

Despite their failings, Bernard and Gage were represented as penitent felons. Lord North's mock confession, too, showed submission to the justice of the sentence. "The penitential appearance of this noble Lord," we are told, "excited compassion in the minds of some of the spectators." But a stampman effigy executed in Massachusetts was presented as the other, less deferential side of vernacular legal culture. This felon was too much the hardened rogue. Quoting English criminal cant, "even on the gallows ... the dying speech would be, come one swing, for with a wry neck and a pissed pair of breaches and all will be over."[73] It is easy to understand

---

[71] *New-York Post-Boy,* May 14, 1770; *New York Mercury,* May 14, 1770; *Virginia Gazette,* June 7, 1770; *The Dying Speech of a Wretched Importer which was Exalted Upon a Gibbet and Afterwards Committed to the Flames at New York* (New York, 1770).

[72] *General Gage's Confession: Being the Substance of his Excellency's Last Conference with his Ghostly Father, Friar Francis* [Broadside, 1775]; *Virginia Gazette,* August 25, 1774; *Boston Gazette and Country Journal,* December 30, 1765; *Essex Gazette,* July 13, 1775.

[73] *Massachusetts Spy,* October 15, 1772.

why American radicals would fabricate submissive mock confessions of political opponents. But why invent insubordinate ones? In some ways, part of mock punishment was self-mockery.

The sovereignty assumed through trials out-of-doors and mock capital punishment had an ironic side. For all its rich cultural detail, it lacked the power of state-directed law. Not surprisingly, then, even an effigy would be seen as willing to "deride and mock at this punishment even on the gallows." If mock punishment was a kind of carnivalesque inversion where extraofficial law replaced official legal norms, then how else to greet the sudden appropriation of legal rights except with humor? Take, for example, the 1765 mock execution of George Grenville, English architect of the colonial customs policy. A report describes "a solemn procession" of the effigy from the courthouse through the North End to the town gallows on Boston's neck. But what happened at the end of the hanging was hardly solemn. The figure was thrown again and again in the air. Grenville's effigy wore a label, drawing upon the hanging ballad tradition: "Your servant, sirs do you like my figure/You've seen one rogue but here's a bigger/Father of mischief how I soar!/Where many a rogue has gone before." Not simply hanged, Grenville was tossed about as he was sent to the devil. "I die ... in the hope," went the fictive confession of an importer, "that the spectators will demolish each other's noses with my legs and arms after my dissolution."[74]

Such an overturning of official legal norms threatened other hierarchies as well. Effigies were gentlemen, sometimes even lords. They were dressed in the clothing of gentlemen. Often this has been seen as an example of plebeian hostility to social elites. But it may just as well suggest an evocative sign of equality under extraofficial law. A Charlestown woman who violated an anti-importation agreement had her effigy placed in the pillory. Although from one of the first families in town, the figure was treated with contempt because "we are not respecting of persons who had violated the resolutions of this province." Not plebeian misrule, but the imposition of equal justice for all, suggested that social hierarchies might be inverted through punishment.[75]

---

[74] *Boston Gazette and Country Journal*, December 30, 1765; *Boston Gazette*, November 4, 1765; *Dying Speech of a Wretched Importer*.

[75] *Virginia Gazette*, July 26, 1770. A number of scholars, including Alfred Young, "English Plebeian Culture," pp. 185–212, and Paul Gilje, *Road to Mobocracy*, pp. 20–21, have identified mock executions with notions of plebeian misrule. Peter Shaw, *American Patriots and the Rituals of Revolution*, offers a psychoanalytic interpretation of Revolutionary symbolism. While arguing that the patriotic movement's ideology was

Examine two mock confessions from the 1770s. Between 1766 and 1771, North Carolina was torn apart by a movement of west country farmers, the North Carolina Regulation, which sought to democratize local government and opposed the inequitable distribution of the tax burden. The Regulators engaged in civil disobedience and limited acts of violence. Declaring that insurrection had broken out in Orange County, Governor William Tryon mustered troops. At the Battle of the Alamance in 1771 nearly three-thousand poorly armed Regulators were defeated by a well-disciplined army of about half that size. Tryon followed his victory by executing a half-dozen Regulators under the Riot Act. American radicals in the northern seaport cities, not surprisingly, saw Tryon's use of the Riot Act as an act of repression masked by law. Isaiah Thomas, patriot printer of the *Massachusetts Spy*, in 1771 accused Tryon in the style of fictive criminal narratives of being a murderer, horse thief, and plunderer. Defenders of Tryon from the coastal town of New Bern, North Carolina, turned the tables. Hanging Thomas in effigy, they included a mock "Last Speech and Dying Words of Isaiah Thomas." Here Thomas becomes the criminal who was "moved and seduced by the devil, who is properly the father of lies, bitter invectives, and scurrilous epithets [issued] against a distinguished gentleman of the most exalted character."[76]

But the story does not end here. Tryon left America and returned with the invading British Army during the American Revolution. He is a kind of counterfigure of the transported felon. In his mock confession, Tryon admits to responsibility for the death of the "innocent, the fatherless, and widows." Like transported felons who faced a death sentence if they returned after their capital crime was commuted to transportation, Tryon could now suffer mock execution: "had I but tarried in my native country when there last, I might, for a little while longer, have escaped this ignominious death." But Tryon was persuaded to return by other members of

---

broadly progressive, he suggests that the mirroring of traditional forms of punishment "could be embarrassingly regressive" (p. 21). Depicting English execution ritual, Thomas Laqueur has portrayed the atmosphere as carnivalesque with few political consequences. "Crowds, Carnival, and the State in English Executions 1604–1868," in *The First Modern Society: Essays in English History in Honor of Lawrence Stone*, eds. A. C. Beier, David Cannadine, and James M. Rosenheim (Cambridge: Cambridge University Press, 1989), pp. 305–356. I have tended to see a greater expression of legal norms than Young, Gilje, or Shaw, and more political meaning than Laqueur.

[76] *Massachusetts Spy*, August 29, 1771; *Virginia Gazette*, August 29, 1771; Marvin L. Michael Kay, "The North Carolina Regulation, 1766–1776: A Class Conflict," in *The American Revolution: Explorations in the History of American Radicalism*, ed. Alfred F. Young, (DeKalb: Northern Illinois University Press, 1976), pp. 71–124.

his gang, Bute, and the devil. The dying speech concludes with a warning to the English generals – Gage, Burgoyne, Howe, and Clinton – "to quit the steps you are now treading, and let my shameful end be the means of turning you from following the damnable advice of North and his cursed ministry."[77]

"We have a hereditary, indefeasible right to a halter," were the words posted on an effigy in 1765. This is a remarkable statement of how emphatically revolutionary Americans asserted the right to judge. Oppressors were labeled "sons of the scaffold" – perhaps a counterpoint to the Sons of Liberty – and as effigies often forced to leave life in precisely such a fashion. Most strikingly, perhaps the most prominent symbol of American opposition to England, the Liberty Tree or Pole, was inscribed with a double meaning as a gallows. Hanged effigies are often referred to as its fruit. Not everyone was comfortable with this double meaning. An opponent of the New York Sons of Liberty criticized the movement for having the Liberty Pole, their "rendezvous made a gallows green." But both Tories and patriots agreed about the iconographic identification of the Liberty Tree with the gallows. In a ballad from 1768, the Liberty Tree was compared to England's Tyburn: "the tree which the wisdom of justice hath rear'd" should not be spared.[78]

What this centrality of scaffold symbolism suggests, of course, is the claim to an American sovereign legal authority over capital punishment. Executions were "the power of the government displayed in its most awful form."[79] But more than that was established. Having inherited a robust vernacular legal culture, common people – both felons and everyday citizens – turned these rituals and narratives into the stuff with which to make their own claims about the law. Vernacular forms of law were invested with a newfound political meaning that could not be ignored.

---

[77] *The Speech of William Tr[yo]n, Esq.* [Broadside] (1776).

[78] *Boston Evening-Post*, September 2, 1765; *Right Hon. William Pitt, Earl of Chatham to the Virtuous and Patriotic Citizens of New York.* [Broadside, 1770]; *Massachusetts Spy*, January 30, 1772; Paul Revere's well-known "View of the Year 1765" depicts an effigy of Andrew Oliver hanging from a tree labeled the "Liberty Tree"; *Liberty, Property, and No Excise: A Poem Compos'd on Occasion of the Sight Seen of the Great Trees (So Called) in Boston ... On the 14th of August 1765* [Broadside, 1765]; *Boston Gazette*, February 19, 1770; "A Parody upon a well-known Liberty Song" (1768) in Frank Moore, *Songs and Ballads of the American Revolution* (New York: D. Appleton, 1856), pp. 41–43.

[79] Nathan Strong, *The Reasons and Design of Public Punishments* (Hartford: Ebenezer Watson, 1777), p. 3.

3

Local Justice, Transatlantic Justice

Joseph Mountain, William Beadle, and Competing Legal Narratives in Connecticut

Through storytelling offenders refashioned themselves. Beyond the rhetorical strategies employed by felons in narratives, apologetics, narrative lacunae, and justification lie larger narratives – those tales whose meanings place political culture in a context for the reader. For eighteenth-century Americans, grappling with the legal consequences of a struggle for independence, these tales underscore the permeability of transatlantic culture. This chapter, a case study, explores how the tale of two offenders captured the problems of their day: religion and race, credit and bondage, and, most of all, the problem of insiders and outsiders at the very moment republican rhetoric posited a brotherhood of citizens.

The first offender, Joseph Mountain, was a mulatto ex-slave executed in 1790 for the rape of a young white girl. Earlier, however, Mountain ran away from his master. He fled to London and pursued a life of crime. In a remarkable execution narrative telling of his experiences as a highwayman in England, Mountain provides a rare glimpse of transatlantic themes mediated through the particular experiences of an African-American felon. Mountain's autobiographical narrative, as well as his pardon petition, raises a number of issues: slavery and liberty, a comparison of English and American treatment of African Americans, debates over capital punishment, and the question of how to construct a republican form of criminal justice. No doubt Mountain was unusually articulate. His own words will be read in intertextual fashion against texts crafted by authoritative figures, including sermons and a charge to the jury.

In 1782, William Beadle killed himself and his family. Born in England, Beadle, like Mountain, was something of an outsider. Nonetheless, he was for some time a respected merchant and an established member of the community. When his fortunes declined, Beadle chose suicide rather than what he believed was the humiliation of poverty. Like Mountain, Beadle wrote remarkably articulate documents placing his crime in context: a five-page will, two letters to an acquaintance totaling sixteen pages, and a variety of other letters. Though these documents did not survive intact, they are quoted by contemporaries. Beadle's writings, too, became the centerpiece of a discourse about transatlantic themes: deism and religious skepticism, the emergence of anonymous market relations, and the impact of the American Revolution on community social structure. Each text must be read as their contemporaries read them against the "texts" of transatlantic issues of race, political economy, sexual and familial relations, and religion.

THE ART OF FLIGHT, THE ART OF WRITING

Two details dominate Joseph Mountain's criminal biography. One was his capture; the other his color. In England, Mountain became a seasoned highway robber. But after the 1790 rape of a young girl near New Haven, he neither fled nor resisted. Even Mountain himself was puzzled by his behavior. "Upon recollection," Mountain later reflected, "I am often surprised that I did not attempt my escape." When the girl's screams attracted neighbors, Mountain had every opportunity to run away before being apprehended. Yet "by some unaccountable fatality I loitered unconcerned." The word *fatality* accurately portrays both his sense that being captured would ultimately be his fate and the fact that the decision was fatal. Mountain was hanged for the rape.[1]

Why did his instincts as a professional criminal fail him this time? What made Mountain choose to remain immobile by his victim's side at the risk of his life? The perplexing question of how he was seized, it appears, was at the root of Mountain's execution narrative. It was not simply the felony itself or a life of crime that needed to be explained. Instead, what the narrative does is juxtapose his wandering – shifting scenes from Philadelphia to London, from France to sailing ships bound for the West Indies – with the paralysis at the moment of the capture. As will be suggested, flight and captivity are two powerful metaphors for Mountain's biography.

---

[1] Joseph Mountain, *Sketches of the Life of Joseph Mountain, A Negro Who Was Executed at New-Haven on the 20th Day of October 1790* (New Haven, 1790), p. 18. On the factors that compel confession, see Peter Brooks, *Troubling Confessions: Speaking Guilt in Law and Literature* (Chicago: University of Chicago Press, 2001).

Secondly, it was a life dominated by color. Mountain was an African American. Most eighteenth-century Americans retained simple standards of racial classification: black or white, slave or free. But Mountain inhabited the ambiguous position between such clearly demarcated definitions. He was not black, Mountain insisted, but like his father, a mulatto. While his father appears to have been a slave, Mountain's mother was freed at age twenty-one. It was commonplace for the execution narrative to claim that the felon came from a good family. For Mountain that meant light skin, his mother's status as a freed woman, and the social position of his masters.

Born in 1758, Mountain claimed that he was raised in the house of Samuel Mifflin. The Mifflins were a prominent Philadelphia family. Thomas Mifflin, who Mountain identified as Samuel's son, would be the first post-Revolutionary governor of Pennsylvania. At the time that Mountain was born, Philadelphia had close to 1,400 slaves in the city. More than 10 percent of the population, black slaves must be seen as part of the city's system of unfree labor that spanned a spectrum from indentured servitude to race-based slavery. Nevertheless, more than any other colonial city, Philadelphia experienced the beginnings of antislavery agitation, largely under the auspices of Quaker leadership. John Woolman urged Friends to free their slaves. In 1770, another Friend, Anthony Benezet, created a school where blacks could receive instruction to prepare for freedom. Quakers were instrumental in the 1775 founding of The Pennsylvania Abolition Society. Such calls for black freedom in Philadelphia, the city that Gary Nash has called the "capital of conscience" of late-eighteenth-century America, must have affected those still enslaved.[2]

But how? The period when Mountain was born represented the high-water mark for black flight. Yet there were other paths. Compare Mountain to his contemporary, Richard Allen. Born in Philadelphia only

---

[2] Gary Nash, "Slaves and Slave holders in Colonial Philadelphia," *William & Mary Quarterly* 30 (1973): 223–256 and *Forging Freedom: The Formation of Philadelphia's Black Community 1720–1840* (Cambridge: Harvard University Press, 1988), pp. 8–37. Two excellent books explore the laboring classes in Revolutionary Philadelphia: Sharon V. Salinger, *To Serve Well and Faithfully: Labor and Indentured Servants in Pennsylvania 1682–1800* (Cambridge: Cambridge University Press, 1987) and Jean R. Soderlund's *Quakers and Slavery: A Divided Spirit* (Princeton: Princeton University Press, 1985) shows how Quaker abolitionist ideology was not always followed in practice. Philadelphia's social elite is described in Thomas M. Doerflinger, *A Vigorous Spirit of Enterprise: Merchants and Economic Development in Revolutionary Philadelphia* (Chapel Hill: University of North Carolina Press, 1986).

two years after Mountain, Allen also began life as an African-American slave. While Mountain could claim membership in the Mifflin household, Allen was raised in the home of another prominent Philadelphian, Attorney General Benjamin Chew. But Chew needed capital and was forced to sell Allen. At the age of seventeen, the very age when Mountain took flight, Allen found himself separated from his parents and younger siblings. Allen's response was very different from Mountain's. Embracing Methodism, Allen dedicated himself to such activities as prayer meetings and missionary work among fellow slaves. After working at odd jobs to provide money for his manumission, Allen would ultimately become the leader of the African Methodist Episcopal Church. The parallels and divergences of Allen's and Mountain's autobiographies are illuminating. Allen worked toward manumission as part of Pennsylvania's gradual emancipation; Mountain chose flight in another country. Allen found solace and community among Methodists, Mountain among prostitutes and highway robbers. While Allen became Philadelphia's most prominent African American, Mountain was hanged for rape at New Haven.[3]

As both Mountain and Allen discovered, being black overwhelmingly shaped identity in colonial America. It determined status, autonomy, a person's role in the labor market, familial relations, and almost every other detail of everyday life. Against appearance and hue, Mountain used language. Nowhere was this clearer than in his very name, Joseph Mountain, with its images of grandeur and power. Joseph is evocative of the biblical figure of the same name who was sold into slavery. Yet Joseph escaped servitude and became one of the most well-to-do men in Egypt. While the biblical Joseph rose by resisting such temptations as Potiphar's wife, the eighteenth-century Joseph followed his lusts and acquired wealth through theft. Yet still the similarity was telling. The biblical Joseph narrative contrasted his own breaking loose from captivity with the inevitable slavery that awaited generations of Hebrews. Similarly, the shift from slavery to free black status was a route for individuals, not, like

---

[3] Billy G. Smith and Richard Wojtowicz, *Blacks Who Stole Themselves: Advertisements for Runaways in the Pennsylvania Gazette 1728–1790* (Philadelphia: University of Pennsylvania Press, 1989); Carol V. R. George, *Segregated Sabbaths: Richard Allen and the Rise of Independent Black Churches 1760–1840* (Oxford: Oxford University Press, 1973); Barbara Clark Smith, *After the Revolution: The Smithsonian History of Everyday Life in the Eighteenth Century* (New York: Pantheon Books, 1985), pp. 139–186. See also Gary B. Nash "'To Arise Out of Dust': Absalom Jones and the African Church of Philadelphia," *Race, Class, and Politics: Essays on Colonial and Revolutionary America* (Champaign: University of Illinois Press, 1986).

rebellion, a collective response to the mass enslavement of blacks. Joseph Mountain's tale then, too, was primarily one of personal liberation.

Historians have shown how important were the naming patterns of free blacks. The first census of the New Haven area in 1790 listed such names as Caesar, Nando, Congo, Pomp, Cuffy, and Sharper. Upon manumission, ex-slaves shed off-handed names like Lucky or literary ones such as Scipio and Othello, and seized control of the naming process. Many chose biblical names. The names in Mountain's family demonstrate such a shift from his father, Fling, to the biblical Joseph. Mountain's name may have simply come from his religious Presbyterian master. Nevertheless, Mountain was undoubtedly a proud man. Like free blacks, Mountain avoided such a familiar form of address as Joe. Naming was a matter of power. A satire published after his execution belittled Mountain by assigning him an old-fashioned slave name, Cuffy Mungo.[4] The narrative itself, then, must be seen as a form of naming: the construction of an image of one's own biography as opposed to categories imposed from the outside. In addition to free blacks, felons were the other eighteenth-century social group to rename themselves. Aliases served not only as a linguistic disguise, but also as a means of inventing a new self. Mountain may have drawn upon both traditions.

But what can be made of the surname Mountain? Surnames were not common for slaves. Free blacks, Gary Nash has argued, saw the surname as a means of establishing identity. They rarely used the last name of their master. Mountain seems to have followed this pattern. Perhaps borrowing the first letter of the Mifflin's name, he created a striking surname. The word *mountain* summons a set of powerful images: strength, potency, independence. Mountains are their own landscape, a refuge. They serve as a geographic counterpoint to urban Philadelphia and London where Mountain was first a slave and later a robber. The mountain as symbol frames the execution narrative. It ends with him "stumbling on the dark mountains of the shadow of death." What could better describe the violent life of dark Joseph Mountain?[5]

[4] *Connecticut Courant*, November 8, 1790.
[5] *The First Census of the United States, Connecticut*, pp. 101–105. Gary B. Nash, "Forging Freedom: The Emancipation Experience in the Northern Seaport Cities, 1775–1820" in *Slavery and Freedom in the Age of the American Revolution*, eds. Ira Berlin and Ronald Hoffman (Charlottesville: University Press of Virginia, 1983), pp. 3–48 and *Forging Freedom: The Formation of Philadelphia's Black Community 1720–1840* (Cambridge: Harvard University Press, 1988), pp. 79–88.

At age seventeen, Mountain left Philadelphia for London with his master's consent. The purpose of this voyage cannot be determined. Mountain arrived in England only a few years after the Somerset Case of 1772. A Virginian, Charles Stuart imported his slave James Somerset to England. Deserting his master, Somerset was later captured and returned to Stuart. As a punishment, Stuart chose to sell Somerset in Jamaica. Lord Mansfield brought Somerset to court under a writ of habeas corpus. In the landmark decision, Mansfield rejected the authority of foreign slave laws in England. The Somerset case was interpreted, somewhat incorrectly, as conferring freedom on any black slave who sets foot on English soil. Mountain's legal status and how he left his master are oddly ignored in his narrative. It is unclear whether Somerset had legal implications for Mountain. Nevertheless, as has been argued, major cases can be psychological landmarks as well as legal ones. Describing the liberating experience of strolling through post-Somerset London in search of amusement, Mountain indeed must have thought that England's air was liberating.[6]

Mountain would not have been the only black face in the city. There were some 10,000 to 20,000 London blacks consisting of nearly 7 percent of the population. Not only were there freed slaves, but black figures were frequently used in the iconography of London's sign boards. Although Mountain may have left behind slavery, it was much more difficult to shake loose the symbolic meaning of color. Blacks were associated with base emotions, such as overheated sexual desire, and portrayed as part of plebian culture. Hogarth's Four Times of the Day, for example, depicted a black man fondling the breasts of a white servant woman. Black figures found their way into Hogarthian landscapes, including the cockfighting pit and the prostitute's boudoir. Mountain slipped into such representational commonplaces in much the same way. At an alehouse, he met two men, Francis Hyde and Thomas Wilson, who traveled about during the day with a hand organ and juggling, but during the night were robbers. They introduced Mountain to their illegal trade. The powerless ex-servant was transformed into a figure who could demand obedience.[7]

Mountain's first attempt at robbery marked a remarkable inversion. Hyde and Wilson were "dressed in white frocks and boots with their

---

[6] Mountain, *Sketches*, p. 2; F. O. Shyllon, *Black Slaves in Britain* (Oxford: Oxford University Press, 1974); David Brion Davis, *The Problem of Slavery in the Age of Revolution 1770–1823* (Ithaca: Cornell University Press, 1975), pp. 469–501.

[7] David Dabydeen, *Hogarth's Blacks: Images of Blacks in Eighteenth-Century English Art* (Athens: University of Georgia Press, 1987).

faces painted yellow to resemble mulattos." Mountain was dressed in the same manner, "with the addition of a large tail wig, white gloves, and a black mask over his face." A kind of racial equality was enforced between the confederates: Mountain's color was masked while the two native Englishmen became mulattos. It appears that such egalitarian social relations, as much as earnings, attracted Mountain to robbery. Ultimately joining a band of highwaymen, Mountain had to undergo a rite of passage before fully entering their fraternity. For eleven days, he robbed alone before returning to the inn where his confederates were waiting. It had been a successful journey, and Mountain came back with a good deal of plunder. He was now accepted: "I shall never forget with what joy I was received. The house rang with the praises of Mountain. An elegant supper was provided, and he placed at the head of the table." The importance for Mountain of the entrance into this fellowship cannot be overestimated. After the celebration, he chose not to return to the roads, but rested among his newfound comrades. "Notwithstanding the darkness of his complexion, he was complimented as the first of his profession, and qualified for the most daring enterprises."

Throughout the narrative, Mountain boasts of his prowess. He refused to be associated with bungling highway robbers who were forced to resort to violence on Tottenham Court Road. With disdain he dismisses another novice whose rite of passage was unsuccessful as "inadequate to the business." But this was more than simply vanity about skill. Pride replaced the moralism of traditional execution biographies as the most prominent theme of the narrative voice. He demands that a Quaker, whom he robs near Manchester, not use the informal form of address: "You must not thou me." Mountain proudly distinguished between highwaymen, who robbed while mounted on a horse, and mere footpads. "The business which now seemed most alluring to me was that of highwaymen. Considering myself at the head of footpads, I aspired to a more honorable profession." The highwayman's horse, which Mountain celebrates in a passage, was not just a means of travel. It was a symbol of power and social station. Like slavery, the use of a horse meant harnessing the brute strength of another.[8]

---

[8] Mountain, *Sketches*, pp. 3–10. On highwaymen, see J. M. Beattie, *Crime and the Courts in England 1660–1800* (Princeton: Princeton University Press, 1986), pp. 148–167; Frank McLynn, *Crime and Punishment in Eighteenth-Century England* (Oxford: Oxford University Press, 1991), pp. 56–82; Peter Linebaugh, *The London Hanged: Crime and Civil Society in the Eighteenth Century* (Cambridge: Cambridge University Press, 1992), pp. 184–218.

Fabricating the self began with Mountain's almost complete identifi-cation with what he calls his "profession." Only after his arrest for rape did this construction take a literary form. Yet the relationship between criminal life and narrative was much more provocative. The eighteenth century might be called the golden age of highway robbery. Tales of such celebrated bandits as Dick Turpin were invested with Robin Hood quali-ties and became part of English folklore. Mountain shaped his life around this genre. Even his manner of accosting victims seemed to have a literary flair: "You know my profession – Deliver!" He would then assume the romantic pose of a gentleman highway robber, taking a prayer book from his pocket and asking them to swear not to report the crime for twenty-four hours. Mountain would have been surprised to be considered what historians call a social bandit. Nevertheless, narcissism pressed him to view his autobiography through narrative lenses. He never failed to read the press reports of his robberies. "I saw a spectacular detail of the trans-action," he recounted with pleasure, "in the newspaper." After a night-time robbery of an old miser's home in Portsmouth, Mountain could not resist gathering the next morning with a crowd of spectators to watch the victim raving at his loss. "I was a spectator at this collection, and now perfectly remember the chagrin of the old man and his wife." Mountain served as both actor and spectator of his own life.

Not surprisingly, then, Mountain's execution narrative has the mark-ings of an oft-told tale. At the celebration following his rite of passage as a highway robber, Mountain recalled "I gave a faithful narrative of my transactions, and produced the plunder as undeniable proof." Nevertheless, though Mountain could read and write, his biography was compiled by someone else. David Daggett, cousin of Yale College President Naphtali Daggett, anonymously published Mountain's tales. Mountain was brought to him to be cross-examined immediately after the rape. Admitted to the bar in 1786, Daggett was a young justice of the peace at the time. Later – and this is another prime example of the seamlessness of learned and vernacular legal culture – he would become Chancellor Kent Professor of Law at Yale and Chief Justice of the Connecticut Supreme Court. Yet Daggett's *Sketches of the Life of Joseph Mountain* shares very little in common with the eighteenth-century law report. Instead, it was intended to be read alongside the ordinary of Newgate's popular tales of highway robbers as a part of a genre of popular crime literature.

Both Daggett and Mountain sharing authorship meant that the narra-tive was double-voiced. As with other African-American texts, black oral traditions and formal white literary traditions coexisted. Borrowing a phrase from critic Henry Louis Gates, the Mountain narrative was itself a "mulatto with a two-toned [literary] heritage." Gates has shown how critical authorial control was for early black writers. In John Marrant's 1785 captivity narrative, a black man held by the Cherokees exerted authority not simply over the text, but his captors' speech as well. Mountain's narrative leveled other voices, such as those of his confederates or the pleas of his rape victim. The psychological motivation, the apologetics, and lack of apologetics are clearly Mountain's. Although, as will be shown later, the narrative fulfills a legal role, there can be no doubt that Mountain – who so well understood his place as an eighteenth-century trope in vernacular legal culture – was the dominant authorial voice.[9]

It was precisely the dominant voice of Mountain that troubled an anonymous satirist attacking the publication of his autobiography. The satire mockingly suggests that some idle person be employed "to visit all the prisons in the state to write the history of the lives and adventures of other renowned heroes who are sentenced to Newgate or [the] gallows." Prisons and the execution narrative, as shall be argued later, must be understood as symbolic counterpoints. Connecticut's Newgate Prison was a converted mine, a place meant to be dark, distant, and forbidding. The publication of Mountain's narrative, on the other hand, brought the criminal underworld to light. Should criminal lives be hidden or exposed? Where does this often voyeuristic uncovering end? The satire calls for publishing accounts of the dissection of felons. Why should surgeons "monopolize the advantages of seeing the heart of a scoundrel?" "The world may be benefitted not only by the lives, achievements, and wise sayings of a villain," the satire sarcastically remarks, "but even by his bowels after death. So that even when dead, his words speak." What it suggests, then, is that the published autobiography serves as a false representation. Probing beneath the outward representation of Mountain, according to the satire, anatomists found a half-dozen devils lodged under the left ventricle of Mountain's heart, all armed with pointed pitchforks.[10]

Questions of inclusion and exclusion belonged not only to Mountain, but to English society as a whole. Protestants reacted angrily to the Catholic

---

[9] Mountain, *Sketches*, pp. 9–11 and Franklin Bowditch Dexter, *Biographical Sketches of the Graduates of Yale College, 1778–1792*, 6 vols. (New York: Henry Holt and Company, 1907), 4: 260–264; Henry Louis Gates, Jr., *The Signifying Monkey: A Theory of Afro-American Literary Criticism* (Oxford: Oxford University Press, 1988), pp. ix–xxviii and 127–169.

[10] *Connecticut Courant*, November 8, 1790; *Connecticut Journal*, December 15, 1790.

Relief Act of 1778, which removed a number of legal restrictions against Catholics. In 1780, as Lord George Gordon presented a Protestant petition to Parliament, London experienced its worst rioting of the century. Lasting for a week, the city suffered £100,000 in property damage and the loss of nearly 300 lives. Two major symbols of justice were attacked. Rioters looted the house of the chief Justice of the Court of King's Beneh, Lord Mansfield, in Bloomsbury and besieged Newgate Prison. Numerous people of color, including Mountain, marched with the mob. A black, Benjamin Bowsey, was a leader of the assault against Newgate. It has been recently argued that the prominent role played by blacks in the riots reflected the disaffection they held in common with plebian London. Yet, here, too, Mountain's narrative was personal. He distanced himself from any collective claims, either racial or plebian: "It was a matter of the most sovereign indifference ... whether the rebellion was just or unjust: I eagerly joined the sport, eagerly rejoicing that an opportunity presented whereby I might obtain considerable plunder in the general confusion."[11]

Mountain soon had another opportunity for plunder. Shortly after the Gordon Riots he met Nancy Allingame, an eighteen-year-old white woman. Against her father's wishes, she married Mountain about six months later. Within three years he went through £500 of her personal property and, after losing her house in Islington, Allingame returned to her father. North of London, Islington was a haunt for highway robbers and other disreputable figures. Was Allingame part of that underworld? What kind of figure was Nancy Allingame? Whether he abused her or not would bear on the feminist claim that rapists often exploit women within legitimate structures prior to their crime. Unfortunately, Mountain says little about his marriage. It does seem, however, that she was a trophy of his prowess, like any seized during his jaunts as a highwayman. The search for sexual inclusion may have been as compelling as his desire to be part of the profession of robbers: "It may appear singular to many that a woman of this description should be in the least interested in my favor;

---

[11] Mountain, *Sketches*, p. 12; Linebaugh, *London Hanged*, pp. 349–356. The best secondary work on the Gordon Riots remains George Rudé, "The Gordon Riots: A Study of the Rioters and Their Victims," *Transactions of the Royal Historical Society*, 6 (1956): 93–114; J. Paul de Castro, *The Gordon Riots* (Oxford: Oxford University Press, 1926). See also Nicholas Rogers, *Crowds, Culture, and Politics in Georgian Britain* (Oxford: Oxford University Press, 1998), pp. 152–75. Contemporary accounts include Thomas Holcraft, *A Plain and Succinct Narrative of the Late Riots* (London, 1780); Thomas O'Beirne, *Considerations on the Late Disturbances* (London, 1780); and William Jones, *An Enquiry into the Legal Mode of Suppressing Riots with a Constitutional Plan of Future Defense* (London, 1780).

yet such was the fact that she not only endured my society, but actually married me."[12]

A restlessness seems to have overtaken Mountain after his separation. There were practical reasons for mobility. He was frightened of being prosecuted for his role in the Gordon Riots. Moreover, it was becoming more dangerous to be a highwayman. Between 1783 and 1787 there was an 82 percent rise in the number of London executions over the previous five years. The rapid increase in the English black population, as refugees from the American War of Independence, may have troubled him. After all, Mountain valued his underworld connections, not those to other African Americans. He left England for France, Spain, and Gibraltar, always working his trade as a highwayman. Later, Mountain became a seaman, voyaging to Philadelphia, Leghorn, Venice, and Saint Kitts. In the course of these travels, he twice visited the coast of Guinea, bringing cargos of black slaves to Jamaica. On May 2, 1789, Mountain landed in Boston and returned to a land where most black men were slaves.[13]

Mountain decided to make his way from Boston to New York. At East Hartford, he stole five dollars from the cabin of a sloop in the Connecticut River. He was immediately apprehended and sentenced to being whipped with ten stripes. The account of Mountain's wounded pride is so striking that it deserves to be quoted at length:

> This was the first time I was arraigned before any court. No event in my anteced-ent life produced such mortification as this; that a highwayman of the first emi-nence, who had robbed in most of the capital cities of Europe, who had attacked gentlemen of the first distinction with success; who had escaped King's Bench prison and Old Bailey, that he should be punished in such an obscure part of the country was truly humiliating.

It was with this deep sense of narcissistic injury, then, that Mountain con-tinued his journey. Only a few days later, Wednesday, May 26, he set out from New Haven to New York. One mile out from town he encountered two sisters. He tried to entice them into a tryst, but they rebuffed him.

---

[12] Mountain, *Sketches*, p. 13; Robert B. Shoemaker, *Petty Crime and the Law in London and Rural Middlesex, c. 1660–1725* (Cambridge: Cambridge University Press, 1991), p. 287; Martha Burt, "Cultural Myths and Supports for Rape," *Journal of Personality and Social Psychology* 38 (1980): 217–230. Mountain's marriage must be seen in light of a 1726 Pennsylvania law that punished a free black marrying a white woman with reen-slavement. Nash and Soderlund, *Freedom by Degrees*, p. 13.

[13] Mountain, *Sketches*, pp. 13 and 16; Michael Ignatieff, *A Just Measure of Pain: The Penitentiary in the Industrial Revolution 1750–1850* (New York: Pantheon Books, 1978), pp. 80–88; Beattie, *Crime and the Courts*, pp. 582–591. Unfortunately, Mountain does not describe in detail is reflections on traveling to Guinea aboard a slave ship. See

Mountain must have seen this as yet another slight to his pride. "They were terrified at my conduct and tried to avoid me." Angered, he seized the older sister. She struggled loose. He then grabbed the younger girl, almost fourteen years old, and threw her to the ground.

Even as the girl's cries attracted neighbors, Mountain remained rooted to the spot. "I still continued my barbarity by insulting her in her distress, boasting of the fact, and glorifying in iniquity." Eliphat Dyer, the judge at Mountain's trial, cited his "after conduct, glorifying in your shame, and even insulting the victim of your brutal lust." The rape was about violence as well as sexual desire. But it was also about representation. Perhaps, then, Mountain waited for arrest because he wanted to tell his tale. Raping a white girl demonstrated Mountain's sexual prowess and, through the narrative, prowess as a criminal. Before being humiliated, Mountain had long boasted of his role as highwayman, and perhaps he even looked forward to the execution narrative as a means of redeeming his pride.[14]

Compare for a moment another African American who was executed in New Hampshire for rape six years later. Thomas Powers, born in Norwich, Connecticut, had a last name as grandiose as Mountain's. But Powers was a slave. While Mountain could trace his crime to exploits as a highway robber, Powers lacked that kind of autonomy. Instead, he saw an early sexual experience as the fictive origins of his rape. Powers was less than eleven years old when "a young woman ... enticing me to her bed, where she was sitting, taught me that awful sin which now cost me my life." Powers continued with a number of sexual liaisons. No direct path lies, of course, from sexual initiation to rape. Nevertheless, Powers's hidden erotic life seemed to serve him, like the criminal underworld for Mountain, as a place of refuge. It seemed that Powers lived a double life: one as a docile and agreeable slave, the other as a sexually independent male. Nowhere does this disassociation appear as sharply as after the rape. Returning to his master's house, Powers did not flee, but sat down as usual and played checkers with the children.

Marcus Rediker, *The Slave Ship: A Human History* (New York: Viking Press, 2007) on this particular experience and W. Jeffrey Bolster, *Black Jacks: African American Seamen in the Age of Sail* (Cambridge: Harvard University Press, 1997) on the particular aspects of seafaring for African American sailors.

[14] Mountain, *Sketches*, pp. 16–18; *Connecticut Courant*, June 7, 1790 and August 16, 1790; *Norwich Packet and Country Journal*, June 11, 1790; Eliphat Dyer's sentencing of Mountain for rape in *Connecticut Courant*, August 23, 1790. The victim, Eunice Thompson, was claimed by various sources to be either thirteen or fourteen years old. According to New Haven records, she was born on June 26, 1776. She had two older sisters, oddly named Thankful and Desire, who were four and five years older than Eunice. *Vital Records of New Haven*, 2 vols. (Hartford: Connecticut Society, 1917), 1:428.

When confronted with the rape, Powers at first denied the crime. Later, he readily admitted it. Why did Powers not choose flight? With few African Americans in New Hampshire, the identification of the attacker must have been straightforward. How could he think that his denial would be believed above the accusation of an injured white woman? Perhaps he constructed a fantasy about himself and the woman – even believing she would remain silent. He asked to speak to his victim, though she refused. Perhaps, like Mountain, he believed in his own innocence, even invulnerability. It was almost as if Powers the rapist was a different person from the Powers who sat across a checkerboard with his master's children. But such contradiction could no longer be sustained. The double life converged in Powers's narrative.[15]

In the eighteenth century, rape was a difficult crime to prove. But not in Mountain's case. Blackstone urged extra caution against conviction based upon "false and malicious witnesses." The burden of proof generally shifted to the alleged victim. Rape prosecutions might be thrown out of court if the woman's character was questionable, if she failed to cry out for help, or if she had not soon afterwards reported the assault. Early Connecticut law, for example, mandated that accusations for rape were only valid if they were promptly made. Courts had special difficulty with accusations of rape when both parties were acquaintances of equal social status. None of these questions, however, could be raised in Mountain's case. "Seldom is such an offence so amply proved," claimed the minister who delivered Mountain's execution sermon. "For seldom is a delinquent of this description so bold and shameless."[16]

Yet Mountain pleaded not guilty. How could he make such a brazen claim to innocence? Like other execution narratives discussed earlier, Mountain's biography was a species of testimony. His defense rested on two assertions. First, though he denied making any excuse, Mountain followed the apologetic tradition of the genre and did precisely that: "There can be no excuse given for me, unless intoxication may be pled in

---

[15] *The Narrative and Confession of Thomas Powers* (Norwich, 1796) and *A Sermon Delivered at Haverhill ... at the Execution of Thomas Powers* (Haverhill, 1796).

[16] Blackstone; *Connecticut Gazette*, August 20, 1790; James Dana, *The Intent of Capital Punishment. A Discourse Delivered in the City of New-Haven, October 20, 1970, Being the Day of the Execution of Joseph Mountain for a Rape* (New Haven, 1790), p. 8. For a discussion of the eighteenth-century American discourse about rape, see Barbara S. Lindemann, "'To Ravish and Carnally Know': Rape in Eighteenth-Century Massachusetts," *Signs: Journal of Women in Culture and Society* 10 (1984): 63–82; Sharon Block, "Rape Without Women: Print Culture and the Politicization of Rape 1765–1815" 89 *Journal of American History* (2002): 849–868.

mitigation of an offence." Mountain's second gambit was even more daring. "I have uniformly thought the witnesses were mistaken in swearing
to the commission of a rape. That I abused her in a most brutal and savage manner – that her tender years and pitiable shrieks were unavailing,
and that no exception was wanting to ruin her, I frankly confess." What
Mountain denied was probably the legal requirement for "some degree
of penetration." Like Levi Ames, he was speaking the language of law.
His strategy was clearly to shift the prosecution to attempted rape The
concern here was not precedent in the strict legal sense, but the habits of
courts. Mountain may have known that courts often preferred to convict
for attempted rape rather than the crime itself.[17]

COMPETING LEGAL NARRATIVES

Our understanding of Mountain would be very different if only his autobiography survived. Fortunately, four other documents shed light on the
different strands of discourse that led to his execution: Judge Eliphat
Dyer's charge to the jury, the sentencing, a pardon petition written by
Mountain, and an execution sermon written by the same minister who
preached about the William Beadle murders, Reverend James Dana.
These four documents either justify the death sentence or question it.
John Adams called Eliphat Dyer, Connecticut Superior Court justice and
tireless land promoter of the Susquehanna Company, "long-winded and
round-about, obscure and cloudy, very talkative and very tedious, yet an
honest, worthy man, means and judges well."

Dyer was true to form. His charge to the jury was an eclectic attempt
to argue that capital punishment was fitting for republican governments.
During the late 1780s, Benjamin Rush had initiated a public debate questioning the legitimacy of the death penalty in the fledgling republic. But
despite disagreements about the type of government, Dyer insisted, all
political forms agree that crimes must be punished. This contradicted
the notion that punishment might follow politics, that there might be
a republican form of punishment as opposed to a monarchical one.
According to Dyer, human passions were unchanging. Dyer traced the
Saxon origins of the jury, concluding with a drawn-out history of the
settlement of Connecticut's wilderness, the rebellion against England, and

---

[17] Mountain, *Sketches*, p. 17; Connecticut Superior Court Records, 27/147–148, August
     1770, Connecticut Archives (Hartford); Edmund Trowbridge, "Notes on Legal Actions
     and Extracts from Cases," Dana Paper, Massachusetts Historical Society (Boston).

the making of the new state. For Dyer, the imagery was one of civilization – not political structures – against savagery.[18]

On Thursday, August 12, Justice Dyer pronounced the sentence before
a crowded courtroom. Here again, Dyer elliptically addressed the debate
over capital punishment. Although Dyer would call for Mountain's death,
his style and words sought to convey a sense of mercy. Dyer spoke to
the prisoner "in a just, pathetic, and forcible manner, and notwithstanding the aggravated circumstances of guilt which appeared, yet such were
the sensations of a feeling heart that the judge could not pronounce the
awful sentence without the most visible emotion." Mountain's lack of
pity was juxtaposed to the pity of the court. Dyer reminded Mountain
that he was relentless despite the victim's screams and tears. Women are
weak and must be protected. "Notwithstanding you had no pity, and
rendered yourself unfit for human society and unworthy of life, yet we
would extend to you every compassionate regard of which your situation
will admit." As a token of his compassion, Dyer permitted Mountain
Sunday public worship at a local church and the aid of a minister as he
prepared for his execution.[19]

Is capital punishment appropriate for either rape or a republican legal
code? What is the meaning of compassion? And what should be the
proper punishment for this crime? These were the issues raised by Dyer's
statements from the bench. Mountain would respond in an intriguing
document, his pardon petition. Addressed to the Connecticut Assembly,
Mountain makes a straightforward plea for mercy: Recognizing he "cannot claim in his favor a virtuous life antecedent to this transaction, nor can
he allege anything in justification of the crime for which he is condemned,
he can only apply to the compassion [underlining in the original] of your
honors." This marks an inversion from the proud highwayman to a condemned felon pleading for mercy. Even more startling is his proposal that
he be sold as a slave and the proceeds of the sale be given to the raped
girl. He would be more "advantageous to society" sold as a slave than
executed. Mountain's entire life had centered on his repudiation of a subordinate status determined by race. Mobility, power, equality – these were

---

[18] Dexter, *Biographical Sketches of the Graduates of Yale College*, 644–647; Charge of
Justice Dyer to Grand Jury, *Connecticut Courant*, August 23, 1790. Benjamin Rush,
An Enquiry into the Effects of Public Punishments upon Criminals and upon Society
(London: C. Dilly, 1787). The next chapter will discuss at length the origins of opposition
to capital punishment.

[19] *Connecticut Courant*, August 23, 1790.

the themes of his autobiography. Yet now Mountain was condemning himself to spend the rest of his life enslaved.[20]

In one sense, however, Mountain did sell his life: through the execution narrative. The proceeds of its sale were to be delivered to the rape victim. But here images were transformed into something that might seem insubstantial. What was sold was not a black man's labor, but a self-defining tale. More troubling still was the fact that rape, a crime of unseen damage, would be met simply with monetary compensation. Nine shillings was the cost of Mountain's autobiography. For some it did not seem like terribly much. "If a villain has murdered a man or ravished a woman who has lost her husband or her reputation, is this not reparation? Does not everybody," it was sarcastically asked, "know that a little money is an excellent substitute for a husband, a parent, or one's own reputation? Wouldn't every female want to be ravished for a few shillings?" Mountain's bargain to sell his life as a slave or the actual hawking of the narrative of his life revealed an odd irony. It not only made the felon himself into a commodity, but eroded the notion of female inviolability as well.[21]

Mountain's petition echoed the innovative instrumentalist notions of punishment that were emerging in the 1780s. But he also understood the emphasis such notions placed upon preventing recidivism. "Should such a measure [Mountain's being sold into slavery] be thought undesirable on the ground that he might, hereafter, commit like crimes," Mountain added, he would "submit to be castrated rather than death." How do we understand this remarkable plea bargaining? On one hand, castration fit the model of symmetry between crime and punishment that was often at the heart of contemporary proposals for reforming criminal law. A sexual crime would be met with sexual retribution; the offending member would be dismembered. Castration was, on the other hand, most certainly a vestige of slave law.

Not surprisingly, then, it was both a reformer and a Southern slave holder who was most famous for proposing castration as a punishment.

---

[20] "Joseph Mountain Pardon Petition," Connecticut Archives, 2nd Series, 4/131, 15 August 1790 (Hartford). Mountain's pardon petition may have stood little chance. Almost unique in my reading of the clemency files of late-eighteenth-century Pennsylvania were letters *against* pardon such as those I found for an African American convicted of rape in 1793. Secretary of Commonwealth, Pardon Books, September 2, 1793, Pennsylvania State Archives (Harrisburg).

[21] *Connecticut Courant*, October 25, 1790 and November 8, 1790; *Norwich Packet*, November 5, 1790. The narrative was later reprinted. *American Mercury*, November 1, 1790.

In his 1779 plan for a new Virginia criminal code, Jefferson suggested that castration was the fitting punishment for rape. Although disallowed by the Crown shortly after being passed and never enforced, the Pennsylvania criminal code of 1700 was celebrated by reformers of the 1780s for limiting capital punishment. It mandated castration and being branded with the letter "R" on the forehead for white rapists after the second offense. Married white men guilty of incest, sodomy, or bestiality would also be castrated. Yet even here, the only instance of a code demanding castration for white offenders paled next to sanctions for blacks passed at the same time. African Americans would suffer death for rape and castration for *attempted* rape against a white woman. The racial component of Pennsylvania's proposed use of castration as a punishment was clear. It only applied when a white woman was the victim of attempted rape; the rape of black women was not acknowledged by early American law. Moreover, capital punishment for the rape of a white woman by an African American was directed not just against slaves but free blacks as well.[22]

Castration was a sanction for black rapists, not whites. It had no precedents in English law. English officials, in fact, considered castration a barbaric punishment. Instead, its origins lay in American slave law. Both slave owners and the authorities, who were often forced to reimburse masters for the loss of an executed slave, opposed death sentences on economic grounds. African Americans were an investment. But while female slaves were valued for their reproductive capacities, the productivity or worth of males did not diminish with castration. A 1705 Virginia statute granted vast discretionary power to the court for punishing a slave with castration. Not "touching his life," it might be employed for incorrigible slaves or those that take flight. In South Carolina prior to 1722, castration was mandated for runaways after the fourth offense. The symbolism was potent. Emasculation was the answer to black claims for mobility or autonomy.

[22] "Joseph Mountain Pardon Petition," Connecticut Archives, 2nd series, 15 August 1790, 4/131; Winthrop D. Jordan, *White Over Black: American Attitudes Towards the Negro, 1550–1812* (Chapel Hill: University of North Carolina Press, 1968), pp. 154–164; Thomas Jefferson, "A Bill for Proportioning Crimes and Punishment" (1779) in *The Papers of Thomas Jefferson*, ed. Julian P. Boyd (Princeton: Princeton University Press, 1954), 2: 492–507. Jefferson's proposal was not always well received. See the letter from Jefferson to Madison, 16 December 1784, 10: 602–606; "An Act Against Rape or Ravishment" (1700), "An Act Against Incest, Sodomy, and Bestiality" (1700), and "An Act for the Trial of Negroes" (1700) in *The Statues of Pennsylvania at Large 1682–1701* (Harrisburg: C. M. Busch, 1893), 17 vols., 2: 7–8 and 77–79.

In 1769, Virginia repealed the 1705 law and replaced it with one limiting castration to attempted rape by a slave against a white woman. According to the new statute, the reason for this change was that castration as a sanction for disobedience was "disproportioned to the offense." What was evolving, then, was an increasingly gendered understanding of castration. North Carolina, too, passed a 1758 act calling for the castration of slaves found guilty of rape. The testicles were the loci not simply of defiance, but also of African-American sexual empowerment. For example, a 1758 North Carolina act called for the castration of slaves found guilty of rape. Ironically, then, Mountain based his plea not upon Connecticut's legal codes, but on an odd mix of reformist notions and the precedent of slave law.[23]

The last argument in Mountain's pardon petition borrows from the movement in the late 1780s to reform criminal law. He doubted "the propriety of capital punishment in any case unless warranted by God." James Dana, minister at the First Church in New Haven, would craft his execution sermon around Mountain's denial of capital punishment as a just sanction for rape. As with his sermon for the family of William Beadle, the sermon for Mountain addressed the issue of culpability. Dana's *The Intent of Capital Punishment* became one of the major late-eighteenth-century apologetic works defending the application of the death sentence. It must be read as part of the discourse of the trial, prompted by Mountain's own repudiation of capital punishment within the broader public debate. Dana favorably compares the 6 capital statutes in Connecticut criminal codes with the 160 for England.

Dana nevertheless faced a dilemma. How could he claim that execution for rape followed divine law when only a few months earlier he had delivered a speech claiming that Christianity abolished Mosaic Law, including slavery? What divine text would legitimize the death sentence? Avoiding the issue of religious sources, Dana offers a pastiche of shopworn arguments: the hanging as a warning to others, the execution as an

---

[23] "An Act Concerning Servants and Slaves" (1705) and "An Act to Amend the Act for the Better Government of Servants and Slaves" (1769) in *The Statutes at Large ... of All the Laws of Virginia*, ed. William Hening, 12 vols. (Philadelphia: Thomas DeSilver, 1823), 3:447–462 and 8:358–361; Winthrop D. Jordan, *White Over Black: American Attitudes Toward the Negro 1550–1812* (Chapel Hill: University of North Carolina Press, 1968), pp. 154–58; Trudier Harris, *Exorcizing Blackness: Historical and Literary Lynching and Burning Rituals* (Bloomington: Indiana University Press, 1984), pp. 29–68. Mountain, however, may have known about a 1783 Connecticut precedent. Convicted of rape, James Gibson of Hartford had his sentence commuted to castration. See *Connecticut Journal*, June 12, 1783.

act of self-defense to protect society through the loss of one member. The commonplace justification of the death sentence for murder was symmetry: The loss of one life demands another. But how could that argument be used with rape? What was lost? Dana suggested that rape meant "an injury so great and irreparable," an assault on female honor.

The theme of rape as irreparable was eighteenth century commonplace. A sermon preached at the execution of another free black convicted of rape in Connecticut only a few years later audaciously argues, then, that rape is worse than murder:

The plunder of the burglar may be recovered, or the loss may be borne; the victim of the murderer may live beyond the grave and the unhappy may with hope soothe their excruciating sorrows; but no means can restore, no mind can sustain the plunder of peace, no balsam was ever found for the ulcer of infamy, no skill can rebuild a ruined family, no artist can repair the dishonor done to a ruined damsel.

Rape was not a crime of the moment. It lingers through loss of reputation and psychological pain. While Mountain used rape as a means to construct his self, injury from the crime served a deconstructive function for the victim. The images from the sermon are telling: bodily decay, an architectural sense of ruin. Such concrete metaphors remade the intangible loss into something tangible. Moreover, rape was multiplied into a repeat offense – not in its act, but in the ability to cause recurring pain.

Dana began by addressing Mountain's pardon petition and ended with the autobiography. It was, ultimately, the narrative that provided the heart of Dana's justification for Mountain's execution. Claiming "very few have been more hardened and vicious offenders," he uses Mountain's boast against him: "Having escaped the vigilance of the civil magistrates in several kingdoms of Europe is this day to be a victim to public justice." With the exception of the petty theft in East Hartford, Mountain lacked an official criminal record. Nevertheless, Dana drew upon Mountain's past as a highwayman to construct an extraofficial portrait of a multiple offender. Citing highway robbery, burglary, rape, gaming, and general debauchery, Dana argued Mountain "merited the punishment you are now to suffer more than twenty times."

Both Dana's sermon and Mountain's autobiography shared common landmarks: Mountain's mobility, "you have gone to and fro in the earth … seeking who you may devour," and the sin of pride. There was a striking similarity in their final arguments. "Those who are so depraved in moral character that they can be neither cured nor endured," Dana stated, "must be amputated for the preservation of the body." Mountain sought clemency through an act of castration/amputation. Such dismemberment was an imagined mock execution, substituting one organ for the body as a whole. For Dana, ironically informed by the narrative, what must be amputated was Mountain himself.[24]

A seamless web of discourse connected Dyer's courtroom decision, Dana's sermon, and Mountain's autobiography and pardon plea. The legal debate was not just about codes, but about the role of capital punishment in a new republic. Dyer and Dana responded to Mountain's narrative through crafting justifications for capital punishment in the very language that was used in the republican idiom about criminal law. A legal public sphere could only be established through a kind of conversation among texts. To read any of these documents alone would have been to miss the point.

CASTING OUT EVIL FROM THEIR MIDST

A woodcut of late-eighteenth-century Wethersfield depicts female reapers gathering the harvest.[25] Behind them lies an idyllic rural scene: cottages, fields, and, of course, the broad river. It seems pastoral, almost biblical – hardly the place where one of early America's most shocking murders took place. Yet it was in Wethersfield where William Beadle in 1794 would kill himself, his wife, and his four young children.

This Connecticut River Valley town was not as untouched by progress as the woodcut makes it appear. With about 3,500 inhabitants, Wethersfield served as an important nexus in New England's commercial economy. Along with the Chesapeake, the Hudson, and the Delaware, the Connecticut River created market-based agriculture very different from the subsistence farming of America's hinterland. The depth of the river at Wethersfield allowed sailing vessels to load produce from the fertile surrounding farmland. In addition, the Connecticut River connected Wethersfield with more than the North Atlantic economy. It reached deep into Massachusetts, where religious revival and political unrest underscored the ways communities might be divided.[26] Religious dissent and

---

[24] Timothy Langdon, *A Sermon Preached at Danbury, November 8th, 1798, Being the Day of the Execution of Anthony* (Danbury: Douglas & Nichols, 1798).

[25] This woodcut might be found in Peter Benes, *Two-Towns: Concord and Wethersfield: A Comparative Exhibition of Regional Culture 1635–1850* (Concord: Concord Antiquarian Museum, 1982).

[26] Henry R. Stiles, *The History of Ancient Wethersfield, Connecticut*, 2 vols. (New York: Grafton Press, 1904) provides an especially rich antiquarian study of the town.

markets dominate the tale of William Beadle in much the same way as they did Wethersfield itself. Criminal narratives were often founded on unspoken broader narratives: economic fluctuations, the disruption of war or poor harvests, or shifting political consciousness. In Beadle's case, it was the religious and economic definitions of community that make his bizarre crime part of a larger social fabric.

Beadle was both an insider and outsider to Wethersfield. To be sure, Beadle was a prominent merchant. Two of the town's leading citizens, Stephen Mix Mitchell and Colonel John Chester, were among his closest acquaintances.[27] Yet by not being native to the town, and mostly by being a dissenter both in theological and economic doctrine, Beadle remained outside the boundaries of the community. Moreover, he seemed to relish a psychological distance from neighbors, a distancing that emerged in its most notable fashion with the murder-suicide. Beadle was not the first self-exile. The local minister began a sermon about Beadle with the Fall of Adam. "Ever since the defection of the first human pair from God," Reverend John Marsh claimed, "there has been a strange propensity in mankind to dispute His authority and find fault with His administration." Beadle was certainly a contentious man who argued with God as surely as with his neighbors. But Marsh's opening image tells more: Wethersfield was Eden, strange serpentine notions from the outside influenced Beadle, and, most important of all, the punishment must be expulsion.[28]

Beadle was loquacious about his crime, silent about his life. Like Joseph Mountain, he constructed a complex and mythic understanding of himself. Unlike Mountain, who crafted an exhibitionist autobiography, Beadle shared this understanding with few others. For any criminal narrative, of course, the first question was what early influences transformed a blameless child into a felon. The anonymous author of letters from Wethersfield reporting on the crime apologized for not being able to respond to this customary query. "Our ignorance of this man ... precluded a possibility of giving you satisfaction on this point. Perhaps no one in this town had more favorable opportunities of obtaining the particulars of his history, yet I could never induce him to mention a single

---

[27] "Will of William Beadle," reprinted in Ezra Stiles, *The Literary Diary of Ezra Stiles*, 3 vols., ed. Franklin Bowditch Dester (New York: Charles Scribner's Sons, 1901), 3: 52–54.

[28] John Marsh, *The Great Sin of Striving With God: A Sermon Preached at Wethersfield, December 13th 1782 at the Funeral of Mrs. Lydia Beadle and their Four Children who were all Murdered by his Own Hands on the Morning of the Eleventh Instant* (Hartford: Hudson and Goodwin, 1782), p. 5.

syllable relating to his age, parentage, or early occupation." Although
Beadle lived in Wethersfield for a decade, he remained enigmatic.

Silence set Beadle apart. But silence does not mean that local gossips
would not weave a fictive biography around him. Their task was not
unlike those who invented Ebenezer Richardson's life almost a quarter-
century earlier. Drawing upon his patrician aloofness and romantic commonplaces, Beadle was thought to be "the natural son of some gentlemen
in England, and that he had been brought up in or near London, and had
been about the court."[29] Such claims to status would have appealed to
Beadle. He was a man described as having "uncommon pride." Born in
Essex, England, he became involved with a deist club in London. In 1755,
he went to Barbados and joined the governor, Charles Pinsold. After
remaining in Barbados for six years, he returned to England and pur-
chased merchandise before coming to New York in 1762. Oddly unable
to settle down, Beadle left New York for various towns in Connecticut,
including Stratford, Derby, and Fairfield. He lived in Fairfield for some
time, married a woman originally from Plymouth who was twenty years
younger, and achieved success as a merchant. By the time he arrived in
Wethersfield, around 1772, he had acquired some £1,200 worth of property. Property, in fact, seemed one of the two ways Beadle sought to sur-
mount the absence of any real lineage. He was one of eighteenth-century
America's self-made men. The other way was deism.

"My person is small and mean to look on," Beadle admitted in a sug-
gestive comment, "and my circumstances were always rather narrow,
which were great disadvantages in this world." Wethersfield rumor-
mongers ascribed to him an illegitimate but distinguished birth. Beadle,
too, tried to invent an aggrandizing, mythic understanding of himself
beyond his small size and small fortune. He saw social inferiors as "a set
of mean wretches as far below him as the moon is below the sun." Beadle's
contempt for his Wethersfield neighbors was striking. In his will, he left
a copy of Montaigne's *Letters* with the note that "the whole town of
Wethersfield is not worth one half the wisdom contained in that book."[30]
During his life, Beadle let this sense of pride be known through stubborn aloofness. "I have great reason to think that my soul is above the
common mold – there are but few men capable of deism. They are when
found," Beadle claimed, "like a diamond among a million pebbles."[31]

---

[29] *A Narrative of the Life of William Beadle* (Bennington: Anthony Haswell, 1794), p. 31.
[30] "Beadle Will," in Stiles, *Diary*, 3: 54.
[31] Marsh, *Great Striving*, p. 22.

"I have renounced all the popular religions in the world, and mean to die a proper deist." Here Beadle's language seems oddly orthodox. He rejected popular religion for firm doctrine. But what makes a "proper deist"? Skeptical about Christianity, Beadle replaced it with a fatalism that reflected his own sense of economic impotence. He claimed man was "a perfect machine ... and he can do nothing but as he is operated upon by some superior power."

Such powerlessness shunted aside moral responsibility. There was no good or evil, no free will. But it also created an overwhelmingly powerful force with whom Beadle could identify. "I really think," Beadle suggested, "that there was never anything done wrong in the world, but believe that all is right – that we are all impelled to say and act everything that we say and act." Beadle left a large collection of writings against both revelation and atheism, attacking the ruling authorities of church and state, and praising suicide. These writings, noted Ezra Stiles who had seen them, "asperse congress, assembly, revelation, and the clergy – they defend suicide and show the deliberate reasons of his resolution on account of reduced circumstances to end the misery of an amiable family."[32]

But was Beadle a "proper deist"? How closely did his own religious *mentalité* conform to normative eighteenth-century deism? Beadle almost certainly read such works as John Leland's *A View of the Principal Deistic Writers*, published in 1757, with his deist circle near London. Leland rejected the authority of revelation. Desacralizing the Bible and troubled by the moral inconsistencies of revealed religion, Leland and other deists saw the history of Christianity as one of corruption. Reason replaced revelation as the centerpiece of belief. With the publication of Ethan Allen's *Reason, The Only Oracle of Man* in 1784, deism in America would soon have a book to rally around. But Beadle, like Carlo Ginzburg's sixteenth-century heretical miller, cobbled together his own personal cosmological system.

Traditional deists saw God as distant and benevolent – or, rather, distant because he had to be benevolent. The evils of human society would have been divinely rooted out if only God were not so transcendent. Beadle's God, however, seemed uncaring at best. Moreover, the deist emphasis on reason shifted power from divine providence to human will. Beadle, on the other hand, saw human beings as bound by fate. "We are all impelled to say and act every thing that we say and act – that a tyrant king or two or three fierce republics deluging three quarters of the world

[32] Stiles, *Diary*, 3: 50.

in blood – that my killing my family – that a man's destroying a nest of wasps ... is as much directed by the hand of heaven as the making [of] this whole world." Without free will, sin could not exist.[33]

A "mercantile deist and gloried in it" was how Ezra Stiles characterized Beadle.[34] It was an odd but significant turn of phrase. In a sense, Beadle was a heretic in his shopkeeping as well as in religion. Credit was common in eighteenth-century America, especially in farming communities. At a mid-century store in Fairfax County, Virginia, for example, more than 80 percent of all purchases were made on credit. Beadle, however, refused credit under any circumstances. Prior to his opening a store in 1773 at Wethersfield, this policy was almost unheard of in colonial America. Beadle announced it under the heading of a "new plan," which was published in the press:

To prevent all distresses and difficulties and inconveniences that attend the common practice of trusting, he is determined not to trust at all – not even a shilling to any person whatever. As he is a stranger in this place, and consequently free from all connections, he hopes this resolution will give no offense, and begs the favor of those who may become his customers to return the compliment. He also hopes that all persons who are convinced of business being done in this manner (considered either as a public or private advantage) will favor him with their countenance and custom, which will be gratefully acknowledged by their humble servant, William[35]

This is a peculiar document. Beadle, it seems, was every bit as doctrinaire about economics as he was about religion. More than simply an economic instrument, credit was a way of establishing a web of personal relations. By denying credit, Beadle was ensuring that he would remain a stranger. In late-eighteenth-century America, social and economic relationships were inextricably intertwined. Beadle describes himself as "a stranger in this place and ... free from all connections."[36] But it was precisely because

<hr />

[33] John Leland, *A View of the Principal Deistic Writers* (London, 1757); Marsh, *The Great Sin*, p. 20. The historical literature on deism remains remarkably thin. See Peter Byrne, *Natural Religion and the Nature of Religion: The Legacy of Deism* (London: Routledge, 1989), pp. 52–110; Herbert M. Morais, *Deism in Eighteenth-Century America* (New York: Russell and Russell, 1960), pp. 85–119; Carlo Ginzburg, *The Cheese and the Worms: The Cosmos of a Sixteenth-Century Miller*, trans. John and Anne Tedeschi (London: Routledge and Kegan Paul, 1980).

[34] Stiles, *Diary*, 3:50.

[35] *Connecticut Courant*, April 27, 1773. Other Connecticut River Valley merchants would adopt limits on credit as the economic situation worsened during the early 1780s. See, for example, Justin Ely of West Springfield and Thomas Hunt of Springfield in the *Massachusetts Gazette*, November 5, 1782 and April 27, 1784.

[36] *Connecticut Courant*, April 27, 1773.

of his status as a newcomer to Wethersfield that credit was so important. How else would he expect to establish himself in a different town? This is especially the case in an economy not yet fully dominated by the cash nexus.

In a sense, Beadle was ahead of his times. He sought anonymous market relations where the only significant factors were the availability of commodities and price competition. As an added attraction, Beadle kept his stock quite full. The goods offered underscore the consumer revolution of the late eighteenth century that prompted customers to demand an increasingly wide array of products, including textiles such as velvets, satins, silk for gowns, and handkerchiefs; durable goods, including brass kettles, spades, shovels, powder and shot, china, pewter, and glass; and a host of stimulants – sugar, coffee, tea, and French brandy.[37]

Beadle's slogan was "as cheap as possible but NO TRUST."[38] His emphasis on the lack of trust between himself and others seems striking. If deism was about distance rather than immediacy, about reason rather than an emotional relationship between God and man, then Beadle's notions of economics were truly deistic. Others did not understand the complex rationale behind his decision not to provide credit. It was attributed simply to avarice. He was "intending to keep his property within his own reach," wrote a neighbor, "believing it always secure while his eye was upon it." But Beadle's concern was about the invisible, not what could be seen.

Around the same time, Adam Smith was writing about the invisible hand that controls the marketplace. Beadle, too, later came to believe that his shop, like his life, was controlled from elsewhere. While he added considerably to his stock, investing in goods rather than real estate, the continental currency taught him that "wealth could take to itself wings and fly away, not withstanding his vigilance." There seems a mocking tone to this report of an overly careful, even distrustful, man who fell victim to currency fluctuations. Inflated prices were paid for his considerable stock. But for Beadle, such losses must have been understood as another example of the power exercised by a capricious and distant master.[39]

---

[37] *Connecticut Courant*, April 12, 1774 and May 28, 1782.

[38] *Connecticut Courant*, November 23, 1773.

[39] See his advertisements in the *Connecticut Courant*, November 23, 1773 and April 12, 1774. The new plan was announced in the April 27, 1773 issue. Marsh, *Great Sin*, p. 32. For a discussion of how credit created webs of social relations, see Ellen Hartigan-O'Connor, *The Ties that Buy: Women and Commerce in Revolutionary America* (Philadelphia: University of Pennsylvania Press, 2009), pp. 161–189. Both the unstable economic situation and the new attractions of expensive consumer goods made credit

After the American Revolution, laissez-faire increasingly challenged older ideas of a regulated economy. Merchants were often caught in the middle of these opposing doctrines. Should prices be set according to the interests of consumers as well as retailers? Or should merchants be allowed as entrepreneurs to set whatever price the market will bear? Ambitious men hoped to pursue their own self-interest. But Revolutionary America also witnessed an outpouring of mutual aid: boycotts, price controls, and the regulation of markets. In addition to the political pressure directed toward merchants to abide by revolutionary sumptuary and price control regulations, shopkeepers had to deal with inflation, an increasingly worthless currency, and the disruption of trade with the West Indies.[40]

In 1782, Boston wholesale prices in hard currency for molasses, rum, and fish rose to nearly twice the level of a decade earlier. But that same year retail prices took a rapid tumble. In his will, Beadle wrote of the burden of worthless currency. Thanks to the depreciation of "Continental trash," he claimed to have lost the considerable sum of £1,200. He was especially angry at the state legislature for the depreciation. Beadle left demands for the assembly to reimburse his heirs or, at least, pay for the rent of his house. Despite his deism, Beadle's will included a clause invoking the wrath of a rather immanent God against any member of the legislature that would not vote to repay his losses: "This is my earnest prayer in these my last hours, that the wrath of the Great God may ... afflict [them] & pursue them till they die, but no further."[41]

During the difficult years following the American Revolution, Beadle was not the only merchant to find himself in dire financial straits. A writer in the *Connecticut Courant* called the devil a fool to try Job with physical

increasingly important in the 1790s. On the increasing demand for gentility, see Richard L. Bushman, *The Refinement of America: Persons, Houses, Cities* (New York: Knopf, 1992).

[40] On competing late-eighteenth-century economic ideologies, see Eric Foner, *Tom Paine and Revolutionary America* (Oxford: Oxford University Press, 1976), pp. 145–182. Colonial Connecticut shopkeepers are described in Jackson Turner Maine, *Society and Economy in Colonial Connecticut* (Princeton: Princeton University Press, 1985), pp. 278–317; J. E. Crowly, *This Sheba. Self: The Conceptualization of Economic Life in Eighteenth-Century America* (Baltimore: Johns Hopkins University Press, 1974); Arthur Harrison Cole, *Wholesale Commodity Prices in the United States 1700–1861* (Cambridge: Harvard University Press, 1938), p. 7; Margaret E. Martin, *Merchants and Trade of the Connecticut River Valley 1750–1820* (Northampton: Smith College Studies in History, 1939); *Connecticut Courant*, April 27, 1795. See also T. H. Breen, *The Marketplace of Revolution: How Consumer Politics Shaped American Independence* (Oxford: Oxford University Press, 2005).

[41] "Letter from a Wethersfield Gentleman" in Marsh, *Great Sin*, p. 32.

afflictions: "Had he set him to retailing goods in a store, He'd hit it – can't do, and patience retain." Beadle clearly lacked the patience of Job. "If a man who has once lived well and done well, falls by unavoidable accident into poverty and then submits to be laughed at, despised and trampled on by a set of mean wretches as far below him as the moon is below the sun … such a man … becomes meaner than meanness itself."[42] Beadle was especially embittered, however, because he had been a strong supporter of the American cause.[43]

Beadle generously subscribed funds for the relief of Boston after the imposition of the Boston Port Bill of 1774. He also agreed to support the tea boycott.[44] In a verse advertisement, he urged women to purchase the remaining stock of tea before the boycott went into effect. "Sweet fair ones though I tell this story/Upon my word, I am no Tory/In spite of all tyrannic tools/I mean to follow virtue's rules." The poem ends with a plea to buy tea before his wife uses what remains. If she, like Eve, would "have a kind of hankering after/This noxious herb [tea] … /With ax or hatchet should lay on." Did Beadle already imagine the axe homicides that would take place seven years later?

This seemingly innocuous poem provides a chilling presaging of the slaughter. Beadle confessed that he had been thinking about murder for the past three years. His business fortunes continued to decline and, according to a local minister, he "chose to destroy himself and his family rather than live in a style below what he vainly imagined became a person of his consequence."[45] But it was not until November 18 that he fully decided to kill his family.

Still, there were doubts. "Shall I really perform the task I have undertaken? I know not 'till the moment arrives. But I believe I shall perform it deliberately and as steadily as I would go to supper or to bed." Planning the murder for that evening, Beadle sent the servant away with the excuse of delivering a letter to a neighbor. She returned, however, sooner than expected. Most likely, Beadle himself delayed. Part of the suspense was the trial of seeing how he, a human machine, would be made to act. Beadle waited for more signs, though none came.

[42] Marsh, *Great Sin*, p. 32

[43] Subscription for the Relief of Boston, 1774 reprinted in Stiles, *Ancient Wethersfield*, 1: 422–428.

[44] Subscription for the Relief of Boston, 1774 reprinted in Stiles, *Ancient Wethersfield*, 1: 422–428.

[45] Marsh, *Great Sin*, p. 27.

"I was determined not to hasten the matter," Beadle wrote, "but kept hoping that yet providence would turn up something to prevent it, if the intent were wrong; but instead of that every circumstance from the greatest to the smallest trifle during the whole of that term [three years] and long before only tended to convince me that the utmost malevolence fortune was, and is, against me on earth." If he delayed, perhaps providence would prevent the act. Did Beadle have in mind the binding of Isaac? James Dana, a minister at Wallingford, was careful to distinguish Abraham's trial and Beadle's tortured musings. The call to sacrifice a son, Dana insisted, came just in this singular case. Nevertheless, the biblical narrative clearly influenced the criminal narrative. Beadle's deliberation for three years paralleled Abraham's journey of three days. Beadle, like Abraham, remained in a state of readiness. For some time, he had carried to bed an axe and a carving knife. Beadle waited. Would his hand bearing a knife be suddenly stayed? Would another sacrificial victim appear? Or this time would the act actually take place?[46]

Just as readers looked to Beadle's writings to decipher an incomprehensible act of violence, Beadle himself saw his life as so many signs and portents. This obsessive self-examination was Beadle's version of the narcissism found in a number of execution narratives. The written word served as a looking glass of the kind Beadle describes:

On the morning of the 6th of December, I arose before the sun, felt calm, and left my wife between sleep and wake, went into the room where my infants lay, found them all asleep; the means of death were with me, but I had not before determined whether to strike or not, but yet thought it a good opportunity. I stood over them and asked my God whether it was right or not, now to strike; but no answer came; nor did I believe ever does to a man while on earth. I then examined myself[;] there was neither fear, trembling, nor horror about me. I then went into a chamber next to that to look at myself in the glass; but I could discover no alteration in my countenance or feelings; this is true as God reigns, but for further trial I yet postponed it.

It was, however, another set of signs, a nightmare of his wife, that convinced Beadle to carry out the murder. Dreaming that Beadle wrote many papers, she envisioned the man wounding himself past recovery, blood emerging from different parts of the body and covering Beadle's papers

---

[46] Marsh, *Men's Sins*, pp. 19, 22, 27, and 33; James Dana, *A Discourse Delivered at Wallingford, December 22, 1782, Occasioned by the Tragical Exit of William Beadle, His Wife, and Four Children at Wethersfield, on the Morning of the 11th Instant by His Own Hands* (New Haven: T. & S. Green, 1782), p. 10.

with blood. She had more dreams: her daughters were killed; she was seized and threatened with punishment but suddenly was able to free herself; she and her children were dead and frozen in the position of corpses.[47]

Beadle justified the murder of his children by claiming that since he brought them into the world, he also had the right to destroy them. But the reason behind killing his wife was less clear. Intending to spare Lydia Beadle, he originally planned to murder the children when she was visiting her family in Fairfield. She, however, returned too quickly. Once again, Beadle revealed the importance of delay and detection in his mental world. Like others suffering from suicidal ideation, he probably hoped to be prevented. Beadle finally decided to kill his wife as well since it would be cruel, he reasoned, to leave her as a survivor. Moreover, they had been bound as a couple through life and should die together.

It would be intriguing to know more about Beadle's married life. Beadle was caught not only between two roles as a merchant in a regulated economy and an increasingly laissez-faire market, but also between two models for the late-eighteenth-century family: patriarchal and companionate forms of marriage. The household mirrored Beadle's cosmos. He was a distant and manipulative figure like his deist God. Perhaps the visit of Lydia Beadle to her family was an escape from a morose man who carried his knife to bed. The distance may have been accentuated by the chronological difference between them. Nearly twenty years separated the fifty-two-year-old Beadle from his wife. If his fate could be determined by providence, their lives might be disposed of by him.[48]

On December 10, Beadle entertained friends. The next morning, he woke the servant and asked that she go to a neighbor, Dr. Porter, because his wife was ill. He struck his wife and each of his four children with an axe as they slept. With a carving knife he then slit their throats. Lydia Beadle, her face covered with a handkerchief, and her son were arranged

---

[47] Marsh, *Man's Sins*, pp. 20 and 23. The letter of a Wethersfield gentleman printed with the Marsh sermon describes the dreams and Beadle's intent, p. 36.

[48] A number of works suggest the changing contours of marriage and domesticity in the late eighteenth century: Jay Fliegelman, *Prodigals and Pilgrims: The American Revolution Against Patriarchal Authority 1750–1800* (Cambridge: Cambridge University Press, 1982); Jan Lewis, *The Pursuit of Happiness: Family and Values in Jefferson's Virginia* (Cambridge: Cambridge University Press, 1983). It is tempting to presuppose that this difference in age might have led to the sort of fears of female insubordination frequently associated with violence against early modern women. Frances E. Dolan, *Dangerous Familiar: Representations of Domestic Crime in England 1550–1700* (Ithaca: Cornell University Press, 1994), pp. 1–19.

with their heads over the side of the bed as if to prevent blood from soiling the bedding. The three daughters were laid side by side on the floor and covered with a blanket. A witness described them as arranged in a row like lambs. What was the reason for the ritualistic cutting of the throat? Why were the faces of the victims covered? Perhaps Beadle wished to heighten the sense of sacrifice. Beadle seated himself in a Windsor chair with a knife and axe on the table before him. Putting pistols in both ears, he fired them at the same time.

For Ezra Stiles, Beadle's murder-suicide was "a mixture of temporary insanity." Perhaps this was just one of Stiles's odd phrases. Nevertheless, the idea of a mixture seems appropriate. Beadle mixed relentless logic with madness, literary production with bloodshed. Despite the idiosyncratic nature of his beliefs, there was an internal logic to Beadle's actions. But the question of sanity was a legal question – and not everyone would agree that Beadle went temporarily insane. Suicide was a crime and the person who commits it *felo de se*, a felon of himself. If he were found *non compos mentis* then he would be spared the punishment meted out to suicides. In Massachusetts, for example, a statute denied a suicide the privilege of burial in a Christian burial ground. Instead, the suicide's corpse was to be laid to rest in a common highway, a cartload of stones serving as a marker.[49] Other jurisdictions relied upon similar sanctions under common law. In addition to denial of a traditional burial, these might include forfeiture of the deceased's estate.

By the end of the eighteenth century, juries increasingly resorted to *non compos mentis* verdicts in order to avoid bringing conviction of the suicide as a *felo de se*. Research examining Massachusetts juries in the early nineteenth century shows a ratio of two and a half *non compos mentis* verdicts for every determination of a felony. In his plan for reforming the penal code, Thomas Jefferson did away with this postmortem determination: "That men in general too disapprove of this severity is apparent from the constant practice of juries finding the suicide in a state of insanity." A number of post-Revolutionary state constitutions, including Maryland and New Jersey, removed common-law sanctions. In the 1790 Pennsylvania Constitution, suicide was reclassified as a natural death.[50] No *mens rea*, no criminal intent, was the legal meaning of Stiles's

---

[49] "An Act Against Self-Murder" (1660) in *Laws of Massachusetts* (Boston, 1772), p. 187; Keith Burgess-Jackson, "The Legal Status of Suicide in Early America: A Comparison with the English Experience," *Wayne Law Review* 29 (1992): 57–87.

[50] Howard I. Kushner, *American Suicide* (New Brunswick: Rutgers University Press, 1991), pp. 1–34. A 1789 suicide by a New Haven law student was found *non compos mentis*

assertion of "a mixture of temporary insanity." Others would disagree. While Beadle's writings were bizarre, they were also well articulated and well organized. A poem about Beadle called his act "a deed so black and yet his mind was sound." This poem, too, clearly addressed questions of legal evidence by arguing that the murder was "deliberate."[51] Just a few days later, a local jury of townspeople decided Beadle was of sound mind.[52]

Burial was the locus of common-law sanctions against suicide. Yet the rituals of inclusion for the victims and casting out for the offender were variations on the common-law theme. The citizens of Wethersfield used the trope of burial as an instrument of symbolic punishment. First, the remains of the victims were placed on display in front of the meeting house. Innumerable spectators paraded in before them, expressing "silent grief," "marks of astonishment," or "furious indignation" against the murderer. This display was ritualistic – a traditional means of mobilizing collective community emotions. Finally, two days after the murder, the family members were buried. The burial was meant to be in "a manner unlike that of the unnatural murder."

There was a large procession and, as customary in eighteenth-century American funerals, each child was borne by youth of the same age.[53] Display of the remains succeeded in mobilizing the community. By the end of the day on December 12, a crowd had gathered. The crowd "grew almost frantic with rage and ... demanded the body of the murderer." But

despite the fact that he, too, left behind nearly a dozen letters about deism (Stiles, *Diary*, 3: 348). Thomas Jefferson, "A Bill for Proportioning Crimes and Punishments in Cases Heretofore Capital," in *The Papers of Thomas Jefferson*, 18 vols., ed. Julian P. Boyd (Princeton: Princeton University Press, 1950), 2: 496. An excellent account of early modern English suicide can be found in Michael MacDonald and Terence R. Murphy, *Sleepless Souls: Suicide in Early Modern England* (Oxford: Oxford University Press, 1990), esp. pp. 15–41 on the legal status of suicides. See also Michael MacDonald, "The Secularization of Suicide in England 1600–1800," *Past & Present* 111 (1986): 52–57 and Lester G. Crocker, "The Discussion of Suicide in the Eighteenth Century," *The Journal of the History of Ideas* 13 (1952).

51 *Poem Occasioned by the Most Shocking and Cruel Murder was ever Represented on the Stage or the Most Deliberate Murder that Ever was Represented in Human Life* [Broadside, 1782].

52 *Connecticut Courant*, 17 December 1782.

53 "Letter from a Gentleman" in Marsh, pp. 34–35. On eighteenth-century American funerals, see Ann Fairfax Withington, *Toward a More Perfect Union: Virtue and the Formation of American Republics* (Oxford: Oxford University Press, 1991), pp. 92–143. On eighteenth-century burial rituals, see John McManners, *Death and the Enlightenment: Changing Attitudes to Death Among Christians and Unbelievers in Eighteenth-Century France* (Oxford: Oxford University Press, 1981) and Michel Ragon, *L'Espace de la Mort: Essai sur l 'architecture. La decoration et l'urbanisme funeraires* (Paris: Albin Michel, 1981).

where should Beadle's corpse be placed? A number of people proposed that the body be buried in a crossroads without any respect and pierced by a stake. This suggestion followed a widespread English folk custom. Death was a moment of reintegration: integrating the deceased into a community of the dead. This departed community mirrored the living community. As a rule, eighteenth-century burial grounds were found just behind the church or meeting house. Neighbors during one's life became neighbors during death.

Burial at a crossroads means remaining excised from the community forever. It is liminal space, a kind of suspension between the community of the living and the community of the dead. To be buried where roads meet is to be sentenced to restlessness, an always unfinished journey. Restlessness, however, implies dangers. Perhaps the purpose of the stake is to fix the corpse in place as well as being an instrument of desecration. It might also have reflected a Massachusetts statute against dueling which mandates burial at a crossroads with a stake through the heart.[54] Yet no one wanted the crossroads to be anywhere near his land. Finally, it was decided to bury the corpse in another liminal space: the bank of the river between high- and low-water marks. The Connecticut River, of course, might be thought of as a kind of highway for Wethersfield. It was the path out of the community, the place where outsiders – seamen and merchants – might be found. Here, too, Beadle would be subjected to drowning daily. But there was a problem with putting the corpse in a place so often frequented. It was removed to a more obscure place. Some time later it would be discovered by children, half-washed up by the rain.[55]

Beadle was treated to a ritualistic counterburial. His corpse was handed out of a window rather than a more respectful passage through a door. Most likely because no human wanted to bear his remains, the corpse was bound by cords to a sled, which was drawn by his own horse. No coffin was used for his funeral, nor did anyone change Beadle's blood-stained clothes. In fact, a bloody knife was bound to his chest. "The body was tumbled into a hole ... like the carcass of a beast."[56]

Over a month later, the trauma over the Beadle murders had still not been healed. "The public at large are very uneasy and something must be

---

[54] "Letter of a Gentleman" in Marsh, *Great Sin*, p. 35. MacDonald and Terrence, *Sleepless Souls*, pp. 44–50 discusses popular culture surrounding the burial of early modern English suicides.

[55] "Letter of a Gentleman" in Marsh, *Great Sin*, pp. 34–35

[56] "Letter of a Gentleman" in Marsh, *Great Sin*, p.35.

done," wrote an anonymous writer surveying the situation, "or a general disquiet will take place." "The guilt of blood staining the land needs some special atonement, and if some special atonement is not made to wipe away the stain" God might demand vengeance against the community as a whole. This writer proposed that Beadle's body be exposed on a gallows near Hartford. His model was the case of an outsider, a Massachusetts slave who poisoned his master and who was hung on a gibbet.[57] There was almost a plea in this proposal, suggesting that only criminal law might provide closure in this case. Through his desperate need for discussion about his deism and economic philosophy, through his murders and the strange compulsion to justify them to others – in short, through his own words and acts – Beadle became an outcast. Once an insider member of the community, he would forever be an outsider: His corpse buried in common ground outside the community.

Mountain began as an outsider, an ex-slave, and a highwayman, but through his discourse demanded as an insider to engage in a dialogue about the place of punishment in a republican society. Nevertheless, the staking out of republican language about punishment had its limits. Although his compelling narrative of past exploits may have satisfied some psychological need, it also portrayed him as both English and a slave – perhaps worthy of either of these two more punitive systems of criminal justice. His offer of castration and slavery was rejected. In the end, Mountain took his traditional role in the ritual of the public execution.

[57] *Connecticut Courant*, January 21, 1783.

4

The Problem of Punishment in an Age of Revolution

During the mid-1780s and throughout the following decade, Americans launched a polemic attack upon English criminal codes. England's rapidly proliferating capital statutes were, however, anything but a comprehensive legal code. These were a disparate collection of laws passed by Parliament over an extended period. Using Blackstonian lenses that saw legal systems as coherent, Americans nevertheless united England's capital statutes into a common "code" with bloodshed as its centerpiece. Moreover, American legal imagining borrowed comparative readings of legal systems to see these capital statutes as representational of society as a whole, claiming that the power of English elites rested upon legalized bloodshed.

It will be suggested in this chapter that Americans imagined an English code before they rewrote their own statute books. Not surprisingly, then, Americans saw the recasting of criminal statutes in the 1780s and 1790s as having representational meaning. American codes were intended as a countercode to what might be found in England. To a significant extent, American state criminal codes abolished sanguinary punishment, and replaced the punishment of public executions with prison sentences. Like early-twentieth-century revolutions, which legitimated themselves through land reform or literacy programs, America intended these codes as an outward representation of the fledgling republic.

The final section of this chapter explores American responses to the French Revolution. Imagining the terror meant coming to terms with law as popular violence. Here again, Americans found themselves faced with a countermodel of radical participatory justice. American criminal law, and especially its new codes, must be seen as emerging in response to these two countermodels. It would be founded neither upon an existing legal order like England's, where the appeal to form and custom masked the violence of Tyburn, nor upon that of Revolutionary France, where the immediacy of politics unleashed the crowd violence of the guillotine.

INVENTING THE BLOODY CODE

Between 1688 and 1815, an immense number of capital crimes dominated English statute books. While in 1688 fewer than 50 offenses were punished with death, by 1776, there were nearly 200. This sanguinary criminal legislation has been called the "Bloody Code."[1] But the word "code" really reflects an assumption that different statutes passed at a variety of different moments contain some sort of kinship. Codes are organized or unified statutes. In fact, however, little connected England's growing number of capital statutes with each other than their recourse to death. No attention was paid to the task of integrating existing criminal penalties and statutory innovation. New statutes fit poorly with traditional common-law crimes. Moreover, England's rapid proliferation of capital statutes in the second half of the eighteenth century was accomplished

---

[1] Frank McLynn, *Crime and Punishment in Eighteenth-Century England* (Oxford: Oxford University Press, 1989), pp. 242–319; Douglas Hay, "Property, Authority, and the Criminal Law" in *Albion's Fatal Tree: Crime and Society in Eighteenth-Century England*, eds. Douglas Hay, Peter Linebaugh, and E. P. Thompson (New York: Pantheon Press, 1975), pp. 17–64; Joanna Innes and John Styles, "The Crime Wave: Recent Writing on Crime and Criminal Justice in Eighteenth-Century England," *Journal of British Studies* 4 (1986): 380–435. Peter Linebaugh, *The London Hanged: Crime and Civil Society in the Eighteenth Century* (Cambridge: Cambridge University Press, 1992), pp. xv–xxvi makes a Marxist argument about the special significance of capital punishment for social control. Two criticisms have been leveled at the idea of seeing capital punishment as having a central symbolic role in Georgian criminal justice. First, its use as a sanction was limited in comparison to other forms of punishment. As has been pointed out by J. M. Beattie, despite the attention received by the proliferation of capital statutes, the most notable change in eighteenth-century punishment is the rise of intermediary punishments such as transportation. J. M. Beattie, *Crime and the Courts in England 1660–1800* (Princeton: Princeton University Press, 1986), pp. 3–14. Most criminal prosecutions, moreover, were for misdemeanors. Robert Shoemaker, *Prosecution and Punishment: Petty Crime and the Law in London and Rural Middlesex, c. 1660–1725* (Cambridge: Cambridge University Press, 1991), pp. 3–18. John Langbein has argued that criminal procedure is largely functional. He rejects the notion of examining punishment for representational meaning. John H. Langbein, "Albion's Fatal Flaws," *Past and Present* 98 (1982): 96–120. Nevertheless, an even cursory examination of the period yields a vast quantity of execution iconography, debates over capital punishment centered on its meaning for society, and an extensive vernacular scaffold literature. There can be no doubt that the symbolic meaning of the death penalty was of signal importance in shaping the legal cultural landscape.

with minimal reflection. Parliament simply tacked on the death penalty to a vast array of offenses because the existing sanctions seemed inadequate. The death penalty was a kind of penal cliché. Blackstone called it a species of quackery that saw the same remedy for every ill: pickpocketing more than a shilling, the theft of shipwrecked goods, or falsifying an entry into a marriage registry.[2]

Criticism of the Bloody Code became commonplace in American writings of the 1780s and 1790s. It was found everywhere: newspapers, periodicals, letters, charges to grand juries, and political pamphlets. Take, for example, this charge to a Philadelphia grand jury: "In England where they boast of the equity and mildness of their legal institutions, and where they allege that neither racks, tortures, nor extorted confessions were ever acknowledged to be any part of their laws, yet their books are crowded with penal statutes which appear to have resulted from the barbarous dictates of revenge ... to inflict the punishment of death alike on persons guilty of murder ... or stealing a trifle."[3] "Their laws like those of Draco," Vermont Chief Justice Nathanial Chipman wrote at the beginning of his law reports, "may emphatically be said to be written in blood."[4]

Americans were not the first to identify the sanguinary nature of England's criminal law. A domestic British critique emerged in the eighteenth century that fueled legal reform movements within England. Nevertheless, America's assessment of English capital punishment was particularly insistent upon linking disparate death penalty statutes into a coherent code. This was a broad assault on the legitimizing claims of English justice insofar as Americans depicted Tyburn as its archetypal symbol. Blackstone spoke of the progress of English law from rude beginnings to a well-developed system of rules. Liberty, Blackstone claimed, was on the march in England. Americans turned this evolutionary narrative

---

[2] William Blackstone, *Commentaries on the Laws of England*, ed. Stanley N. Katz, 4 vols. (Chicago: University of Chicago Press, 1979), 4:17. Blackstone's project of legitimizing existing British law stumbles over his portrait of criminal statutes: "But even with us here in England, where our crown-law is with justice supposed to be more nearly advanced to perfection; where crimes are more accurately defined and penalties less uncertain and arbitrary; where all our accusations are public, and our trials in the face of the world; where torture is unknown and every delinquent is judged by such of his equals against whom he can form no exception, not even a personal dislike – even here we shall occasionally find ... [some laws] that seem to want revision and amendment." (*Commentaries*, 4:3).

[3] [Boston] *Independent Chronicle*, February 14, 1793.

[4] Nathanial Chipman, *Reports and Dissertations* (Rutland: Anthony Haswell, 1793), pp. 132–133.

upside down by underscoring the profusion of capital statutes added to English law in recent times.

Why did Americans turn with such a vengeance to inventing the Bloody Code? This discourse must be placed in the context of American Revolutionary polemics. As David Brion Davis has shown so well, British writers taunted Americans for being inconsistent. This charge centered upon the American institution of slavery. "How is it that we hear the loudest yelps for liberty," Samuel Johnson remarked, "among the drivers of Negroes?" In the 1774 English satirical print, "The Bostonians in Distress," a cage of the type used for slaves was depicted hanging from a Liberty Tree. The American metaphor of enslavement by England was countered with the image of Americans as slaveholders.[5] In turn, Americans responded by pointing toward the Bloody Code.

Slavery was a discrete system, largely sectional, and seen as affecting only those not born as free descendants of Englishmen. Americans argued that the Bloody Code struck at the core of England's own unfettered populace. Inventing the Bloody Code meant imagining an entire system of governance based upon violence masked through legal sanction. Americans identified capital punishment as central to the organization of English society. In England, Nathaniel Chipman wrote, the "multitude are restrained by fear." England was portrayed in much the same way as Blackstone depicted primitive societies. An anonymous American essayist in the mid-1790s, for example, borrowed Aztec imagery to represent English law as a kind of evil deity: "It is to this idol that whole hecatombs of human sacrifices are yearly offered up. The worshipers of it, like the worshipers of the sun, seem to think the more pure and unspotted the victim, the more acceptable it will be to their God."[6]

"The rulers of eighteenth-century England cherished the death sentence," Douglas Hay has told us.[7] American polemicists cherished the fact that the English cherished the death sentence. Repeatedly turning to the task of quantifying the victims of England's Bloody Code, American newspapers kept count of executions. The number, they always noted,

[5] David Brion Davis, *The Problem of Slavery in the Age of Revolution 1770–1823* (Ithaca: Cornell University Press, 1975), pp. 273–284; Duncan J. MacLeod, *Slavery, Race, and the American Revolution* (Cambridge: Cambridge University Press, 1974); "The Bostonians in Distress" (1774) in ed. J. A. Sharpe, *Crime and Law in English Satirical Prints 1600–1832* (Cambridge: Chadwycke-Headley, 1980), p. 96.

[6] Chipman, *Reports and Dissertations*, pp. 132–133; [Philadelphia] *New World*, 2 November 1796.

[7] Hay, *Albion's Fatal Tree*, p. 17.

was rising. A Pennsylvania periodical claimed that the frequency of executions almost doubled between 1780 and 1785. According to the *New York Journal*, the number of hangings rose to 600 between 1771 and 1790. "They string up monthly numbers of their fellow mortals," complained a newspaper writer in 1784.[8] No other country in the civilized world, it was often stated, had as many executions as England, no other city as many as London. "In London," wrote an essayist in 1788, "there are more executions than in any other city in the world. 10, 15, and sometimes 20 victims of justice may be seen suspended together."[9] London's Old Bailey alone, according to one anonymous American polemicist, claimed more capital convictions than all of the United States.

Writing in 1787, Benjamin Rush estimated that 70,000 felons were executed in England since 1688. Rush's figures were an exaggeration. An historical examination of executions in England suggests that fewer than 2,000 people were hanged during that period.[10] Nevertheless, capital punishment was peaking during the decade Rush wrote. It was impossible to deny, moreover, a much greater number of capital convictions – though more than half of these resulted in pardons – and the centrality of capital punishment in late-eighteenth-century English legal culture. What remains most telling about Rush's statement, however, is the terminus a quo for his statistics: the Glorious Revolution. This date marked a critical turning point in the traditional Whig history of English liberty. But the irony of capital punishment undercut any such self-congratulatory claims.

What did Americans learn from the Bloody Code? The word code embodies a pair of aspects: a body of laws and an array of symbols. As a code, it might be decoded. Most eighteenth-century Anglo-American discussions of punishment centered on deterrence. But for many Americans in the 1780s and 1790s, Tyburn told more about the nature of English law and society than it communicated about the risks of crime. In the 1760s and early 1770s, as has been shown, Americans learned how to imagine a legal system as the outward representation of a society. Here that lesson was applied to the symbolic meaning of English punishment. In order to distance themselves from England, Americans plumbed

---

[8] *Pennsylvania Mercury*, November 26, 1784.

[9] *Pennsylvania Mercury*, November 27, 1788. See also Zechariah Swift, *A System of the Laws of Connecticut* (Windham: John Byrne, 1795), p. 243.

[10] Benjamin Rush, *An Enquiry into the Effects of Public Punishment upon Criminals and upon Society* (London: C. Dilly, 1787), p. 17; V. A. C. Gatrell, *The Hanging Tree: Execution and the English People 1770–1868* (Oxford: Oxford University Press, 1994), pp. 7 and pp. 616–619.

English criminal procedure as a sharp point of differentiation between themselves and their mother country. Americanization of criminal justice took place because Americans imagined England as a legal cultural other. Opposition allowed Americans to change, something quite difficult in the inherently conservative common-law tradition. Decoding England's criminal codes, in other words, was the first step in fashioning their own codes.

This decoding, imagining criminal law as representational, identified extensive reliance upon capital punishment as what made English culture unique. Why did England's existing legal regime rest upon a Bloody Code? And why was America spared? Two arguments were made, one founded upon an examination of English society and the other upon English political governance. England's harsh criminal codes, the first argument went, emerged as a response to crime. Unlike America, England suffered from real deep-seated social problems. "Any country where their laws are very sanguinary and severe ... the morals of that state are very bad."[11] English law, according to Connecticut Judge Jesse Root, "was adapted to a people grown old in the habits of vice where the grossest enormities and crimes were practiced."[12] It was suitable for what William Bradford called "an old, corrupted, and populous country." A youthful society like America need not rely upon capital statutes. "Such a code of criminal law," wrote Samuel Williams in 1794, "is wholly unfitted to the uncorrupted state of the people in America."[13] This argument rested upon the familiar revolutionary tropes of virtue and corruption. Cruelty, luxury, and dissipation touched all parts of English society. These produced a kind of crime unknown in America.

The second explanation laid the blame directly at the authorities' doorstep. An essay published in Pennsylvania in 1785, for example, denied that the English were more depraved than any other people. It was simply that the government had provided an example of rapaciousness and brutality for its citizens. Through taxes, moreover, it reduces "subjects to states of starvation – thus, from an impulse of the first law of nature urging them to steal."[14] The Bloody Code was evidence of a brutal elite.

---

[11] *Pennsylvania Packet*, September 1, 1786.

[12] Jesse Root, *Reports of Cases Adjudged in the Superior Court and the Supreme Court of Errors from July 1789* (Hartford: Hudson & Goodwin, 1798), pp. iii–iv.

[13] Samuel Williams, "The Natural and Civil History of Vermont" (1794) in *American Political Writings during the Founding Era 1760–1805*, 2 vols., eds. Charles S. Hyneman and Donald S. Lutz (Indianapolis: Liberty Press, 1983), 2:969.

[14] *Pennsylvania Packet*, February 14, 1786.

One version of this critique saw executions as the natural outgrowth of the institution of monarchy. To be sure, whatever the precise source for the Bloody Code, the governing authorities were responsible for planting Tyburn at the core of their existing legal regime. Rather than deter crime, its cruel display bred callousness. A common American image in this discourse was pickpockets operating among spectators gathered for executions.

English social critics echoed American imaginings of the Bloody Code. Menasseh Dawes, for example, blamed both British society and its ruling elite. The rise of property, creating "an artificial state of civilization," has led to luxury and dissipation. Dawes described England as caught in a "maze." A lawless underclass breeds violence while a self-interested patrician class rests upon the legal violence of capital punishment to sustain an inequitable distribution of property. But Dawes was not hopeless. He was heartened by American criticism of sanguinary punishment. English liberty will rise like a phoenix from its ashes in America, "an old empire will mature in a new one" where legal reform will do away with sanguinary punishment.[15]

Americans did not simply critique English society. Around Britain's gallows Americans crafted a myth about their own relationship to English legal culture. In the beginning, went this oft-repeated myth, was William Penn, who chose to repudiate the English dependence upon the death penalty and in 1700 drafted a criminal code with only one capital statute for premeditated murder. But in 1718 Queen Anne repealed Penn's law and with "high-handed measures ... [drove] our ancestors into an adoption of the sanguinary statutes of the mother country."[16] "The natural tendency of this policy was to overwhelm an infant colony, thinly inhabited, with a mass of sanguinary punishments hardly endurable in an old, corrupted and populous country."[17]

Like all instances of myth making, the Penn narrative relied upon some rather striking lapses of historical memory. Pennsylvania's code included branding as well as castration for a second rape offense. African Americans were subject to a two-tiered criminal justice system. For rape of a white woman, buggery, and burglary, the penalty was death. Attempted rape

[15] Menassah Dawes, *An Essay on Crimes and Punishments* (London: C. Dilly, 1782), pp. xxii-xxviii.
[16] "An Act Against Murder" (1700); *The Philadelphia Monthly Magazine or Universal Repository*, January 1798, pp. 45–48.
[17] *The Philadelphia Monthly Magazine or Universal Repository*, January 1798. Robert J. Turnbull, *A Visit to the Philadelphia Prison* (Philadelphia: T. Phillips and Sons, 1797), p. 2.

of a white woman might be punished by castration.[18] To some extent, the use of castration and a parallel legal system with capital penalties for African Americans reflected Pennsylvania's partial eschewing of the death sentence for European colonists. These allowed colonial authorities to increase enforcement of two potential sources of disorder, youths and slaves, without recourse to capital punishment for the remainder of its citizenry. Given the Penn myth, it was ironic that the Crown found castration a cruel and unusual punishment unknown in common law. The Crown called these sanctions exceptional and demanded repeal.

Drawing upon the trope of native virtue and foreign corruption, Americans re-imagined Native American law. Just a few years earlier, Americans justifying conquest of Native American land would conjure up primitivism, even savage images. Now justifying revolution, they referred to Indian law as "plain and equitable." Rush, for example, claimed Native Americans would only resort to executions for intertribal murder but never for homicide within a tribe. The counterpart to this convention was the long-standing critique of England's transportation of felons to America as a breach of the duty to teach virtue to one's offspring. "What mother ever sent thieves and villains to accompany her children?"[19]

What America did, then, was construct a legal cultural myth inverting Blackstone's historicist reading of the common law. For Blackstone, the Norman conquest threatened native Saxon liberties; notions of legal liberty went underground in the form of common law and ultimately prevailed. According to the Penn myth, however, the outsiders were Englishmen whose sanguinary laws were rooted in Gothic tribal traditions and imposed upon the colonies. Blackstone's narrative celebrated common law above more code-centered continental legal systems. Codes, not common law, were valorized as the centerpiece of the Penn myth.

Here lies another irony. American polemicists conveniently ignored America's most significant experiment in code making: seventeenth-century New England codes. These codes were unsuitable for all sorts of

---

[18] *The Statutes at Large of Pennsylvania 1682–1801*, 17 vols. (Harrisburg: C. M. Busch, 1896–1915), "An Act Against Rape and Ravishment" (1700), II: 7. "An Act for the Trial of Negroes" (1700), II: 77–79.

[19] Robert Coram, *Political Inquiries, To Which Is Added a Plan for the Establishment of Schools Throughout the United States* (Wilmington, 1791), p. 53; Benjamin Rush, *Considerations on the Injustice ... of Punishing Murders by Death* (Philadelphia: Matthew Carey, 1792), p. 7. W. Winterbotham, *An Historical, Geographical, Commercial, and Philosophical View of the United States*, 4 vols. (London: J. Ridgway, 1795), 2: 106–107 argues that Native American law was governed by notions of familial rights. *Virginia Gazette*, May 24, 1751.

reasons: They were overtly religious and included a significant number of capital punishment provisions. Adultery was a capital crime in the first Massachusetts code, for example, but not in England. Although perhaps never implemented in practice, the *Laws and Liberties of Massachusetts* of 1648 established the death penalty for a rebellious son.[20] American rhetoric ignored, too, that colonial legislators had, like England, increasingly come to rely upon the death penalty, although not to the same degree. Such selective legal memory had its uses. Juxtaposing the Bloody Code against the mythic Penn code, Americans were able to reject the English law that they once identified with – and in its stead reinvented an independent legal self.

The notion of a code formulated in rhetoric, iconography, and mythic narrative during the 1780s may have animated the large-scale statutory reform of criminal law in the 1790s. In just a few short years, Americans recast their criminal codes. Punishment was fixed in proportion to the crime, and the number of capital statutes radically diminished. But it is important to note that America's reformed codes had their origins in a grand act of intertextual reading that cast England's pastiche of different capital statutes as a single unified criminal code. Only later did this imaginative reading become actualized with American reformed codes serving as counterpoints to those of England. Making real codes, however, did not end the idea of criminal law as mirroring society. With their newly crafted reform codes in place, Americans understood their *own* system of punishment as representative of a more virtuous republic and, therefore, also serving as an inherent continuing repudiation of the Bloody Code.

"SANGUINARY LAW IS A POLITICAL DISTEMPER"

New revolutionary and post-revolutionary state constitutions reflected Americans' willingness to shape their own governing systems.[21] Not surprisingly, however, they also trumpeted a departure from England's sanguinary criminal code. In many ways, these constitutions and the criminal codes themselves served as outward legitimating representations of the American Revolution. In much the same way as revolutionary states in the twentieth century would point to their health programs or literacy

[20] David T. Konig, *Law and Society in Puritan Massachusetts, Essex County 1629–1692* (Chapel Hill: University of North Carolina Press, 1979).

[21] James Wilson, Charge to the Grand Jury of the Circuit Court for the District of Virginia, May 23, 1791 (Richmond) in Maeva Marcus and James R. Perry, *The Documentary History of the Supreme Court, 1789–1800* (New York: Columbia University Press, 1986), I: 189.

programs, the nascent American republic identified its revolution with the transformation of its criminal law.

Recasting criminal statutes, one American observed in 1783, meant establishing mild laws that would with the "same act benefit yourselves and latest posterity and excite the applause of admiring nations." Take, for example, the 1776 Maryland Constitution, which stated that "sanguinary laws ought to be avoided, as far as is consistent with the safety of the state."[22] Similar restrictive statements may be found in the Vermont Constitutions of 1777 and 1786 and the Massachusetts Constitution of 1780, among others.[23] These implied the central role of legislative statutes rather than common law in remaking the landscape of the criminal justice system. Georgia's 1798 Constitution called for legislative revision of criminal law within five years.[24] Other constitutions identified a shift from sanguinary punishment to terms of incarceration. Delaware's 1792 Constitution, interestingly, even demanded that "in the construction of jails a proper regard shall be had to the health of prisoners."[25]

Such statements reflect a remarkable outpouring of constitutional imperatives for legislatures to reform state criminal laws. Nowhere, perhaps, can this be seen more clearly than in the reform manifesto found in New Hampshire's Constitution of 1784:

All penalties ought to be proportioned to the nature of the offence. No wise legislature will affix the same punishment to crimes of theft, forgery, and the like, which they do to those of murder and treason; where the same undistinguishing severity is exerted against all offenses the people are led to forget the real distinction in the crimes themselves, and to commit the most flagrant with as little compunction as they do those of the lightest dye; for the same reason a multitude of sanguinary laws is both impolitic and unjust. The true design of all punishments being to reform, not to exterminate, mankind.[26]

---

[22] *Rudiments of Law and Government Deduced from the Law of Nature, Particularly Addressed to the People of South Carolina but Composed on Principles Applicable to All Mankind* (Charleston: John M'Iver, 1783), p. iv; "Maryland Constitution" (1776), art. XIV in *The Federal and State Constitutions, Colonial Charters, and Other Organic Laws*, ed. Francis Newton Thorpe, 7 vols. (Washington: Government Printing Office, 1909), p. 1688.

[23] "Vermont Constitution" (1777), sec. XXXV; "Vermont Constitution" (1786), art. XXXIV; "Massachusetts Constitution" (1780); "A Declaration of the Inhabitants of the Commonwealth of Massachusetts," art. XII in Thorpe, *Federal and State Constitutions*.

[24] "Georgia Constitution" (1798), art. III, sec. 8 in Thorpe, *Federal and State Constitutions*.

[25] "Delaware Constitution" (1792), art. I, sec. 11 in Thorpe, *Federal and State Constitutions*.

[26] "New Hampshire Constitution" (1784), "Bill of Rights," art. XVIII in Thorpe, *Federal and State Constitutions*.

In a similar fashion, state constitutions announced their abandonment of various vestigial feudal aspects of English common law. New York's 1777 Constitution did away with attainder and corruption of blood.[27] Attainder mandated forfeiture of an estate and the extinction of civil rights for those sentenced to death. Under the same circumstances, corruption of blood created a bar to inheritance or transmission of estates. Nathaniel Chipman saw these rules as essentially feudal whose purpose was to transfer estates to the Crown. The New Jersey Constitution of 1776 and the Vermont Constitution of 1786 ended common-law forfeiture of estates for suicide.[28] Such clauses were not simply the instructions of constitutional conventions to legislatures. As reformers complained, for example, it took some time for Pennsylvania to act upon the constitutional clause calling for a less sanguinary form of punishment.[29] The inclusion of these statements in documents of fundamental law indicates their representational significance. State constitutions were, in a sense, ideological vehicles. By signaling differences with English criminal law, states were announcing the special character of justice in fledgling American republics.

Pennsylvania was presented as the centerpiece of the American experiment in creating a reformed criminal code. In 1786, Pennsylvania abolished the death penalty for a number of crimes, including burglary and sodomy.[30] A 1794 statute left only first-degree murder as a capital offense.[31] Both statutes replaced sanguinary punishment with incarceration and labor at public works. Built in 1790, Philadelphia's Walnut Street Prison with its separate cells became a model for others embarking upon a criminal justice system with prison rather than capital punishment as its cornerstone.[32]

---

[27] "New York Constitution" (1777), art. XV in Thorpe, *Federal and State Constitutions*.

[28] Chipman, *Reports and Dissertations*, pp. 131–132; "New Jersey Constitution" (1776), art. XVII; "Vermont Constitution" (1786), chap. II, sec. XXXV in Thorpe, *Federal and State Constitutions*.

[29] The Society for Alleviating the Miseries of Public Prisons, *Extracts and Remarks on the Subject of Punishment and Reformation of Criminals* (Philadelphia: Zachariah Paulson, 1790), pp. 3–4.

[30] An Act Amending the Penal Laws of This State, ch. MCCXLI (1786); *The Statutes at Large of Pennsylvania 1682–1801* (Harrisburg: Pennsylvania State Printer, 1896).

[31] An Act to Reform the Penal Laws of the State, chap. MDXVI (1790).

[32] David J. Rothman, *The Discovery of the Asylum: Social Order and Disorder in the New Republic* (Boston: Little, Brown and Company, 1971), pp. 79–108; Albert Post, "Early Efforts to Abolish Capital Punishment in Pennsylvania," *Pennsylvania Magazine of History and Biography* 68 (1944): 38–53; Michael Meranze, "The Penitential Ideal in Late Eighteenth-Century Philadelphia," *Pennsylvania Magazine of History and Biography* 108 (1984): 419–450; Negley K. Teeters, "Public Executions in Pennsylvania," *Journal of the Lancaster Historical Society* 64 (1960), 87–165; Michael Meranze, *Laboratories of Virtue: Punishment, Revolution, and Authority in Philadelphia 1760–1835* (Chapel

These changes were lauded by those critiquing English criminal statutes. The self-congratulatory rhetoric was remarkable. Connecticut jurist Zephaniah Swift, for example, urged that philosophers and governments study Pennsylvania's reformed criminal code. "The world has never before witnessed such an example of benevolence in the mode of punishing criminals nor has punishment ever before produced such salutary effects." Comparing the achievement of Pennsylvania's legislature to those of Alexander the Great and Julius Caesar, he hastened to add that the former's is greater.[33] In a charge to a jury, Chief Justice Thomas McKean of Pennsylvania imagined offenders praising its criminal justice system as well: "The criminal law of this state is so pregnant with justice, so agreeable to reason, so full of equity and clemency that even those who suffer by it cannot charge it with rigor."[34]

Pennsylvanians heralded their reforms as what one legislator called a "novel experiment."[35] Serving as leading spokesmen for Pennsylvania's criminal justice system, William Bradford and Benjamin Rush spread its fame across the Atlantic. Visitors from Europe, like the duc de Rochefoucauld-Liancourt, flocked to see the Pennsylvania experiment. They often added their own accounts. An anonymous visitor from Paris spoke of its implementation as "an exalted honor ... [and] a bright example [shining] across the Atlantic to illuminate some kingdoms in Europe ... to expel the remaining hades of our Gothic darkness."[36] Another traveler in 1791 called Pennsylvania's reform a "mighty revolution."[37]

Hill: University of North Carolina Press, 1996), pp. 78–83; Robert R. Sullivan "The Birth of the Prison: The Case of Benjamin Rush," *Eighteenth-Century Studies* 31 (1998): 333–344; Mark E. Kann, *Punishment, Prisons, and Patriarchy: Liberty and Power in the Early American Republic* (New York: New York University Press, 2005); Ronald J. Pestritto, *Founding the Criminal Law: Punishment and Political Thought in the Origins of America* (DeKalb: Northern Illinois University Press, 2000). Jack D. Marietta, *Troubled Experiment: Crime and Justice in Pennsylvania, 1682–1800* (Philadelphia: University of Pennsylvania Press, 2005). More generally, see Mathew W. Meskell, "The History of Prisons in the United States from 1777–1877," *Stanford Law Review* 51 (1999): 839–865. Rebecca M. McLennan's important recent study of the history of prisons moves forward the contradictions of mixing labor and punishment. It examines the ideological foundations of the prison in the nineteenth century, and underscores the importance of considering the broader intellectual currents, such as antislavery or progressive Era reform. Rebecca M. McLennan, *The Crisis of Imprisonment: Protest, Politics and the Making of the American Penal State, 1776–1941* (Cambridge: Cambridge University Press, 2008).

[33] Swift, *System of Laws*, p. 294.
[34] William Cobbett, *The Democratic Judge of the Equal Liberty of the Press* (Philadelphia: William Cobbett, 1798), pp. 42–45.
[35] *Pennsylvania Packet*, September 1, 1786.
[36] *Pennsylvania Mercury*, November 26, 1784.
[37] *Pennsylvania Mercury*, August 23, 1791.

Americans, too, came to tour the new Philadelphia prison. A visitor from Richmond noted with approval how prison authorities had transformed the bar room where alcohol was once served into an office for keeping records about inmates. He called current reliance upon capital punishment in other states as much proof of barbarism as medieval combat.[38] Imprisoned for libel, William Cobbett complained about the constant press of visitors. What "infinite satisfaction," he mockingly wrote, for prisoners to be "exhibited to traveling philanthropists as a living monument of American mildness and humanity."[39] Philadelphia's Society for Alleviating the Miseries of Public Prisons served as the center of a web of transatlantic correspondence about Pennsylvania's experiment. It sent an anti–capital punishment pamphlet to a member of New Jersey's Council of State and to the Massachusetts Attorney General.[40]

Americans congratulated themselves on reforming their codes. "Instead of 160 [capital crimes in England], there are only nine" such offenses in Vermont. No one, this observer hastened to add, has been convicted of any of these. Not all comparisons were so simple. Just as Americans had come to contrast their codes with England's Bloody Code, states compared their own system of punishment with each other and, especially after 1786, with Pennsylvania's.[41] No more crime exists in Pennsylvania with its mild criminal code, a Boston newspaper pointed out in 1793, than in Massachusetts.[42] James Wilson saw reform of criminal law codes as critical for the health of the country. Sanguinary law was a "political distemper" of the most dangerous kind because it corrupted the people through laws, "the very source from which the remedy should flow."[43]

For the success of the experiment, too, it was important for reform prisons and codes to be copied. Those state legislatures recasting their criminal justice system feared that mild punishment would attract offenders. Irish immigrants were said to be coming to Philadelphia with the idea that if caught, they would at least be well housed. Localities were still accustomed to the old system of sanguinary punishment combined with

---

[38] *Pennsylvania Mercury*, August 23, 1791.

[39] Cobbett, *Democratic Judge*, p. 99.

[40] Minutebook of Philadelphia Society for Alleviating the Miseries of Public Prisons, May 8, 1787 to October 9, 1809, Historical Society of Pennsylvania, 22.

[41] Samuel Williams, *The Natural and Civil History of Vermont* (Walpole, New Hampshire: Isaiah Thomas and David Carlisle, Jr., 1794), p. 351.

[42] [Boston] *Independent Chronicle*, February 14, 1793.

[43] James Wilson, Charge to the Grand Jury of the Circuit Court for the District of Virginia, May 23, 1791 (Richmond) in Marcus and Perry, *The Documentary History*, I: 189.

warning out. An examination of the pardon books in the Pennsylvania Archives shows that during the 1790s, clemency was often granted on the condition of leaving the state. In 1795, a Rhode Island court whipped a thief with the warning that returning to town would mean a death sentence. Virginia found itself compelled to pass a statute against anyone importing a felon into the commonwealth.[44]

Not all states fully eschewed sanguinary or public punishment. While Rhode Island's 1798 "Act to Reform the Penal Code" introduced different degrees of homicide, it still included such traditional punishments as sitting on the gallows for sodomy and branding for counterfeiting. A 1791 Vermont statute set the punishment for horse theft as branding with the letters "H.T." on the forehead and cropping the ears.[45] Nevertheless, codes and prisons had become the outward face of a republican movement to reform criminal justice. "Capital punishments," Benjamin Rush wrote, "are the natural offspring of monarchical governments."[46] Although monarchies relied upon inflicting terror against their population, harsh criminal sanctions were unnecessary in a republic. During the mid-1780s, Americans invented the English Bloody Code within a polemical framework. Just a few years later other codes would be invented as part of a broad and actual attempt to repudiate sanguinary punishment. Tyburn served as London's iconographic centerpiece. Walnut Street Prison was Philadelphia's.

But the critique of sanguinary punishment was only one strand of imagining justice. The other was public participation in interpreting and implementing criminal law. Nothing better illustrates the tensions centered on public participation than two documents published within one year of each other. A 1787 Vermont law declared it a crime to defame a court of justice or criticize any sentence or proceeding. This statute was clearly influenced by the outbreak of Shays' Rebellion in western Massachusetts. Not only was a harsh set of sanctions mandated for the offense, but it was also quite discretionary. It might be punished with

---

[44] [Philadelphia] *Independent Gazette*, July 10, 1787; Pardon Books, Secretary of the Commonwealth, Pennsylvania State Archives, Harrisburg, Pennsylvania; "Daniel Pendleton" (March 1795), Judicial Records, Rhode Island State Archives, Providence, Rhode Island; *New York Daily Gazette*, January 6, 1789.

[45] "An Act to Reform the Penal Laws" (1798), ed. John D. Cushing, *The First Laws of the State of Rhode Island*, 2 vols. (Wilmington: Michael Glazier, 1983), 2: 585; "An Act in Addition to an Act Entitled 'An Act for the Punishment of Theft'" (1791), *Statutes of the State of Vermont Revised and Established* (Bennington: Anthony Haswell, 1791), p. 282.

[46] Rush, *Considerations on the Injustice*, p. 18.

fine, imprisonment, disenfranchisement, or even banishment. Some, however, believed courts should be subject to criticism. A letter published in
a Pennsylvania newspaper in 1788 claimed that justices are "merely the
trustees of the people, and the people, or their constituents, have a plain
unquestionable right to expect at all times and on all occasions their
guardianship."[47]

A broad debate emerged in the late 1780s and 1790s about the respec-
tive roles of judges and juries in determining criminal culpability. While in
the 1760s, juries often retired to taverns to determine verdicts, by the late
1780s, segregated space was designated in newly designed courtrooms
for jury deliberations. In fact, as was the case in a 1786 Ipswich murder
trial, the defense raised a challenge to a jury verdict in a tavern where the
juniors "inquired people's opinions out of doors." Professional lawyers
tended to prefer handing the power of finding guilt and calibrating the
sentence to judges. Only the judiciary has a position in society, noted
lawyer James Kent argued, to "exempt them from the baneful influence
of faction." According to a writer in 1790, trial by jury without judicial
appeal would surely be "nothing less than a Bastille barricaded by the
strongest injunction of legal dignity." In contrast, a popular appeal was
made toward juries determining the degree of punishment. Questions of
sentencing, the argument went, were questions of experiential knowledge, not law. The solution often found in the reformed codes was to limit
discretion. "If the appointment of punishments should not in all cases be
perfectly equitable, they will at least be certain."[48]

Who will judge was a critical subject of debate. Should judges be
appointed by the executive, chosen by the legislature, or elected by the
people? Pennsylvania, for example, shifted from a system of governor-
appointed judges to a fixed term of seven years. Figures like Benjamin
Austin attacked the role of professional elites in shaping law. It is important, however, not to see Austin as reflecting simple antilegalism. In fact,
he was part of a radical critique concerned with the integrity of law
that focused on the openness of legal knowledge. Laws should be plain,
intelligible, and accessible to the average person. One consequence of
the notion of openness was an attack upon judicial discretion, which

[47] "An Act for the Punishment of Defamation" (1787), *Statutes of the State of Vermont*, pp.
47–48; *Pennsylvania Mercury*, 24 June 1788.
[48] Martha J. McNamara, *From Tavern to Courthouse: Architecture and Ritual in
American Law, 1658–1860* (Baltimore: Johns Hopkins University Press, 2004), pp.
43–44 and 55–56. James Kent, *An Introductory Lecture to a Course of Law Lectures*
(New York: Francis Childs, 1794), p. 11; *Gazette of the United States*, July 10, 1790.
Pennsylvania Mercury, April 14, 1786.

was troubling for both its reliance upon judges and English common law.[49]

"What people in their senses would make judges ... depositories of the law," stated a South Carolina pamphlet in 1783, "when the easy, reasonable method of printing at once ... divulges it to those who ought in justice to be made acquainted with it." Knowledge of the law indicated consent. An editorial criticizing the closing of the Senate doors in 1792 stated that only being convinced of the reasonableness of law, not blind obedience, distinguished free individuals in a republic from slaves. Perhaps one of the most common representations of this radical belief in open law was the depiction of judges' scarlet robes or, as one writer called them, "harlequin dress." Robes were seen as masking the simple in a flowing curtain of cloth. Laws must be "ripped of their treble attire of which they are now so beautifully garnished, reduced to their natural simplicity."[50]

But how to reform law was not the only issue. The idea of substituting capital punishment for incarceration and labor raised other ideological concerns. Prisoner labor included the manufacture of nails as well as marble for tables and tombstones. For artisans, making labor into a punishment was seen as degrading. "What right has the government to disgrace the necessary and honorable occupation of any citizen by making it the employment of convicts?" "Shall the freedom of our artisans, manufacturers, and tradesmen ... continue to be held so cheap as to be valued at less than the twentieth part of the price of an African slave?" Moreover, prisons eroded the boundaries between slavery and freedom. Incarcerated felons were called "public slaves." To celebrate a civic fête in 1793, Bostonians opened the prison doors so those incarcerated might sense liberty."[51]

---

[49] Gordon S. Wood, *The Creation of the American Republic 1776–1787* (Chapel Hill: University of North Carolina Press, 1969), p. 161; Benjamin Austin, *Observations on the Pernicious Practice of the Law* (1786) (Boston: Joshua Belcher, 1814).

[50] *Rudiments of Law and Government Deduced from the Law of Nature, Particularly Addressed to the People of South Carolina* (Charleston: John M'Iver, 1783), p. 37; *National Gazette*, 8 August 1792; *New York Journal and Patriotic Register*, 16 February 1793; [Boston] *American Herald*, April 17, 1786; *New York Journal and Patriotic Register*, February 16, 1793. See *The People the Best Governors or a Plan of Government Founded on the Just Principles of Natural Freedom* (1776), pp. 39–40; "To the Independent Electors of the City of New York," [Broadside, 1788]; John B. Dressler, Jr., "The Shaping of the American Judiciary: Ideas and Institutions in the Early Republic" (Ph.D. dissertation, University of Washington, 1971). See Williams, *Natural and Civil History*, p. 140, for example, critiques the reliance on common law.

[51] *Porcupine's Gazette*, June 2, 1798; *Independent Gazetteer*, April 3, 1790; *New York Journal and Weekly Register*, August 28, 1788; *Pennsylvania Mercury*, April 1, 1788; *Boston Gazette*, January 24, 1793.

The great expense of maintaining prisoners was seen as falling largely on the industrious class of artisans and tradesmen. Such arguments drew upon the classic American artisan distinction between producers and nonproducers. An anonymous 1790 letter blamed the idea of the penitentiary on "speculative citizens." This phrase embodies a pair of meanings: embracing speculative ideas and economic speculating. But there was an intriguing twist. Forcing working men to bear the economic burden of prisons was to compel them to labor more in order to support a penal system that protected the property of the well-to-do. "We think it unjust that the bread necessary for the support of our children," the letter continues, "should be taken from us by arbitrary laws to support the convicts from the jails of Europe."[52]

Reform-minded Americans crafted new criminal codes that abolished a preeminent role for capital punishment. This reform might be called a bourgeois legal revolution. It focused on capital punishment, considered a feature of monarchical governance, and did away with feudal remnants in legal procedure. Newly recast criminal codes were the outward representation of the fledgling American republic. There was, however, another aspect of popular legal imagination that was neutralized by this reform: the role of the common people in interpreting and implementing criminal law.

IMAGINING LAW AS VIOLENCE

In 1792, Ezra Stiles and the chief justice of South Carolina exchanged thoughts about building a monument to the three regicide judges who took refuge in New Haven after sentencing Charles I to death almost a century and a half earlier. By erecting the monument opposite Yale College, students would be constantly reminded of the need to sacrifice themselves for liberty.[53] Coming the same year as the execution of Louis XIV, this proposal had clear political meaning. Two years later, Stiles would publish his history of the three judges. Putting a king to death for treason, Stiles wrote, is "glorious work."[54]

Stiles's celebration of regicide was part of a large-scale debate over the execution of the French monarch. For Stiles and others, regicide was

---

[52] *Independent Gazetteer*, April 3, 1790. For other statements reflecting this economic concern, see *Pennsylvania Mercury*, March 6, 1788, September 6, 1788, and November 10, 1789.

[53] *National Gazette*, December 15, 1792 and January 30, 1793. See also the letter opposed to the monument's construction, *Norwich Weekly Register*, January 30, 1793.

[54] Ezra Stiles, *A History of Three of the Judges of Charles I: Major-General Whalley, Major-General Goffe, and Colonel Dixwell* (Hartford: Elisha Babcock, 1794), p. 228; Edmund S. Morgan, *The Gentle Puritan: A Life of Ezra Stiles 1727–1795* (New Haven: Yale University Press, 1962), pp. 444–462.

a respectable part of the Anglo-American political tradition. Americans were "descendants of old king-killing Oliverians."[55] Commonly, recourse to tyrannicide was traced from Brutus through the English Civil War. Do we consider the tribunal that executed Charles I "cut-throats?"[56] Despite this historical pedigree, however, it was difficult to square a defense of revolutionary regicide with America's less violent revolution, especially when the American Revolution resulted in a well-publicized shift in its criminal justice system away from sanguinary punishment.

American partisans of the French Revolution, then, needed to invent a "bloody" American Revolution, an American revolutionary experience centered on executions, in order to draw parallels between American and French revolutionary cultures.[57] To do this, America's legal history needed to be re-imagined. The American Revolution did have its share of sanguinary punishments. During the struggle to free the colonies from England, asserted a 1795 tract responding to a Francophobic Federalist clergyman, loyalists were treated to cruel sanctions such as tarring and feathering without a proper trial. "We likewise confined and banished men, confiscated their estates, and even hanged those who took an active part against us – think of those things before you lament the fate of a paltry king."[58]

No example of American willingness to employ capital punishment as an instrument of revolution was more frequently cited than the 1780 execution of British officer Major John André as a spy. An extensive sentimental literature arose around the trial and execution.[59] André was portrayed

---

[55] *Pennsylvania Packet and Daily Advertiser*, April 23, 1790.

[56] See, for example, *Massachusetts Magazine* 8 (1795): 363; *New York Journal and Patriotic Register*, April 20, 1793; and *National Gazette*, April 20, 1793.

[57] Much work still needs to be done on the debate about the French Revolution in America. Although a preliminary treatment, David Brion Davis, *Revolutions: Reflections on American Equality and Foreign Liberations* (Cambridge: Harvard University, 1990) provides the most thoughtful discussion of the subject. Ruth H. Bloch, *Visionary Republic: Millennial Themes in American Thought 1756–1800* (Cambridge: Cambridge University Press, 1985), pp. 150–186; Charles Downer Hazen, *Contemporary American Opinion of the French Revolution* (Baltimore: Johns Hopkins University Press, 1897). For this section, I have drawn upon a number of dissertations, see Judah Adelson, "The Vermont Press and the French Revolution" (Ph.D. dissertation, New York University, 1961); Richard Schuyler Schadt, "The French Revolution in Contemporary American Thought" (Ph.D. dissertation, Syracuse University, 1960); and Alan Blau, "New York City and the French Revolution 1789–1797: A Study in French Revolutionary Influence" (Ph.D. dissertation, City University of New York, 1973).

[58] James Sullivan, *The Alter of Baal Thrown Down or the French Nation Defended Against the Pulpit Slander of David Osgood* (Boston: Chronicle Press, 1795); *New York Journal and Patriotic Register*, 6 July 1793.

[59] *Major André* [Broadside, 1780]; William Dunlap, *André: A Tragedy in Five Acts* (New York: Swords, 1798). Philip Freneau, a strong French sympathizer, portrayed André in a

as a sensitive soul, a true gentleman who loved sketching and theater, and who faced death with consummate courage. Much was made of the lady folk he left behind in England. André charmed his captors. According to an often-told tale, André requested to be shot like a soldier rather than hanged like a common felon. But Washington insisted upon the gallows. "Did you ever learn the history of André?" went the rhetorical question. "Was Louis more amiable than André who all his enemies admired? Was Louis more innocent ...?" But the King of France, like André was sentenced to death. This anonymous writer claimed that in order to support the French, it was necessary to "recall to the memory of Americans their own actions in past time."[60] "Without such men as those who condemned André, we should now be a province of the British empire, without such men as those who condemned [Louis] Capet, France would have been as Poland."[61]

As has been argued, André substituted as an object of capital punishment for Benedict Arnold. While negotiating with Arnold the betrayal to the British of West Point, a fort commanding the entrance to the Hudson River, André was caught with incriminating documents. Arnold or André must be executed, Hamilton lamented, and "the former was out of our power."[62] But Americans might *imagine* the execution of Arnold. In Philadelphia, for example, an effigy of two-faced Arnold dressed in uniform was led through the streets. Behind him stood a devil dressed in black robes with a pitchfork ready to toss Arnold into Hell.[63] A similar mock execution took place in 1780 at Hartford. Such use of Arnold effigies continued in Guy Fawkes fashion through the early 1790s.[64]

If Americans did not resort to public beheading like the French, they asserted the centrality of executions in their imagination. A 1793

---

less sympathetic fashion as a figure willing to trade American lives for aristocratic favor. Philip Freneau, *The Spy* (1780). Kenneth Silverman, *A Cultural History of the American Revolution: Painting, Music, Literature, and Theatre in the Colonies and the United States from the Treaty of Paris to the Inauguration of George Washington 1763–1789* (New York: Columbia University Press, pp. 377–382. Robert A. Ferguson, "Becoming American: High Treason and Low Invective in the Republic of Laws," in *The Rhetoric of Law*, eds. Austin Sarat and Thomas R. Kearns (Ann Arbor: University of Michigan Press, 1994), pp. 103–134 provides a provocative account of the André affair.

[60] *New York Journal and Patriotic Register*, June 17, 1793; *National Gazette*, March 20, 1793.

[61] *National Gazette*, May 15, 1793.

[62] Ferguson, *Becoming American*, p. 112.

[63] *Pennsylvania Packet*, October 3, 1780.

[64] *Pennsylvania Packet*, January 16, 1781; Charles Royster, "'The Nature of Treason': American Revolutionary Virtue and American Reactions to Benedict Arnold," *William & Mary Quarterly* 36 (1970): 163–193.

pro-French writer compared Arnold's desired execution to the death of Louis XVI. They were "similar in almost everything except that Louis was stopped at Varennes and is dead, but his prototype [Arnold] escaped to the enemy." Both were honored by their country, both were traitors, and both, of course, deserved death. The "prototype of Louis Capet is Benedict Arnold."[65] "If you abhor the conduct of Arnold, you must excuse the execution of Capet."[66] In other words, American Revolutionaries were no different from the French. Imagined or mock executions during the American Revolution simply reflected the lack of available objects for punishment. As one pro-French writer stated, "Don't we enjoy the death of Caesar in theater?"[67]

But revolutions are not perfect theater. King George III was too far away to play his part in an execution spectacle. "In this country," noted a defender of French revolutionary regicide, "we are not so rich as to have any royal blood."[68] "If George had been among you in 1779, what would you have done?"[69] For one anonymous author, the French provided legal due process for Louis XVI, unlike imagined American regicide. Would Americans have tried George III by "a Congress and executed him with a guillotine? No they would have given him a martial law, considered him a tyrant, a usurper, and a spy, tried him by a court martial, and hung him on a gibbet."[70] At the heart of this argument is the difference between a domestic revolution, as in the case of France, and a rebellion against a colonial power. America had no aristocracy to uproot. Nevertheless, rebellion against a king, according to pro-French polemicists, was a species of regicide. "We rose up against the king which was much the same" as killing him.

A 1793 writer, for example, compared the American destruction of royal images to the guillotining of Louis XVI: "A statute of him [George III] which stood in this city was demolished, made into bullets, and fired against his troops. Whether the head was first taken off I do not remember but … it was hewn to a stump."[71] William Cobbett expressed his fears of American Jacobinism by pointing to the beheading of a statue of Pitt in Charleston. Those who decapitate a monument might also embrace

---

[65] *National Gazette*, May 15, 1793.
[66] *New York Journal and Patriotic Register*, June 15, 1793.
[67] *National Gazette*, April 17, 1793.
[68] *New York Journal and Patriotic Register*, July 6, 1793.
[69] *New York Journal and Patriotic Register*, November 2, 1793.
[70] *National Gazette*, May 15, 1793.
[71] *New York Journal and Patriotic Register*, July 6, 1793.

the guillotine. As Richard Lee wrote shortly after the execution of the French monarch, George III, too, has long deserved to die. Regicide is a necessary prerequisite, wrote Benjamin Franklin Bache, to becoming a republic. "Monarchy is established in blood and can be overturned only by blood."[72]

Pro-French Americans invented a regicide tradition for the American Revolution. Just as revolutionary Americans themselves in the 1760s and 1770s fabricated a vernacular legal culture of mock executions in order to transform politics out-of-doors into a kind of sovereign tribunal, so did defenders of regicide re-imagine these acts as America's killing of a king. Both the American and French regicide tradition were claimed to be grounded in legal norms. "Louis perished under the sword of law."[73] No more rigorous standard was applied to the French monarch than might be employed to judge an ordinary felon. Having betrayed his people, Louis XVI was guilty of treason. One argument made was that Louis XVI was a public servant. Implying a contrast with the cruel English punishment of burning alive for petty treason, it asserted the right of Frenchmen to guillotine a servant who betrayed his master through murder.[74] Echoing this claim, Stiles labels it another species of petty treason, parricide, against the nation that bore him.[75] "To kill a king is like killing another man."[76]

Here political Francophiles followed a set of tropes that seemed remarkably similar to those surrounding the American invention of the English Bloody Code. French kings had made their citizens "liable to the rack and the stake ... [to] the Bastille and the gallows." They would be "everyday sacrificed on the gibbet, the scaffold, or the rack." Men were "dragged from their families daily and broken alive on the wheel without even the form of a trial, and their orphans and widows dared not to inquire into the fate of a father or a husband or bestow one tear on their catastrophe lest they should mix their blood with its kindred gore on the wheel of torture."[77]

---

[72] William Cobbett [Peter Porcupine], *History of the American Jacobins* (Philadelphia: William Cobbett, 1796), pp. 24–25; Richard Lee, *An Answer to the King of England's Manifesto Against France* (1793), p. 14; *General Advertiser*, September 14, 1791; *New York Journal and Patriotic Register*, July 6, 1793. See also the suggestion that regicide is a redemptive act: *National Gazette*, May 11, 1793.

[73] *New York Journal and Patriotic Register*, November 2, 1793.

[74] *New York Journal and Patriotic Register*, July 6, 1793.

[75] Stiles, *History of Three Judges*, p. 233–34.

[76] *National Gazette*, May 15, 1793. See also, for example, *National Gazette*, April 20, 1793.

[77] *New York Journal and Patriotic Register*, April 20, 1793 and September 3, 1791; Sullivan, *Alter of Baal*, pp. 20–26.

It was increasingly difficult to argue, however, that old regime France was sanguinary while turning a blind eye to a Jacobin government that embraced with a fury capital punishment as an instrument of policy. How could England be criticized for Tyburn while justifying French use of the guillotine? How could those who celebrated America's shift away from capital punishment come to terms with the terror? Supporters of France found themselves facing a serious dilemma. The solution was to argue that America and France were fundamentally different. People "protected by the mild laws of a plentiful Republican country" lack the historical experience of a brutal old regime.[78] Moreover, American supporters of the French Revolution saw terror as a species of official punishment turned back against those who invented it.

The guillotine itself was said to be an invention of the French ruling class. Its original purpose was to be a sanguinary instrument for executing felons, "heightening the horror of the act." In short, this representation of the guillotine echoes American claims about England's use of the scaffold. Just as England's rulers built their social order upon a regime of capital punishment, the French aristocracy reveled in the guillotine's bloody imagery. Take, for example, one imagined tale about the place of the guillotine in aristocratic circles. It was their custom to have a guillotine brought to the dinner table around the time of dessert. Around the table were arranged figures of French radicals, such as Condorcet or Brissot, and around the neck of each was tied a vial of red liquid. To the delight of guests, when the effigy was guillotined, the blood-like liquid flowed. Many would dip their handkerchiefs in it and exclaim, "How sweet is the blood of patriots." This tale included a telling detail: The effigies were tried by an actual magistrate who joined the guests. Its meaning is clear. While regicide embodied law as justice, a monarchical regime had turned law into violence.[79]

Opponents of France, often Federalists, were endowed as well with an imaginative reading of regicide. But they discounted the notion that revolutionary executions were founded upon legal norms. Regicide was an

---

[78] *National Gazette*, April 20, 1793.

[79] *New York Journal and Patriotic Register*, April 10, 1793. On the origin of the guillotine, see Daniel Arasse, *La Guillotine et L'imaginaire de la Terreur* (Paris: Flammarion, 1987). Sentimental references to the gloom of the Bastille were also a commonplace part of this literature. See, for example, *New York Journal and Patriotic Register*, January 4, 1792 and April 24, 1793; Margaretta Faugeres, "On Seeing a Print, Exhibiting the Ruins of the Bastille" in *The Posthumous Works of Ann Eliza Bleeker in Prose Verse to which is Added a Collection of Essays, Prose, and Poetical by Margaretta V. Faugeres* (New York: T. Saunders, 1793), pp. 329–332.

act of the mob. Ignoring the trial of Louis XVI, Francophobic polemicists saw the monarch's execution as a mindless act of participatory justice. Revolutionary tribunals were composed of "robbers, spies, and the sans-culotte sultans of the Revolutionary Committees – angels of death."[80] French Revolutionary justice, mocked a Francophobe, was "martial law." How could "our [American] Jacobins so much pant" for it while they "despise jury trials and all the solemn form of [the] … common law?" No higher principles united France's terror with the law-dominated American Revolution. "The iron reign of self-created clubs controlling law," wrote one Federalist, "calls forth abhorrence."[81] Law was not real law, but terror under the mask of legal power controlled by the mob.

As the terror continued, even supporters lost faith in crowd justice. One pro-French writer had to admit that regicide and terror "originated in the licentious frenzy of a mob, intoxicated with a drought to which they had become unaccustomed [liberty] or it was the oppressed breaking their yokes on the necks of the oppressors."[82] This argument was echoed by Paine. He blamed revolutionary terror on an old regime of sanguinary punishment common to monarchical regimes. French mobs learned how to enforce cruel sanctions from a state that invented the execution of Damien. The lower orders, wrote Paine, are the objects of systematic judicial terror, and "they inflict in their turn the examples of terror they have been instructed to practice."[83] A fundamental shift had occurred in the interpretation of popular justice. In the 1770s, the mob was celebrated as proof of English liberty. The crowd in the French Revolution, however, became transfigured into something savage, almost bestial, and, even for some American supporters of the French Revolution, a misbegotten creature formed through centuries of oppression. Popular participatory justice was now unthinkable.

What is so striking about the polemic battle between American opponents and defenders of regicide is the way bloody images run amok. A Francophilic writer complained that "imagination is on the rack to rouse the passions and paint in glowing colors the horrors and cruelty of a revolution."[84] An instrument of criminal sanction has been turned against

---

[80] *New York Gazette and General Advertiser*, September 2, 1797.

[81] *Columbian Centinel*, April 15, 1797; George Richards, *An Oration on the Independence of the United States* (Portsmouth: John Melcher, 1795), p. 30.

[82] *New York Journal and Patriotic Register*, April 3, 1793.

[83] Thomas Paine, *The Complete Writings of Thomas Paine*, ed. Philip S. Foner (New York: Citadel Press, 1969), pp. 266–267; Eric Foner, *Tom Paine and Revolutionary America* (Oxford: Oxford University Press, 1976), pp. 97–98; Gordon Wood, "A Note on Mobs in the American Revolution," *William & Mary Quarterly* 23 (1966): 635–642.

[84] *New York Journal and Patriotic Register*, September 13, 1797.

the imagination. France was depicted as a valley of death. "See this land strewed over with bloody carcasses torn to pieces," wrote an anti-French writer, "mutilated, beheaded, these heaps of bones, of limbs, of heads." The ghosts of victims cried out from the earth for justice.[85] So powerful were these images that they dampened the remaining echoes of execution imagery as the lingua franca of popular politics. To be sure, there were still a few uses of the guillotine in much the same fashion as the Liberty Tree a few decades earlier. Joel Barlow might still write a song in praise of the guillotine to be sung to the melody of "God Save the Queen": "God Save the Guillotine, Till England's King and Queen." New York's Tammany shocked the city by displaying a guillotine with a beheaded wax figure.[86] But these were the exceptions, not the rule.

Two graphic images, especially, were juxtaposed to each other: a head without a trunk and the multiheaded hydra. Francophobes, of course, represented the guillotine through the victim. "The guillotine works as constant as a sawmill and a human head is too frequently held trunkless."[87] Anti-Jacobin polemic conjured up an apocalyptic vision of heads in search of bodies and bodies hoping to be reunited with their heads: "There a head stripped from the rest of the body rolls before us, bites at us, muttering these words: butchering legislators, what have you done with my body and limbs? Why have you thus mangled and separated us?"[88] The headless body may be seen as a metaphor of a nation shorn of its ruler. The hydra is a counterimage: a monster dominated, truly becoming monstrous through its swollen heads. To be sure, monarchy as an institution – rather than the individual monarch – consists of more than one head. "Though the royal head is the head of a hydra," wrote an American of the beheading of the French king, "yet by lopping off this one they are dismayed and have stupefied the monster."[89] As has been shown, the hydra symbol was a common figure in French Revolutionary iconography. Americans, too, adopted this imagery. In democratic societies, toasts were made to the dismemberment of the hydra.[90]

[85] *New York Gazette and General Advertiser*, September 2, 1797. Also, *New York Journal and Patriotic Register*, December 25, 1793.

[86] *Porcupine's Gazette*, September 23, 1797; *New York Journal and Patriotic Register*, 30 April 1794; *New York Columbian Gazetteer*, March 27, 1794.

[87] *Vermont Gazette*, February 7, 1794.

[88] *New York Gazette and General Advertiser*, September 2, 1797.

[89] *New York Journal and Patriotic Register*, July 6, 1793.

[90] *New York Journal and Patriotic Register*, July 6, 1793 and December 25, 1793. On Democratic-Republican societies, see Paul Goodman, *The Democratic-Republicans of Massachusetts: Politics in the Young Republic* (New York: Columbia University Press, 1964); Alfred F. Young, *The Democratic-Republicans of New York: The Origins 1763–1797*

Both headless trunks and hydras were mythical monsters, deformed and mutilated. These were bodies in pain that reflected a body politic in pain.[91] Whatever the purposes of evoking them – to establish credentials as either victims or revolutionaries – the underlying logic remained the use of capital punishment as violence. American legal reformers feared the effect of hangings on how the common people imagined justice. Violence from capital punishment according to legal form might spread to executions at the hands of the mob. In 1794, New York embarked upon the first step toward nonpublic capital punishment. It instituted a lattice screen that would hide the execution from the crowd. Only three years later an anonymous New York commentator would express the hope that revision of the sanguinary code would allow "the public eye [to be] screened from such scenes of horror."[92] The revision of New York's penal code to provide less capital punishment, it was hoped, would allow "the public eye ... [to be] screened from such scenes of horror."[93]

As French Jacobins embraced the terror and heirs to the American Revolution witnessed a reformation of criminal codes that repudiated the broad use of capital punishment, it was clear that these two paths diverged. No matter how central execution imagery might have been to the American Revolution, by the mid-1790s this paradigm seemed increasingly foreign. The French Revolution effectively cast doubts upon faith in participatory crowd justice. Never again would mock executions seem so mock.

Joel Barlow was a student of Ezra Stiles, the Yale College educator with a penchant for regicide, and a lawyer. His first volume of *Advice to the Privileged Orders*, published in 1792, contains a complex vision of law. On one side, criminal law was nothing but a mask for power. Judges enforce elite interests. Draconian laws "enshrine the idol of property in

(Chapel Hill: University of North Carolina Press, 1967); Eugene Perry Link, *Democratic-Republican Societies 1790–1800* (New York: Columbia University Press, 1942); Lynn Hunt, *Politics, Culture, and Class in the French Revolution* (Berkeley: University of California Press, 1984), pp. 87–122.

[91] Dorinda Outram, *The Body and the French Revolution: Sex, Class, and Political Culture* (New Haven: Yale University Press, 1989), pp. 106–123.

[92] John Drayton, *Letters Written During a Tour Through the Northern and Eastern States of America* (Charleston: Harrison Bower, 1794), pp. 23–24; *New York Journal and Patriotic Register*, August 19, 1797. Louis Masur, *Rites of Execution: Capital Punishment and the Transformation of American Culture 1776–1865* (Oxford: Oxford University Press, 1989) discusses the emergence of nonpublic executions to the early nineteenth century.

[93] *New-York Journal and Patriotic Register*, August 19, 1797.

a bloody sanctuary and teach the modern European that his life is of less value than the shoes on his feet." Barlow sees society in a perpetual state of internecine warfare between classes. Under such circumstances, the moral boundaries between crime and punishment become porous. Property crime against the well-to-do is justified as "reprisals." Although at times the state must employ sanctions, "every punishment is a new crime because the society itself is the source of all crimes." As such, it loses its legitimacy to punish. Nonetheless, Barlow sees the use of the guillotine in the French Revolution as a temporary expediency. In a state of war, "there is an apology for human slaughter."[94]

Despite this grim view of criminal justice, Barlow praises America's experiment in legal reform, especially attempts to abolish sanguinary punishment. Criminal justice should not be founded upon terror. He calls for a radical openness in legal knowledge. Only a minimal number of laws should exist, their language transparent. These should be principles every man could discern as just. Local ministers of justice should be created who constantly instruct citizens about legal duties and rights, making "law as the friend of every man." If an *individual* is unaware of a statute, it becomes an ex post facto law. Barlow, therefore, demands two types of consent, collective and personal, in order to establish a binding law. How do we square these two seemingly contradictory examples of imagining of law – Barlow's depiction of law as the battlefield of old enmities and his naïve belief that law might be a familiar friend? For Barlow, legal order depended upon social structure. Old regime law and French Revolutionary justice were species of martial law. In America, where property was more evenly distributed, law was moving toward becoming nonsanguinary and founded upon pure consent.[95]

To be sure, while such a radical polarization of law either as martial or as internalized by ordinary citizens was not embraced by the majority of Americans in the early 1790s, there was general agreement about what forms of criminal justice not to follow. The English Bloody Code and French Revolutionary terror were countermodels. Barlow's vision of criminal law founded upon consent, however, fell by the wayside as American legal reformers focused upon these countermodels to define themselves. American radicals of the 1790s nonetheless continued the

---

[94] Joel Barlow, "Advice to the Privileged Orders in the Several States of Europe" in *The Works of Joel Barlow*, 2 vols., ed. William K. Bottorff (Gainesville: Scholars' Facsimiles, 1970), 1:9, 87; Samuel Bernstein, *Joel Barlow: A Connecticut Yankee in an Age of Revolution* (Portland: Ultima Thule Press, 1985), pp. 12–32.

[95] Barlow, "Advice to the Privileged Orders," pp. 57, 94, 115–118.

tradition of making critical and political readings of the criminal law. The thrust in the 1760s was the creation of a national American legal consciousness. But, this time in the early 1790s, it was not simply England that was the critical object. Radical critics pointed to criminal law as bolstering the unequal distribution of economic power. What, after all, were statutes against theft other than a defense of property? Why were felons almost always poor rather than the well-to-do? And why, it was asked, did society need to be founded upon the sanctioned violence of punishment? The early 1790s witnessed the birth of a class analysis of the criminal law. Yet unlike the national anti-English critique of the 1770s and 1780s, this class critique never influenced the remaking of official justice. Instead pushed toward the margins of the dominant legal discourse, it remained only as a legacy for disenfranchised nineteenth-century radical critics. Yet unlike the national anti-English critique of the 1770s and 1780s, this class critique never influenced the remaking of official justice. Instead pushed toward the margins of the dominant legal discourse it remained only as a legacy for disinfranchised nineteenth-century radical critics.

Much like felons who reconstructed their lives through their own narratives, America in its revolutionary age had its own project of self-fashioning. It rehold the story of its beginnings, and promoted the idea of the penitentiary and a gentle way of punishment as core to its revolutionary ideals. This was a political narrative intended to trumpet the acheivements of the Revolution and mobilize support for the fledgling republic from abroad. Drawing upon a language of law crafted in the crucible of mass politics, and upon a self-consious identification as a republic, America distinguished itself from both English and French approaches to criminal justice. Punishment, state-sanctioned violence, posed problems in the age of revolution. But it is also created possibilities.

5

The Statute Imagined

John Young and the New York Protest Against the Surgeons

The last two decades of the eighteenth century comprised the golden age of American legal reform. Reformers called for replacing frequent clemency under harsh laws with milder codes and fewer pardons. The prisons, not the gallows, became the most important instrument of retribution. In the words of Michel Foucault, penal reform meant the rise of a "gentle way of punishment." Influenced by debates in neighboring Pennsylvania, New York State also chose this path. America hoped to prove to itself and the world that after its critique of English sanguinary punishment, the republic would prove to be a place where new laws might be designed for those experiencing the regeneration of the American Revolution in the new world. As J. Hector St. John de Crèvecoeur would describe it, America would now be a place of refuge, the "great American asylum."[1] Alexis de Tocqueville called America "the classical land of penitentiaries."[2]

The American Revolution, like all wars and upheavals, brought in its wake social instability and crime. In 1799, New Haven lawyer David Daggett published an oration entitled *Sunbeams May Be Extracted from Cucumbers – But the Process Is Tedious*. A Federalist, Daggett borrows Swiftian imagery to criticize Jefferson and other pie-in-the-sky social reformers – those who believe the experience of revolution might alter fundamental social relations. In this oration, Daggett mocks American

[1] J. Hector St. John Crèvecoeur, *Letters from an American Farmer* (London: Davies and Davis, 1783), p. 52.
[2] Alexis de Tocqueville, *Écrits sur le système pénitentiaire en France et à l'étranger*, 2 vols., ed. Michelle Perrot (Paris: Gallimard, 1984), 1:67.

Revolutionary theories of criminal law founded upon consent rather than the threat of official violence. "We are seriously told," Daggett complains, "that men are to be governed by reason. Instruct men and there will be an end to punishment." But how can we expect, Daggett wonders, highway men, burglars, and murderers to change their character? How should we protect ourselves until they do?

This chapter is about one law where the tension between the reliance upon sanguinary sanctions and the republican aversion to those sanctions manifests itself. It explores the origins and implementation of a 1789 New York statute that provided for the dissection of statutes. The American genesis of dissection as a means of retribution took place in the midst of a rhetorical commitment to penal reform. While from the middle of the eighteenth-century English statutory law directed that murderers' cadavers be delivered to the surgeons, New York's Anatomy Act marked the first codification of this practice in America. However, the New York Anatomy Act does *not* make explicit the role of dissection as legal retribution. According to the act's preamble, the statute is meant to prevent grave robbing. Using the cadavers of executed felons for medical study would ensure a sufficient number of anatomical specimens. Nevertheless, the Anatomy Act was more than simply a pragmatic means of furnishing surgeons with corpses. Applying to executed murderers, arsonists, and burglars, the act created a new sanction to be added to the death sentence. New York's Anatomy Act had faces: It sought to prevent anatomists from desecrating cemeteries and, although silent about the implications for criminal justice, it introduced dissection into America's retributive apparatus.

The reticence of the statute is equaled by that of its framers. There are no surviving records of legislative debates that might aid in understanding New York's Anatomy Act. Neither have private papers yielded clues about its purposes. In fact, it remains impossible to know the identities of either its proponents or its detractors. The essential documents required for the kind of close textual analysis favored by legal historians do not exist. The Anatomy Act has become so shrouded in silence that it fell out of most standard New York collections of statutes within a few decades of its passing. Even if legislative sources were available, they would not fully explain the significance of dissection as an innovative mode of punishment. For debate over the role of dissection did not take place in legislatures and courtrooms. Shaped by a tradition of popular protest against anatomy, the debate also extended to late-eighteenth-century streets and alleyways.

Consequently, the focus must be on how the act was *read* by eighteenth-century Americans. In this story we have a glimpse of surgeons demanding cadavers, free black outrage over the desecration of their burial ground, anxious governing authorities, and a major antidissection riot brought about by the statute's implementation. Perhaps the most prominent actor was the legal imagination. If New York legislators evoked dissection as a consequence of capital punishment for murder, they must have relied upon the English precedent for punitive dissection. Anatomical dissection was considered more frightening, and consequently more of a deterrent, because it was unseen. Imagined retribution, such as dissection, emerged as a dominant form of punishment in the late eighteenth century as American states shifted from sanguinary sanctions to incarceration with prison walls. But the architects of the Anatomy Act were not the only ones engaged in the project of legal imagination. The common people, as we shall see, read into the lacuna of language the idea that dissection mandated under the Anatomy Act was most certainly punitive – and even more punitive than traditional capital punishment.

Reading the statute comes through reading a case in order to bridge the chasm between the printed statute and its implementation. John Young, hanged for murder at New York City in 1797, was one of the first Americans to be sentenced to postmortem dissection under the Anatomy Act. His execution evoked widespread protest. By following the controversy surrounding the little known incident, it becomes possible to understand how eighteenth-century New Yorkers interpreted and confronted the introduction of dissection into American legal practice. The Young episode underscores the popular view of dissection as a punitive instrument. As shall be seen, contention over Young's sentence had important implications for the future of the Anatomy Act.

This exploration of the case, then, is intended as another expedition into the intertextual reading of criminal law – whether it be through the transatlantic reading of two criminal tales together as interpreted through political lenses – as was the case with Ames and Richardson, reading Mountain's and Beadles's self-representation in light of unpacking their puzzling responses to their own crimes, reading punishment as a decipherable text – or, as we see with John Young, reading a statute in intertextual comparison with British punitive dissection as seen through the eyes of contemporaries. Any attempt to decode interpretive meaning must take into account the social and economic structures that shape perception. In the matter of punitive dissection, these proved to be especially important. Dissection raises questions about the willingness of society to permit the violation of certain individual rights. Although most eigh-teenth-century Americans acknowledged the fact that dissection meant desecrating the dead, they often acquiesced to the anatomical use of society's outcasts. Dissection reflected a process of social definition. Who would be the surgeon's victims? Who are the custodians of the dead? What is the significance of visibility for inflicting pain? Such questions illuminate the contours of late eighteenth-century society, for, as has been argued, imagining law also means imagining a civic culture.

POPULAR PROTEST AND THE MAKING OF A LAW

Punitive dissection did not come easily to America. New York's Anatomy Act emerged out of a rancorous debate over the rights of the dead. By taking to the streets in extralegal crowd action, antidissection forces ironically set the stage for the creation of this remarkable statute. As described in this chapter, intense popular opposition to dissection evoked a crisis requiring legislative intervention. It was a chain of events – the development of American anatomical study, the increased frequency of grave robbing, and the role of popular protest in contending against dis-section – that compelled New York's legislature to adopt the Anatomy Act. The American origins of punitive dissection are intertwined not just with the quest for anatomical specimens, but also with the protests it evoked.

Although America's first public anatomical lectures took place in the 1750s, few corpses were dissected in the colonies. With the American Revolution, however, three changes led to a marked increase in the demand for cadavers. First, the Revolutionary War brought into the profession new surgeons who desired experimental material to main-tain their skills. The Revolution, secondly, created a growing concern for building an indigenous medical education system that would free students from attending British schools. A number of new medical col-leges were established. Harvard's was founded in 1782 and the one at Dartmouth in 1797.[3] Finally, the approach to anatomical training had

---

[3] The rise of anatomical studies in America is examined in Jonathan Harris, "The Rise of Medical Science in New York 1720–1820" (Ph.D. dissertation, New York University, 1971); Edward B. Krumbhaar, "Early History of Anatomy in the United States," *Annals of Medical History* 4 (1922): 271–287; Frederick C. Waite, "The Development of Anatomical Laws in the States of New England," *New England Journal of Medicine* 233 (1945): 716–726; Whitfield J. Bell, Jr., "Science and Humanity in Philadelphia 1775–1790" (Ph.D. dissertation, University of Pennsylvania, 1947). For the social meaning of dissec-tion, see Ruth Richardson, *Death, Dissection, and the Destitute* (London: Weidenfeld and

changed. Students no longer simply watched their teacher perform a dissection before the entire class. The new method required each individual to gain practical experience through "frequent dissections of dead bodies with his own hands."[4]

Attempts to satisfy this growing demand for cadavers met with popular opposition. Although resentment was strongest in the port cities of Boston, New York, and Philadelphia, it could be found wherever surgeons dissected cadavers. The birth of Philadelphia's antidissection protest coincided with the beginnings of advanced anatomical study in America. In 1765, William Shippen, Jr.'s laboratory was attacked by a mob. When in 1771 a Worcester apothecary acquired the cadaver of a hanged felon, he faced an angry crowd that gathered outside of his house. The rioters demanded the corpse and, after receiving it, put the now-decaying remains on display. That night the crowd again marched to the apothecary's home. Blowing horns and ringing bells, they ended the evening by hanging a dead dog in his doorway.[5]

By the 1780s, tension between surgeons and citizens had reached major proportions. In Philadelphia, there was a sense that "the theater for dissecting dead bodies has become ... a terror to the citizens."[6] Friends of the deceased guarded the Quaker burial ground, and mourners made grisly searches to see if corpses remained in their graves. Both Baltimore and New York had serious antidissection riots in 1788. New York's riot would end in bloodshed. By the time the Anatomy Act was drafted at the end of the decade, it would be quite clear that something had to be done about mounting public protest over dissection.[7]

Why did the common people fear the surgeons? What made them willing to risk imprisonment or even their lives by attempting to rescue lifeless corpses? And what can we learn from popular antipathy toward

Nicolson, 2001) and Michael Sappol, *A Traffic in Dead Bodies: Anatomy and Embodied Social Identity in Late Nineteenth-Century America* (Princeton: Princeton University Press, 2002).

4 John Jones, *The Surgical Works of John Jones* (Philadelphia, 1795), p. 12. On the new enthusiasm for anatomical dissection, see the letter of William Hamilton to Peter Helms (October 25, 1793), manuscript collection, New York Academy of Medicine (New York).

5 See Shippen's denial of grave robbing in *The Pennsylvania Chronicle*, January 8, 1770. On the Worcester riot: *The Boston Gazette*, February 25, 1771 and Dirk Hoerder, *Crowd Action in Revolutionary Massachusetts 1765–1780* (New York: Academic Press, 1977), p. 52.

6 *Pennsylvania Mercury*, March 8, 1788.

7 *Pennsylvania Mercury*, May 8, 1788; *Pennsylvania Packet*, 25 April 1788; *Maryland Gazette*, June 5, 1788. New York's Doctors' Mob riot of 1788 is described later in this chapter.

dissection? To answer these questions, it is necessary to recognize the dread with which criminals greeted the sentence of dissection. A member of the House of Lords declared in 1786 that he had seen hardened felons show no emotion upon being sent to the gallows, but when informed of dissection, "their countenance changed, they grew suddenly pale, trembled and exhibited a visible appearance of horror." "I was in a cold sweat," a highway robber supposedly wrote about the fear of dissection that he experienced while awaiting execution at Boston in 1788, "my knees smote together and my tongue seemed to cleave to the roof of my mouth." Sentenced to dissection in 1791 under New York's Anatomy Act, Whiting Sweeting blamed dissection – not the threat of capital punishment – as the motive behind his escape attempt.[8] Peter Linebaugh has suggested that antidissection sentiment had its origins in "a compound of Christian and quasi–pagan beliefs" such as the possibility that the dead will be revived. Alternatively, Paul Gilje asserts its origins lie in the greater emotional ties that marked the rise of romanticism. Yet neither of these arguments explains the absolute horror that felons felt toward the surgeons.[9] Rather than being rooted in either a religious *mentalité* or a

---

[8] T. C. Hansard, *The Parliamentary History of England*, vol. 26 (London, 1803), cols. 195–202. Felons' fear of dissection is also described in an English proposal to dissect every executed criminal, Public Record Office [London], HO 42/6, April 26, 1785; *Pennsylvania Mercury*, January 12, 1790; *Vermont Journal*, November 4, 1789; Whiting Sweeting, *The Narrative of Whiting Sweeting, Who was Executed at Albany, the 26th of August 1791* (Philadelphia, 1792), pp. 53 and 72. Sweeting, coincidentally, was sentenced by the same judge who presided over the trial of John Young. Yet with the support of friends, Sweeting was able to prevail upon the surgeons not to dissect his corpse.

[9] Peter Linebaugh, "The Tyburn Riot Against the Surgeons," in *Albion's Fatal Tree: Crime and Society in Eighteenth-Century England*, eds. Douglas Hay, et al. (New York: Pantheon, 1975). pp. 102–106; Paul Gilje, "The Common People and the Constitution: Popular Culture in Late Eighteenth-Century New York City," in *New York in the Age of the constitution 1775–1800*, eds. Paul Gilje and William Pencak (Madison: Fairleigh Dickinson University Press, 1992). Despite their creative attempts at reconstructing the meaning of popular opposition to anatomy, both Linebaugh and Gilje leave many questions unanswered. Using material collected by folklorists, Linebaugh's pioneering essay underscores the complex web of beliefs surrounding the public execution. Nevertheless, it remains unclear how many of those beliefs – such as identifying therapeutic powers with the executed criminal's corpse – contributed to popular protest against dissection. Moreover, the lessons derived from the Tyburn antidissection riots remain difficult to apply to other cases of popular antipathy to the surgeons. Linebaugh, for example, argues that the common people believed that dissection would prevent the executed felon's revival. This popular notion, he continues, was based on the "practical reality" of half-hanged felons surviving their execution. Yet why do the common people also vehemently object to grave robbing in instances where revival is impossible? Does the waning of religious commitment or denominational distinctions (Linebaugh employs evidence from Irish Catholics) influence belief in resurrection? Why were recidivist criminals, who easily ignored Christian

newfound sentimentalism, this trepidation was more visceral than theological. It involved creating a mental image of dismemberment. Those threatened by dissection conjured up images of sharpened knives and lacerated flesh. As one critic of New York's antidissection protest pointed out, the concern seemed to center on the body instead of the soul.[10] And, in fact, when rioters took possession of dissected cadavers, they confirmed this emphasis on the visual by displaying the dismembered corpses. The crowd in the New York Doctors' Mob of 1788 protested indignities done to the dead, but at the same time exposed half-dissected remains. Similar exhibitions were made during the 1771 Worcester riot and, as we shall see, in the affair of John Young.[11]

In addition to this visceral reaction, opposition to dissection freely cast itself in the ideological trappings of late eighteenth–century American politics. Popular antidissection protest was seen as through comparative lenses – with the implication that a republican government should provide rights for those deceased. "Nothing appears more shocking to human nature … ," wrote a New Yorker in 1792, "so much as violence used towards the dead."[12] Just as protesters might riot when common law was violated, so might they take to the streets against this transgression. Critics of dissection pointed out that burial places of all countries were considered sacred and, as was noted after New York's 1788 antidissection riot, even "savages protect their dead."[13] Although the grand jury report on the New York riot chided the populace for their use of violence, it admitted the legitimacy of antidissection protest: "Men seem prompted by their very nature to an earnest desire that their deceased friends be decently interred."[14]

---

ideas about damnation, terrorized by dissection? And if a pragmatic fear of death underlay resurrectionist opposition to dissection, why was anatomy more frightening than an execution? Gilje's provocative essay suggests that participants in the 1788 Doctors' Mob riot may have been influenced by new romantic notions of death. Yet in the first half of the eighteenth century, long before such values became dominant, Englishmen took to the streets to protest dissection. And, as will be discussed, free blacks – though not among the New Yorkers most influenced by the rise of romantic sensibilities – were in the vanguard of antidissection agitation.

[10] *Boston Gazette*, April 28, 1788.

[11] *Boston Gazette*, April 25, 1788; *The Minerva and Mercantile Evening Advertiser*, August 19, 1797.

[12] *Greenleaf's New-York Journal and Patriotic Register*, August 8, 1797.

[13] *Pennsylvania Packet*, April 25, 1788 and *Greenleaf's New-York Journal and Patriotic Register*, March 3, 1792.

[14] The grand jury report on the Doctors' Mob of 1788 may be found in the [New York] *Daily Advertiser*, May 10, 1788.

If unwritten or natural law demanded protecting the dead, it is not surprising that surgeons were envisioned as unnatural. An "unnatural business" was the euphemism used by one opponent to refer to dissection.[15] By examining the inner workings of corpses, anatomists exhibited a greater measure of inquisitiveness than some thought proper. Critics often ignored the importance of anatomical practice in medical training. Instead, they argued that dissection was just "to gratify the curiosity of a herd of unthinking and unprincipled physical students."[16] The reputation of physicians as free thinkers contrasted with religious obligations to honor the deceased. A New York citizen complained in 1792 that bodies were "being violently dragged from the silent mansion to become a subject of mirth to a licentious set of men and the laughter of fools, who cut and mangle a body."[17]

Antidissection rhetoric employed a universalist language portraying anatomy as a violation of nature. Nevertheless, this did not mean that opponents reacted identically to every case of dissection. Communities were most concerned with their own dead. While desecrating the grave of someone with connections might kindle a riot by friends and relatives, opponents of dissection could be silent when the victim seemed more distant. No protesters gathered when the corpse of a New York black, executed for rape in 1763, was turned into "a raw head and bloody bones by [the] ... tribe of dissectors."[18] Crowd action depended upon mobilizing popular anger. The identity of the anatomized corpse was an important ingredient for recruiting a mob.

[15] *Pennsylvania Mercury*, May 3, 1788.
[16] *Pennsylvania Mercury*, May 3, 1788; [New York] *Daily Advertiser*, February 16, 1788. Also, see the report in the *Pennsylvania Journal and Weekly Advertiser*, February 22, 1786, which reflects this argument. It describes the loss of six slaves who threw themselves into the sea when a slave ship captain sought to gratify his curiosity by having a dead black dissected on deck. Michael Sappol, *A Traffic of Dead Bodies: Anatomy of Embodied Social Identity in Nineteenth-Century America* (Princeton: Princeton University Press, 2002) provides a particularly thoughtful glimpse at the significance of anatomy for constructing collective and individual self-regarding.
[17] *Greenleaf's New-York Journal and Patriotic Register*, March 3, 1792. Elaine Scarry, *The Body in Pain: The Making and Unmaking of the World* (New York: Oxford University Press, 1985), pp. 27–59 and 204–205 discusses the inversion of medical science as it becomes an instrument of pain. See also W. R. Fanu's examination of Hogarth's portrayal of anatomy in "The Rewards of Cruelty," *Annals of the Royal College of Surgeons* 21 (1957): 390–394; Catherine Gallagher and Thomas Laquer, *The Making of the Modern Body: Sexuality and Society in the Nineteenth Century* (Berkeley: University of California Press, 1987); Giovanna Ferrari, "Public Anatomy Lessons and the Carnival in Bologna," *Past and Present* 117 (1987): 50–106.
[18] *New York Gazette*, November 28, 1763.

There was a hierarchy for the eighteenth-century dead as surely as there was one for the living. At the pinnacle of this hierarchy stood respectable white citizens interred in churchyards. Burying the deceased in the shadow of a church meant extending the sanctity of the chapel to the cemetery. It also reflected an attempt to bind the fate of the dead with a community of believers. Encircled by a fence or wall and dotted with inscribed gravestones, the church burial ground identified which corpses belonged to that community. There was no doubt that these dead had defenders. When the incidence of grave robbing increased, church members hired watchmen and might marshal the threat of crowd actions.[19]

Unlike the churchyard dead, those of the poor, blacks, and strangers were more vulnerable to grave robbers. Their remains were relegated to a separate paupers' burial ground. The cemetery for New York's poor at Pottersfield, located behind the almshouse, was frequented by surgeons' assistants in search of cadavers. Often buried without proper coffins, corpses in Pottersfield were more easily disinterred. The poor also could not afford those methods used to ward off grave robbers, such as placing a corpse temporarily in a vault or hiring watchmen. Most importantly, however, the less well-to-do simply made better victims. Robbing a grave at Pottersfield instead of one in a churchyard would not elicit the wrath of an organized religious community. Moreover, the lower classes did not dispense patronage, support medical colleges, or govern hospitals.[20]

Inequalities existed even among those interred at Pottersfield. Unable to bury their dead in white churchyards, the city assigned blacks a segregated section of the cemetery. This topographic configuration and black powerlessness made them the ideal victims of anatomists. Blacks were the most common source of cadavers in eighteenth–century New York. "I rather believe," wrote a New York proponent of anatomy in 1788, "that the only subjects procured for dissection are the productions of

---

[19] Claudia Heaton, "Body Snatching in New York City," *New York State Journal of Medicine* 43 (1943): 1861–1865; David C. Humphrey, "Dissection and Discrimination: The Social Origins of Cadavers in America 1760–1915," *Bulletin of the New York Academy of Medicine* 49 (1973): 819–827; F. C. Waite, "Grave Robbing in New England," *Bulletin of the Medical Librarians Association* 33 (1945): 272–294. The discussion of the hierarchical topography of death has benefitted from Michael Rogan, *The Space of Death*, trans. Alan Sheridan (Charlottesville: University of Virginia Press, 1983).

[20] Julius Calvin Ladenheim, "The Doctors' Mob of 1788," *Journal of the History of Medicine and Allied Sciences* 5 (1950): 23–43.

Africa or their descendants ... and if those characters are the only subjects of dissection, surely no person can object."[21]

Yet the free black community did object. In February 1788, free blacks
petitioned the city to restrain medical students from robbing their burial
place in Pottersfield. They argued that the surgeons "under the cover of
night, and in the most wanton sallies of excess ... dig up the bodies of
the deceased, friends and relatives of the petitioners, carry them away
without respect to age or sex, mangle their flesh out of wanton curiosity and then expose it to beasts and birds." With discontent mounting in
their community, free black leaders brought forward a proposal for an
alternative source of cadavers. This proposal, a critical precursor to the
Anatomy Act, urged limiting dissection to criminals.[22]

Free blacks had their own reasons for opposing such "sallies of excess."
Among these may have been the persistence of African traditions of rev-
erence toward the deceased.[23] Perhaps, too, free blacks were troubled by
what inequality among the dead meant for the living. Segregated cemeteries
and victimization by anatomists seemed emblematic of their failure to gain
equal rights. In the late 1780s free blacks found themselves in an ambiguous position between the status of full citizens and that of slaves. Only
three years before the petition against grave robbing, the New York legislature appended to a gradual slave emancipation bill an amendment that
would have denied free blacks the right to vote. The entire measure was
defeated, but debates clearly demonstrated how tenuous was the free black
claim to the privileges accorded to whites. The small size of the free black
population as compared to the city's slave population contributed as well
to its sense of insecurity. In 1790, there were 1,011 free blacks as opposed
to 2,369 slaves. During the 1780s and 1790s, the free black community
was terrorized by attempts to kidnap members and sell them as slaves.[24]

---

[21] *New York Daily Advertiser*, April 23, 1788. See the reference on the African-American
cemetery in the *Minutes of the Common Council of the City of New York 1784–1831*,
19 vols. (New York: 1917), 2:134.

[22] See the letter of a free black in the [New York] *Daily Advertiser*, February 16, 1788;
February 4, 1788 petition to the Common Council in "Petitions 1700–1795," Records of
the City Clerk, New York, quoted in I. N. Stokes, *The Iconography of Manhattan Island*,
6 vols. (New York: 1928), 6:46.

[23] Daniel R. Roediger, "And Die in Dixie: Funerals, Death, and Heaven in the Slave
Community 1700–1865," *Massachusetts Review* 22 (1981): 163–183; Melville J.
Herskovits, *The Myth of the Negro Past* (Boston: Beacon Press 1941), pp. 197–206.
Sterling Stuckey, *Slave Culture: Nationalist Theory and the Foundations of Black America*
(New York: Oxford University Press, 1987), p. 59 has found that American slaves drew
upon Central and West African burial customs as late as the 1850s.

[24] Arthur Zilversmit, *The First Emancipation: The Abolition of Slavery in the North*
(Chicago: University of Chicago Press, 1967), pp. 139–152; Rhoda G. Freeman, "The

Free black opposition to dissection, therefore, must be understood as part of a larger attempt to distance themselves from the status of slaves. Dissection resembled the punishing of rebellious slaves with dismemberment. It also served as a reminder of the ways that the bodies of blacks, dead as well as living, might be subject to exploitation. The dissection of free blacks was founded on a racist premise similar to those marshaled to justify slavery. By using black corpses as anatomical specimens, the surgeons implied that blacks – more than any other group – lacked the sensibilities to protect their dead. Just the opposite was true. As their petition to halt grave robbing showed, free blacks demonstrated an extraordinary devotion to deceased friends and relatives.[25]

This persistent commitment to the dead shaped free black political priorities. During the last two decades of the eighteenth century, Philadelphia's and New York's newly established Free African Societies requested private burial grounds as one of their initial acts. These cemeteries, quite possibly sought to stem grave robbing, and the 1788 petition were part of a concerted free black defense against dissection. Collective political action had one notable success: The petition calling for the dissection of executed felons may have been the first time that an American black proposal was transformed into law. Why was New York's legislature willing to meet black concerns and adopt a suggestion from free blacks as the centerpiece of the 1789 Anatomy Act? Oddly, the failed attempt in 1785 at emancipating New York slaves could have contributed to white politicians' growing awareness of free blacks as a political group. Although the legislature sought to deny liberated blacks the

---

Free Negro in New York City in the Era Before the Civil War" (Ph.D. dissertation, Columbia University, 1966), pp. 1–25 and pp. 64–90. Gary Nash, "Forging Freedom: The Emancipation Experience in the Northern Seaport Cities 1775–1820," in *Slavery and Freedom in the Age of the American Revolution*, eds. Ira Berlin and Ronald Hoffman (Charlottesville: University of Virginia Press, 1983), pp. 3–48; Shane White, "'We Dwell in Safety and Pursue Our Honest Callings': Free Blacks in New York City 1783–1810," *Journal of American History* 75 (1988): 445–470. More generally on the status of Northern free blacks, see Shane White, *Somewhat More Independent: The End of Slavery in New York City 1770–1810* (Athens: University of Georgia Press, 1991).

[25] Viewing it as a species of political quietism, later black activists have been troubled by the traditional black emphasis on the dead (see Roediger, "And Die in Dixie," pp. 163–164). Gary Nash counters that criticism by suggesting that free black attempts to acquire graveyards reflect their African religious heritage and creates a sense of identity. As suggested here, however, their concern with the dead – overshadowed by the threat of dissection – was also an expression of pragmatic politics. Gary Nash, *Forging Freedom: The Formation of Philadelphia's Black Community 1720–1840* (Cambridge: Harvard University Press, 1988), p. 45.

franchise, the heated debate over this question underlined the potential importance of free black votes.[26]

Nevertheless, black antidissection protests alone did not prompt the passage of the Anatomy Act. It was, ironically, a riot over the dissection of a white woman that impelled the legislature to adopt the free black proposal calling for the anatomical use of executed felons. New York whites had not taken to the streets to oppose the desecration of the black burial ground at Pottersfield. But in the spring of 1788, when grave robbers dared to disinter a white woman from the yard of Trinity Church, anger among whites erupted. "The internments not only of strangers and the blacks had been disturbed," wrote an outraged New Yorker, "but the corpses of some respectable people were removed."[27] Anatomists had violated a taboo as important as that against disinterring the deceased. They had failed to respect the hierarchical spatial arrangements that circumscribed late-eighteenth-century death. It was a mistake to confuse Trinity Church's burial place, segregated and attached to an important religious institution, with a black cemetery situated in the midst of paupers' graves. The result of such an error was the Doctors' Mob of 1788.

The riot began one Sunday, April 13, 1788, when a small group of boys playing outside the city hospital arranged themselves so that they could stare in the window. An irate anatomist then took an arm and used it to frighten one of the boys away. This child ran to his father and told him the story. Shocked, the father, who was a stone mason, and a group of friends decided to examine the grave of the boy's recently interred mother. The coffin was empty. Within a short time, furious workmen assembled and marched to the hospital. There they found some half-dissected bodies, which they exposed to the public in order to demonstrate the surgeons' cruelty.[28] Through displaying these cadavers, rioters drew

[26] *New York Packet*, April 25, 1788; Ralph G. Victor, "An Indictment for Grave Robbing at the Time of the 'Doctors' Riot' of 1788," *Annals of Medical History* 2 (1940): 366–370. On Trinity Church's segregationist burial policy, see Stokes, *Iconography*, 5:1265.

[27] *New York Packet*, April 25, 1788; Ralph G. Victor, "An Indictment for Grave Robbing at the Time of the 'Doctors' Riot' of 1788," *Annals of Medical History* 2 (1940): 366–370.

[28] Narratives of the Doctors' Mob include Ladenheim, "The Doctors' Mob of 1788," 23–43; Linda Grant DePauw, *The Eleventh Pillar: New York State and the Federal Constitution* (Ithaca: Cornell University Press, 1966); and Paul Gilje, *The Road to Mobocracy: Popular Disorder in New York City 1763–1834* (Chapel Hill: University of North Carolina Press, 1987), pp. 78–83. Yet for the most part, these narratives fail to address the motives behind what Sean Wilentz calls "seemingly bizarre" antidissection agitation (*Chants Democratic: New York City and the Rise of the American Working Class 1780–1850* [New York: Oxford University Press, 1984], p. 64). An exception is Paul Gilje's "The Common People and the Constitution." The version here is drawn largely from accounts

upon a traditional means of enlisting others in their protest: using the sight of dismembered corpses to evoke a visceral sense of outrage against dissection. For much of the riot's first day, protesters searched the hospital and surgeons' homes for more remains. Anatomical instruments were ruined and specimens destroyed. Rioters also seized and intimidated a number of medical students.

The next morning, when passions might have waned, there was a renewed demand for the inspection of anatomists' houses. Fearing a complete breakdown of order, Governor George Clinton called out the militia. The mob met the militia on its way to the jail, where the anatomists were confined for their safety, seizing and destroying the troops' firearms. At the prison, the remaining militiamen attempted to defend the surgeons. This small company boasted a stellar cast, including Clinton, John Jay, Alexander Hamilton, and Baron von Steuben. The militia and its luminaries met the rioters in a pitched battle, during which Jay and von Steuben were wounded. Using a motley collection of weapons ranging from staves of picket fences to stray stones, the crowd proved itself a formidable force. The militia commander, unable to turn back the rioters, withdrew his troops to a strategic distance and ordered them to fire. These volleys, followed by a charge with fixed bayonets, killed three rioters and wounded a half-dozen others. The Doctors' Mob, which began as a limited exercise in politics out-of-doors, ended poorly with a riot of surprising magnitude and fatalities.

Although both primary and secondary accounts of the Doctors' Mob end with the quelling of the riot, it should be recalled that antidissection sentiment remained strong. The militia that paraded through New York City streets the following day demonstrates the absence of a clear denouement. It was composed not of local militiamen, many of whom had failed to report for duty or surrendered their weapons, but of troops from the surrounding counties. More than a military victory was required; the authorities needed to deal with awakened fears over dissection. Rumors had spread that dead bodies were being exported to Europe, and there was talk of boarding foreign ships to search for them. One humorist suggested that the dread of surgeons was so great that an Irish militiaman in New York insisted upon being buried with his sword in order to protect himself.[29]

---

in contemporary newspapers, including the *New York Packet*, April 25, 1788 and the *Massachusetts Sentinel*, April 23, 1788. See the intriguing letter of a militiaman in the *Massachusetts Spy*, May 1, 1788.

[29] *Pennsylvania Packet*, April 28, 1788; *Boston Gazette*, May 5, 1788.

Nor was it unlikely that anatomists would soon forget the abuse they suffered at the hands of rioters and return to robbing graves. The demand for cadavers seemed a durable feature of life in the major port cities. Baltimore experienced a dissection riot in 1788, and in nearby Philadelphia, indignation was mounting against anatomists. New York's political leaders may have suspected that further desecration of cemeteries would provoke another Doctors' Mob. In fact, three years later, renewed grave robbing prompted a call for an encore of the 1788 riot. A letter appearing in a New York newspaper asked, "Where are those who boldly stepped forward in the former disturbance?" Its author flatly stated that if there was another riot "I will willingly join them, for I abhor and detest the inhuman practice" of dissection.[30]

New York's political leaders saw that only by providing a reliable source of anatomical specimens would it be possible to permanently stem antidissection protest. Acknowledging the legitimacy of popular opposition to grave robbing, they also conceded the legitimate reasons why anatomists acquired cadavers.[31] Consequently, the legislature adopted a statute that did more than simply punish grave robbers. Citizens of Philadelphia and New York, however, chose a different approach by proposing legislation that would inflict stiff penalties for the theft of corpses. These suggestions included rewards for capturing grave robbers, whipping and imprisonment, and retaliating by dissecting anatomists after their death.[32] One Philadelphian even pointedly remarked that unauthorized dissection was a capital offense in Spain.[33] Yet New York's legislature not only wished to punish grave robbers, but also to end the need to rob graves. For that reason, the Anatomy Act was based on a notion first proposed by free blacks. It introduced into America the first legislation for setting aside executed felons as anatomical specimens.[34]

---

[30] *Greenleaf's New-York Journal and Patriotic Register*, May 3, 1792.

[31] The growing respectability and professionalization of medicine contributed to the New York legislature's willingness to provide cadavers. In 1797, the same year as the John Young controversy described here, John Jay requested and received legislative support for an anatomical museum at Columbia (ed. Charles Z. Lincoln, Messages from the Governors, (Albany, 1909), 2: 389; Stokes, *Iconography*, p. 1339.

[32] *Pennsylvania Mercury*, March 8, 1788 and May 3, 1788; *Pennsylvania Packet*, April 25, 1788; *Greenleaf's New-York Journal and Patriotic Register*, May 3, 1792.

[33] *Pennsylvania Mercury*, May 3, 1788.

[34] After the Doctors' Mob, the notion of using felons as anatomical specimens gained wide currency. See *Pennsylvania Packet*, April 25, 1788. In the *Pennsylvania Mercury*, May 3, 1788, a reader suggested that "There are bodies which might be procured for this purpose – candidates for the gallows or wheelbarrow – persons devoid of every principle of justice who have forfeited bonds of friendship and consanguinity."

Enacted within a year of the Doctors' Mob, the Anatomy Act of 1789 recognized the riot's influence upon its genesis. The bill's official title was "An Act to Prevent the Odious Practice of Digging up and Removing for the Purpose of Dissection, Dead Bodies Interred in Cemeteries or Burial Places." It acknowledged the fact that grave robbing had "occasioned great discontent ... and in some cases disturbed the public peace and tranquility." The law's provisions were quite simple. Those executed for murder, arson, or burglary could be handed over to the surgeons for dissection. Any body snatcher might be sentenced at the judge's discretion, the law warned, to standing in the pillory, a fine, and/or imprisonment.[35]

Both the surgeons and their opponents won important concessions. Anatomists were granted a source of cadavers "in order that science may not ... be injured by preventing the dissection of proper subjects." Antidissection protesters were reassured by harsh penalties for grave robbers. Yet a careful reading of the law indicates that its architects conceded the possibility of further extralegal activity. The sentence of dissection could only be implemented at the judge's discretion. Fearing that protest might erupt over the dissection of a particular felon, the authors of the Anatomy Act left it to the court to decide who should suffer that fate. This clause presumably permitted the authorities to defuse a potential riot.

Interestingly, the act failed to determine the exact penalties for grave robbing. Specifying neither the maximum fine nor the length of the prison sentence, it allowed the judge to levy *any* fine or jail term. Arguably, a grave robber might be excused from prison or, on the other extreme, punished with a life term. The Anatomy Act was highly unusual, perhaps unique, in granting justices such wide powers in sentencing. It contradicted the idea of legal reformers that it was the legislature's responsibility to provide sharply defined penalties. According to reformers, statutory law – not the whims of unelected judges – should determine the proper measure of punishment that matched the crime.[36]

---

[35] "An Act to Prevent the Odious Practice of Digging up and Removing for the Purpose of Dissection, Dead Bodies Interred in Cemeteries or Burial Places," January 6, 1789, New York, Chap. 3 in *Laws of the State of New York*, 3 vols. (New York, 1792), 2:219 and *Laws of the State of New York ... From the First to the Twelfth Session* (New York, 1789), 2:390. The Anatomy Act, interestingly, is not included in all printed versions of the New York code.

[36] Gordon S. Wood, *The Creation of the American Republic 1776–1797* (Chapel Hill: University of North Carolina Press, 1969), pp. 291–305.

Why, then, did New York's legislature abdicate this prerogative and leave it to the discretion of judges? Legislators might have hoped to sidestep the issue of how grave robbers should be punished. In the wake of the Doctors' Mob, they must have found it difficult to satisfy the popular clamor for harsher penalties. More importantly, such authority gave judges the flexibility to modulate the punishment according to the status of the victim. Just as the rioters of the Doctors' Mob differentiated between black graves and those in Trinity's churchyard, the legal system could make similar distinctions when determining a sentence for grave robbing. Such flexibility allowed the authorities a way to respond to popular unrest. By choosing a rigorous punishment, they could neutralize antidissection protest.[37]

Significantly, through incorporating the pillory among other punishments for body snatching, the Anatomy Act provided a role for the antidissection crowd. Sentencing a grave robber to the pillory would expose the felon to the full wrath of the populace. The extralegal crowd, not the wooden stocks, was the central feature of the punishment. Here, too, the Anatomy Act ran counter to reformist trends. Although during the late eighteenth century the populace's role in punishment was increasingly curtailed, this clause in the Anatomy Act represented a daring attempt to harness popular antidissection sentiment as part of the legal process.

The framers of the Anatomy Act probably understood the risk they took by including extralegal crowd action within the arsenal of penalties marshaled against grave robbers. It must have been included because, quite simply, no other punishment would be as effective. After the Doctors' Mob riot, grave robbers most likely feared the populace more than the authorities. In addition, without a modern police force at their disposal, the authorities had to rely heavily upon fear as a deterrent for a crime committed through stealth. Faced with the difficulty of guarding cemeteries against the stealth of grave robbers, New York's legislature drew upon the specter of the antidissection crowd. If that specter appeared a bit too real, the pillory need not be used. Like consigning a felon's cadaver to the surgeons or the fine and imprisonment that could be leveled against grave robbers, the Anatomy Act specified that the pillory might be invoked only at the judge's discretion.

Although the Anatomy Act was meant to prevent another antidissection riot, it also introduced a new punishment into New York's criminal

---

37 In Connecticut, where discretionary power was made explicit, the court could order the dissection of an executed felon "if they think proper on consideration of the character of such person." Connecticut State Archives [Hartford], IV:49, 1788.

codes. Those executed for murder, arson, or burglary could receive – at the judge's discretion – an additional sentence of dissection. Did the authors of the bill recognize the importance of dissection as an instrument of retribution, or were executed felons simply a convenient source of cadavers? Unfortunately, the intent of the Anatomy Act's framers cannot be known. Contextual evidence, however, does suggest that they must have realized that the dissection of felons also could be used as a form of retribution. The Anatomy Act's closest precedent in Anglo–American law was England's 1752 act mandating the dissection of executed murderers. Widely known in America, the English law unambiguously saw dissection as a punishment. Its purpose, the law flatly stated, was to add "some further terror and peculiar mark of infamy ... to the punishment of death."[38]

New York's Anatomy Act also seems to have served as the model for a number of American statutes passed in the 1790s that mandated punitive dissection. In 1790, the United States Congress gave federal judges the right to include dissection when imposing the death penalty for a murder committed in a military garrison or other federal domain. New Jersey promulgated a 1796 law that, at the court's discretion, allowed for the dissection of convicted murderers. Incorporating clauses that permitted the sentence of dissection only at the court's discretion, both laws echoed the language of the 1789 New York statute. Unlike the Anatomy Act, those statutes passed in the 1790s were not reticent about identifying dissection as a legal deterrent. Neither the New Jersey bill nor that of Congress mentioned the benefits to medical science. Instead, the New Jersey law was entitled "An Act for the Punishment of Crimes" and the federal statute "An Act for the Punishment of Certain Crimes." These statutes also recognized the dangers of popular resistance to punitive dissection. They attached stiff penalties of a hundred-dollar fine and one-year imprisonment to any attempt at rescuing a felon's cadaver from the

---

[38] "An Act for Better Preventing the Horrid Crime of Murder" (25 Geo. II, c.37, 1752). The English Murder Act is treated in Leon Radzinowicz, *A History of English Criminal Law and Its Administration from 1750*, 5 vols. (New York: 1948), 1: 206–207; Linebaugh, "Tyburn Riot," pp. 76–78; and J. M. Beattie, *Crime and the Courts in England 1660–1800* (Princeton: Princeton University Press, 1986), pp. 525–530. Not only was the knowledge of the Murder Act widespread in America (see, for example, the *Virginia Gazette*, 14 August 1752), but as described earlier, it became part of vernacular legal culture. In addition, less than three years prior to the passing of New York's statute, William Wilberforce attempted to expand England's Murder Act by mandating punitive dissection for other crimes. This proposal passed the House of Commons, but was vetoed by the House of Lords. Hansard, *Parliamentary History*, 26 cols. 195–202.

surgeons. Whether it was a self-conscious addition to the criminal code, New York's Anatomy Act stood midway between an English precedent and a lineage of American laws that identified dissection as a mode of punishment.[39]

Punitive dissection was favored for a number of reasons. It provided for an additional punishment that distinguished between one capital sentence and another. According to Blackstone, "In very atrocious crimes, other circumstances of terror, pain and disgrace are superadded ... [such as] public dissection." This may have been an important consideration in constructing the Anatomy Act. A 1788 New York statute imposed the death sentence for treason, murder, stealing from a church, buggery, burglary, breaking into an inhabited house, arson, forgery, counterfeiting, and malicious maiming. Passed in the shadow of such a severe law, the Anatomy Act singled out certain crimes that posed a risk to life – murder, burglary, and arson – for postmortem retribution. Moreover, by delivering the executed criminal's corpse to the surgeons, the authorities were also able to curtail public demonstrations favorable to the felon. Eighteenth–century retributive dissection took place in laboratories and hospitals. Such a privatized punishment allowed for a level of control that appealed to both legal reformers and conservatives.

Punitive dissection's greatest attraction was its strength as a deterrent. It was supposed to frighten hardened criminals more than the threat of hanging. During the 1780s, when the Anatomy Act was framed, there was a growing dissatisfaction with the effectiveness of public punishment. Drawing on Edmund Burke's notion that imagining the unknown has a greater impact than that which is actually observed, a new approach to punishment developed that stressed the advantages of hidden retribution.

---

[39] The New York Anatomy Act appears to have been widely known. See, for example, the unusual reporting in the *Pennsylvania Mercury*, February 3, 1789; "An Act for the Punishment of Certain Crimes," April 30, 1790; U.S. Statutes, chap. IX in *Acts Passed at the First Congress of the United States of America* (Philadelphia, 1795), pp. 176–188; "An Act for the Punishment of Crimes," March 18, 1796; New Jersey R.S. 257, 4 in William Patterson, *Laws of the State of New Jersey Revised and Published Under the Legislature* (Newark, 1800). "An Act Against Dueling," June 30, 1784 in *The Perpetual Laws of the Commonwealth of Massachusetts from the Commencement of the Constitution in October 1780 to the Last Wednesday in May 1789* (Boston, 1789), p. 213 was another early statute with a dissection clause. It ordered the corpse of a slain duelist to be either buried near the gallows with a stake driven through its chest or delivered to the surgeons. A proposal for this law (*Boston Post-Boy*, November 15, 1773) argues that if the duelist's corpse "should be anatomized as in the case of murder in England, it would operate more effectively on the passion of shame than as it now stands." Still, the New York Anatomy Act was the first American statute mandating punitive dissection for common felons.

By concealing punishment, its terrifying dramaturgy was internalized and magnified. Benjamin Rush's *Enquiry into the Effects of Public Punishment,* published in 1787, provided the most important American exposition of how a science of sensibilities may be applied to legal process. Enacted only two years later, the Anatomy Act was drafted in the midst of ferment over the relationship between the imagination and retribution. Although the architects of the Anatomy Act left no record of what shaped the decision to evoke dissection as a punishment, punitive dissection must have seemed the perfect instrument to conjure up frightening images of the unseen. The graphic nature of dissection ensured that it would exercise a powerful hold over the imagination.[40]

POPULAR PROTEST AND THE UNMAKING OF A LAW

John Young never thought he deserved to be a major figure in a sensational murder trial and a candidate for the surgeon's knife. He blamed this fate on a web of credit and debt that remains difficult to reconstruct. Young's troubles began when he transferred his music publishing firm from Philadelphia to New York. Lacking sufficient capital, he entered into two partnerships. His first associate claimed that Young owed him a large amount of money and seized his possessions. The second partnership, even more disastrous, ended with Young being sent to debtors' prison for four months. Imprisonment was a bitter experience for Young. His second partner, Young believed, had taken advantage of the arrangement in order to learn how to operate the publishing business alone. Furthermore, Young's economic difficulties worsened during his stay in jail.[41]

Upon release, Young was pressed to pay a note owned for his previous lodgings. He attempted to stall by disputing the amount and, as claimed in one letter, it was necessary to further delay payment because he had been robbed. Young promised to send money as soon as possible: "I have

---

[40] Edmund Burke, *A Philosophical Inquiry into the Origin of Our Ideas of the Sublime and the Beautiful* (Notre Dame: University of Notre Dame Press, 1968), pp. 57–70; Steven Wilf, "Imagining Justice: Aesthetics and Public Executions in Late Eighteenth-Century England," *Yale Journal of Law & the Humanities* 5 (1993): 51–78.

[41] There has survived an unusually rich historical record detailing Young's involvement with debt. These include lawsuits for debt: *John Young v. Christian Bacher,* September 8, 1796 and *John Young v. Eliza Miller,* January 13, 1797, Mayor's Court Docket, Manhattan County Archives, New York; letter of John Young to Eliza Miller and letter of John Young to Abigail Birdsail, March 2, 1797 in *Greenleaf's New-York Journal and Patriotic Register,* August 30, 1797. See Young's own account in John Young, *Narrative of the Life, Last Dying Speech, and Confession of John Young* (New York, 1797), pp. 2–5.

not a dollar but as I borrow it, nor do I expect any till my first musical number comes out, which is now printing. I would be sorry to hold five dollars in my pocket without letting you have four of them." His creditors were not sympathetic. On April 1, 1797, Young was again placed in jail. He could not raise funds for bail because creditors maintained a hold over his property. Although after seven weeks in prison he was allowed to go free, once again Young remained encumbered by debt. There was little chance of resuscitating the printing business. Young became a musician who earned his living by playing at private houses.[42]

Returning from just such a performance at the home of Aaron Burr, Young met with an unpleasant surprise. A creditor had obtained a court order that directed Deputy Sheriff Robert Barwick to take him into custody. Barwick willingly accompanied Young to several places while the prisoner attempted to raise money for bail. Finally, as it grew late and the sun began to set, Barwick refused to go elsewhere. A desperate Young then pulled himself loose and drew his pistol, shooting Barwick through the left chest. Moments later, the deputy sheriff was dead.[43]

In his printed confession, Young failed to express remorse over the murder. He ignored that genre's traditional call for repentance and its formulaic declaration of contrition. Instead, Young transformed the literary form of the dying speech and last confession into an attack on those who used credit to destroy the honest working man. Clothing himself in the garb of artisan republican rhetoric, Young appealed to the sympathy of those fellow New Yorkers who had also suffered at the hands of creditors. During the middle 1790s, there was increasing popular agitation for debtor reform. In the spring of 1797, the New York legislature debated the bankruptcy law with "considerable warmth." As Bruce Mann has so elegantly shown, Americans of all classes in the 1790s were more willing to ascribe insolvency to failed risk taking than to moral weakness in repaying legitimate debts. Young attempted to cast his predicament as part of this larger issue. He dubbed debtors' prison an American Bastille, and his last warning – so different from the customary admonition to avoid wrongdoing – was not to let your papers fall into the "hands of those tolerated leeches that call themselves sheriffs' officers."[44]

---

[42] Letters of John Young to Eliza Miller and letter of John Young to Abigail Birdsail, March 1 and 2, 1797 in *Greenleaf's New-York Journal and Patriotic Register*, August 30, 1797; Young, *Narrative*, pp. 2–5.

[43] Young, *Narrative*, p. 6; *Greenleaf's New-York Journal and Patriotic Register*, July 1, 1797; *New York Magazine or Literary Repository* (July 1787): 389.

[44] Letter of James Greenleaf to Aaron Burr, March 17, 1797 in *The Papers of Aaron Burr 1756–1836*, microfilm edited by Mary-Jo Kline; Young, *Narrative*, pp. 2–5. The

By portraying himself as a common man who had fallen prey to rapacious creditors, Young shrewdly sought to mobilize popular sympathy and transform himself from a criminal into a victim. Unlike blacks disinterred from Pottersfield, he was not an anonymous victim. Throughout the summer of 1797, the sad tale of Young's crime, trial, and execution captured public attention. While Young's published last confession provided New Yorkers with a firsthand account, his minister penned a portrait of Young's life in prison. New York's newspapers and gossips debated whether Young deserved his fate. As Young campaigned to muster sympathy, dissection once again became a public issue.[45]

Unfortunately for Young, the court's sympathy lay with the murder victim. Barwick left a widow and nine children. At the trial, the deputy sheriff was portrayed as an indulgent man who was willing to accompany Young for three hours during an elusive search for bail. According to Chief Justice Robert Yates, the murder was an outrage carried out with a prepared weapon against a law officer. There was little Young could do against such damning arguments. He denied saying that Barwick would never take him into custody. Rather, Young insisted, he repeatedly warned the deputy sheriff to keep his distance. It was only because Barwick rashly ignored this advice and rushed forward that the death occurred. Through such claims, Young hoped that the murder charge would be reduced to manslaughter. There were at least a dozen witnesses testifying against his version of the incident. On Young's side, he had the testimony of a lone mulatto woman. Although defended by such distinguished attorneys as Aaron Burr, Henry Brockholst Livingston, and Nathaniel Pendleton, the trial did not go well for Young. On Friday, August 4, the judge expressed his hope that the accused might experience in another world the mercy that justice denied him in this one. Then came the terrifying sentence: Young was to be "hanged by the neck until dead."[46]

---

importance of debt in late-eighteenth-century New York society has been examined in Alfred Young, *The Democratic Republicans of New York: The Origins 1763–1797* (Chapel Hill: University of North Carolina Press, 1967). Bruce H. Mann, *Republic of Debtors: Bankruptcy in the Age of the American Independence* (Cambridge: Harvard University Press, 2003).

[45] Christopher Flanagan, *Conversation and Conduct of the Late Unfortunate John Young* (New York, 1797).

[46] Minute Book of the Supreme Court of Judicature, Manhattan County Archives [New York], July 28, 1797; Young, *Narrative*, pp. 6–7; *Greenleaf's New York Journal and Patriotic Register*, August 8, 1797; *The Minerva and Mercantile Evening Advertiser*, 5 August 1797. The strategy of Young's defense is described in the [Newark] *Sentinel of Freedom*, August 9, 1797.

When the judge passed the sentence of death, he forgot to include the order for dissection. Young had to be recalled to the courtroom in order to learn that his body would be given to the surgeons. A sympathetic verse tract depicting the ghost of John Young returning in search of his grave was published posthumously. It was modeled on the vernacular legal literary genre of hanging ballads. In the poem, Young's ghost complained with less-than-haunting verse about the leveling of a second sentence: "But pity whither hadst thou fled to mourn/When the firm tongue my sad decree which gave/Bade me (though once dismist) again return/ To tell me I was denied a grave." Young's poetic specter and the ordinary people of New York did not question the justice of his conviction. Only Young continued to claim his innocence. Rather, they were troubled by the imposition of punitive dissection. "Was I punish'd to avenge the dead?" Young's ghost asked. "Or was it that the living might be taught to look upon the murder's doom with dread?"[47]

Even if the Anatomy Act remained reticent about dissection's punitive character, those in workshops and streets knew what the sentence meant. Young would be denied a grave. Shorn of the gravestone's stolid promise of a memorial, his body would be hacked into minute and virtually unrecognizable pieces. "No grieving friend ... shall mark ... his tomb and whisper 'here he lies.'" The sentence served as a symbolic form of annihilation. It was, in the words of one eighteenth-century New Yorker, a "sentence of unnecessary barbarity." This language echoes claims that England's Bloody Code was legalized vengeance. New York citizens, including the city's Freemasons, urged that he be spared dissection, for such vengeance was "doubtless murder." The Masons also offered to bury his dissected remains. But even this was not allowed.[48]

Dissection was a shaming punishment. Bernard de Mandeville had once marveled at the way poor people considered dissection a disgrace to surviving relatives. After the dishonor of being hanged for murder, he caustically commented, dissection was certainly not much of a scandal. Young and many of the common people, however, were convinced that being handed over to the surgeons meant a special humiliation. Young was concerned about "the odium that ... exist[s] in the mind of so many." He abstained from describing his parents in the last confession so that they should "avoid the taunts of unfeeling men."[49]

[47] Margaretta V. Faugeres, *The Ghost of John Young* (New York, 1797), p. 4.

[48] Faugeres, *Ghost*, p. 4; *New York Gazette and General Advertiser*, August 14 and 17, 1797.

[49] Bernard de Mandeville, *An Enquiry into the Causes of the Frequent Executions at Tyburn* (London, 1725), pp. 26–27; Young, *Narrative*, p. 2.

Young spent his last days as a model prisoner. He asked that God forgive the witnesses who gave false evidence against him. As a gesture of compassion, he left a bequest of fifty dollars for the education of Barwick's children. Although perhaps not sufficiently remorseful about ridding the world of a deputy sheriff, Young expressed sorrow over making a widow and nine partly orphaned children. "He was truly weary and heavy laden. His head seemed to be waters and his eyes a fountain of tears. For, like the penitent David, he often watered his couch with them." The evening before the execution, three friends joined him around ten o'clock and remained with him, singing and praying until two in the morning. Then, in the stillness of a summer night, Young peacefully dozed off.[50]

The condemned might have slept peacefully, but all around him, New York City was stirring. Governor John Jay had heeded the county sheriff's appeal for a military presence in the city. While the request was based upon a possible rescue attempt, Jay was anxious to comply for another reason. He believed it important that the "authority of the law should be seen to bear down [on] all opposition, and that on such occasions it should be rendered particularly solemn and impressive." Perhaps, too, memories of being wounded by a rock during the 1788 Doctors' Mob contributed to the governor's resolve.[51] Jay was serious about meeting possible crowd protest with force. General orders dispatched on August 13 directed all grenadier and light infantry companies, together with a cavalry corps, to be readied in the city. A lieutenant colonel was placed in command and instructed to keep the peace. These troops were not merely for show. Each soldier was issued twelve rounds of ammunition and ordered to "suppress any insurrection or riot [that] should arise." By eight in the morning, hours before the hanging, soldiers had already been deployed around the jail. They were commanded to wait there "until the time came to accompany Young to the place of execution."[52]

Startled New Yorkers awoke to find that their city was bustling with military maneuvers. "It is an extraordinary circumstance," wrote one citizen in a New York newspaper, "that the militia should be called out to

---

[50] Flanagan, *Conversations and Conduct*, pp. 3–4.

[51] Letter of John Lansing to John Jay (NNC-SC 7137), August 15, 1797; letter of John Jay to James Kent (N:3092), August 15, 1797 in the John Jay Papers, Columbia University, New York. On Jay's experience in the Doctors' Mob, see Sally Jay letter, April 17, 1788, John Jay Papers; *Massachusetts Spy*, May 1, 1788.

[52] The General Orders, August 13, 1797 may be found in *Greenleaf's New York Journal and Patriotic Register*, August 19, 1797 and the *New York Gazette and General Advertiser*, August 17, 1797.

attend the execution of a man convicted of murder, when no solid reason can be urged for its defense." Who was responsible for what New York's inhabitants considered martial law? Some blamed a "nerveless sheriff" and called for his replacement. Others argued that accountability ultimately rested with "imbecility on the part of the executive."[53] Calling out the militia was the governor's decision. Jay had chosen to deploy the militia rather than relying upon the sheriff's *posse comitatus*. Not surprisingly, Federalists and Antifederalists exchanged harsh words about Jay's role in the affair. Federalists suspected that Jay's opponents might be lurking behind the John Young controversy. They were probably right. Young's lawyers, publicists, and even Margaretta Faugeres, the author who conjured up his poetic specter, were all Republicans. Publisher Thomas Greenleaf, *bête noire* of the Federalists, used his newspaper to rally support against Young's dissection.[54]

Young seems to have recognized the importance of such an anti–Jay network. He defended himself with the rhetoric of artisan republicanism. This idiom, articulating the rights of the common man, fit nicely with the universalist language of antidissection protesters. It strengthened his identification with artisans who might serve as the backbone of his defense against the surgeons. Yet through employing partisan politics in his cause, Young undermined his larger claim to a communitywide antidissection consensus. The politicization of antidissection protests meant that Young's cause might be represented as a factional instrument aimed at the Federalists. Or, as one New Yorker called the controversy, "one of the quick-sighted maneuvers of Antifederalism – it is a specimen of the malignity and low cunning of that disorganizing sect."[55]

By mid-morning on Thursday, August 17, Young's friends had returned to help him prepare for the end. Meanwhile, the authorities, increasingly nervous about public sentiment, decided to move the execution to a field near the hospital. They hoped that the surgeons would be able

---

[53] *Greenleaf's New-York Journal and Patriotic Register*, August 17, 1797, August 19, 1797, and August 30, 1797. A letter from a New York citizen (August 30, 1797) argued that even the British government avoids military intervention.

[54] Faugeres lent her poetic talent to artisan and Antifederalist causes. See, for example, her ode in George Clinton, *Oration Delivered on the 4th of July 1798 Before the General Society of Mechanics and Tradesmen* (New York, 1798). Young, *Democratic Republicans* describes the political role of Faugeres (pp. 362–363) and Greenleaf (p. 393). Also, ed. Dumas Malone, *Dictionary of American Biography*, 10 vols. (New York, 1931), 2:314–321 and 6:312–313.

[55] *New York Gazette and General Advertiser*, August 21, 1797; Wilentz, *Chants Democratic*, pp. 61–101.

to whisk away the body to their laboratory and that the risky business of transporting the coffin across town could be avoided. It was dangerous enough just to bring the condemned to the place of execution. Even with a full contingent of soldiers there might be trouble. The condemned, too, sensed the precariousness of the situation. Possibly hoping for the rumored rescue attempt, Young insisted upon walking.[56]

Young sought one final opportunity to muster popular sympathies. Dressed in a white outfit bound with black, he drew upon the symbolic repertoire of Anglo–American executions. White apparel meant that the condemned continued to protest his innocence. He also composed a penitential hymn for the occasion. Once again, Young was unlucky. The militia escort included a military band that played lively marching tunes as the procession made its way to the scaffold. Young's hymn could not be heard above the sound of musical instruments. Later, there were complaints about such incongruous music. As one critic remarked: "Had an accidental witness ignorant of the occasion ... met the procession this morning, he must have considered it the celebration of some festival." Young's attempt at popular theater had turned into a farce.[57]

Still worse for Young, other kinds of theater were also taking place. Relatives of the victim chose their own symbolic appeal to the populace. Barwick's family, perhaps including all nine children, came to attend the execution. They stood as a silent rebuke to Young's play for gaining sympathy. The state, on the other hand, was determined to remind Young and the spectators of its power. Its troops eclipsed the view of the condemned. When the procession finally arrived at the scaffold, the soldiers formed a hollow square around it. For one bystander, it appeared that the government had adopted the full trappings of a despotic regime as they arranged themselves in the traditional Roman phalanx. The sheriff must have been reassured by the formidable presence of so many armed men dividing the condemned from the crowd.[58]

The execution did not take long. Young addressed a few words to the minister, sang a psalm, "and with great composure pulled his cap over his face." With the rope tied around his neck, the sheriff granted Young an additional quarter-hour to pray. Then, as the late afternoon

---

[56] *Greenleaf's New York Gazette and Patriotic Register*, August 19, 1797; *The Minerva and Mercantile Evening Advertiser*, August 17, 1797.

[57] *The Minerva and Mercantile Evening Advertiser*, August 17, 1797; *New York Gazette and General Advertiser*, August 18, 1797. See Peter Gassner's 1854 recollections of his father's role as a militiaman guarding Young in Stokes, *Iconography*, 5:1315.

[58] *Greenleaf's New-York Journal and Patriotic Register*, August 19, 1797.

sun dwindled, the executioner did his work and Young was hanged until dead. The crowd had been notably silent during the execution. Most likely, onlookers simply drifted away as the corpse was placed in a coffin. In order to avoid any unnecessary injury to the feelings of the persons who had assembled to see the execution, the body was conveyed to Pottersfield.[59]

Young would have only a brief rest in the city's burial ground at Pottersfield. Clearly, the authorities must have become timid in the face of popular opposition. They abandoned the earlier plan of delivering the corpse directly to an adjacent hospital as being too dangerous. Instead, it was thought safer to avoid so bluntly indicating any connection between the hanging and the surgeons. The anatomists' assistants would have to come like common grave robbers to the cemetery to disinter the corpse. At a late hour of the night they removed the cadaver and carried it to the anatomical theater. There, the anxious surgeons conducted the dissection in "as secret [a] manner as the nature of the business would admit."[60] The surgeons ordered that the dismembered remains be buried, but their assistants grew apprehensive that these might be discovered. They could imagine angry workmen digging up the hospital's yard searching for the corpse. Perhaps the assistants were worried that the incident might become a repetition of the 1788 riots. At that time, workmen armed with stones and bricks had threatened anatomists' lives – who knows what they might do now? Better, the assistants believed, to commit the corpse to the bottom of the river. Yet in their alarm and confusion, they failed to attach the necessary amount of weights to sink the corpse-filled sack.[61]

Early the next morning the sack was found washed ashore at New Market Slip. Angered by the sight of Young's mutilated remains, the

---

[59] *Greenleaf's New-York Journal and Patriotic Register*, August 19, 1797 and August 23, 1797; *Philadelphia Daily Advertiser*, August 19, 1797; letter of the surgeons John B. Hicks and Richard S. Kissman in *The Minerva and Mercantile Evening Register*, August 22, 1797. The contemporary estimate of 10,000 spectators at Young's execution, which would constitute slightly less than 30 percent of the city's population, must be used with caution (*Greenleaf's New-York Journal and Patriotic Register*, August 19, 1797).

[60] *The Minerva and Mercantile Evening Advertiser*, August 22, 1797 and *Greenleaf's New-York Journal and Patriotic Register*, August 21, 1797.

[61] Letter of William Turk in *Greenleaf's New-York Journal and Patriotic Register*, August 23, 1797; *New York Gazette and General Advertiser*, August 22, 1797. Fear over a repetition of the Doctors' Mob riot may have been heightened by the fact that the surgeon John Hicks, who had been accused of grave robbing in 1788, was involved in the Young dissection. After each incident, he published a defense of his conduct. [New York] *Daily Advertiser*, August 17, 1788 and *Greenleaf's New-York Journal and Patriotic Register*, August 23, 1797.

discoverers removed them from the sack and put them on display. The cadaver, which "consisted of most of his fleshy parts," was exposed to arouse popular indignation. It is possible to envision the gathering crowd of bristling working men and women as news of the event spread. Despite this provocation, Young's execution did not become an encore of the 1788 Doctors' Mob. Although the possibility of a riot existed, Jay's show of force appears to have been successful in stemming crowd action. Only after this added humiliation, then, did Young find his final resting place. He was buried in a simple grave near Long Island's East River shore.

The uproar over Young's hanging failed to evolve into a major riot. Yet it did represent a turning point for the Anatomy Act. By protesting John Young's fate, New Yorkers had crafted a powerful rejection of punitive dissection. The Anatomy Act may not have been written with the intent of introducing dissection into American criminal codes, but that was how the statute was deciphered from the vantage point of the streets. It was seen as the transplantation of British draconian punishment into the new republic. Such popular hermeneutics identified the Anatomy Act with retribution as surely as if it was engraved in the text. After the Young episode, it could no longer have been possible to read the act without considering this change in meaning. Ignoring the reticent preamble of the Anatomy Act, politics out-of-doors had inserted its own interpretive coda. Moreover, the protests demonstrated that the act was unable to fulfill its avowed aim of circumventing antidissection unrest. By selecting the protagonist of the execution spectacle as the surgeons' victim, the act had, in fact, provided a public event around which antidissection sentiment could crystallize. Yet the Young affair uncovered a still deeper contradiction about the legal imagination. If dissection could serve as a potent deterrent because it was reproduced in the imagination of the populace, then that same horrifying imagery might evoke popular anger over its imposition. Punitive dissection, even when concealed in a surgeon's laboratory, was simply too vivid.

It is not surprising, then, that the Anatomy Act does not appear to have been invoked after the Young episode. Emerging out of one antidissection protest, the Anatomy Act suffered an irreversible decline after the furor of 1797. Although the presence of armed soldiers assured Young's execution, the protesters may have ultimately won. Not wishing to risk another confrontation over dissection, the authorities seem to have abandoned the practice of supplying surgeons with the cadavers of executed felons. Around the same time, other changes rendered the statute obsolete. With a 1796 reform of the penal code that removed capital sentences for burglary and arson, executed criminals could provide few corpses. In order to meet their growing demand for bodies, anatomists were forced to look elsewhere. By the early nineteenth century, both punishment and anatomy repudiated the methods of the Anatomy Act. Anatomists quietly acquired the cadavers of the vagrant poor, while penal reformers did away with the spectacle of the scaffold. Both punishment and anatomy became more hidden.

The story of the Anatomy Act is full of ironies. Anatomical science, meant to serve the living, was inverted to become a punishment inflicted upon the dead; the black initiative calling for the dissection of executed felons was only accepted after New York whites staged an antidissection riot; and the statute, which sought to end antidissection unrest, instead contributed – and ultimately fell victim – to such protests. Yet there was one irony more striking than any other. The genesis of punitive dissection in America took place just as the country was beginning to embark upon a course of criminal law reform. It must have seemed paradoxical that the threat of a riot over the dissection of an executed felon, not an infrequent occurrence in England, should come to post–Revolutionary America. Although American legal reform condemned the sanguinary nature of English law, New York lawmakers had almost certainly borrowed from a 1752 English statute the notion of dissecting felons.

New York's Anatomy Act had an ambiguous relationship to the recasting of criminal law statutes in the Early Republic. A political reading of criminal law, with its republican thrust of making sanctions less public and sanguinary, had resulted in a novel statute where sanctions relied upon the imagination. But the other side of this newfound debate over criminal law identified a core role for the public, engaging in legal interpretation, transparency in criminal law procedure, and the marshaling of the common people to defend rights. Both these approaches had their roots, as we have seen, in a revolutionary blossoming of law-talk. Perhaps, then, the Anatomy Act's sleight-of-hand about its purposes is not so strange. The statute's reticent text mirrors a reticent mode of punishment. Yet reticence demands elucidation. During the John Young episode, ordinary New Yorkers uncovered the Anatomy Act's punitive aspect. Strikingly, it is their rendering of the act that has proved most significant.

Conclusion

Out of the American Revolution emerged a newfound legal culture grounded upon imaginative visions of criminal justice. Creating legal rhetoric tied to popular politics, the use of law as an instrument of political mobilization, the fabrication of legal language and symbolism accessible to the common people, the demand for the transparency of criminal law process, seeing criminal law as the mirror of society, and the recasting of statutes away from sanguinary punishment marks a notable departure from existing early-eighteenth-century Anglo-American conceptions of criminal law.

Most legal histories of America's foundational period have engaged in an archeology of knowledge that has yielded a past remarkably consonant with our present. The search has been for our *official* legal ancestry – in statutory material transplanted from England, common-law norms, and the rulings of courts. Yet it is often the plethora of unofficial responses to law at all levels of society that formed the backbone of late-eighteenth-century American legal culture. An explosion of law talk in the form of print and ritual was simultaneously used to communicate legal decision-making, ignite political mobilization, and mock both the powerful and the powerless. It made law the lingua franca of late-eighteenth-century America.

We are so used to mining the past for its genealogical beginnings – such as the origins of various rights or even the kernel of legal procedures – that we have failed to realize that perhaps the most significant feature of American legalism of the period was how it *read* law in an intertextual fashion. Comparison between otherwise unrelated cases, between an American law and its British parallel, and between the competing legal regimes clustered around the Atlantic are all examples of an insistence upon legal intertextuality with a political twist. Americans had learned this lesson well. By the early 1770s, as we saw in the cases of Ebenezer Richardson and Levi Ames, even ordinary garden-variety criminal cases might be seen as embodying the politics of criminal law.

Intermingling popular politics with the language of criminal law challenged professional hegemony over legal issues. Newspapers, treatises, and well-circulated descriptions of trials all contributed to the creation of a legal public sphere. Nevertheless, the use of law as a language of political mobilization would have been much less successful were it not for the existence of vernacular legal culture, such as execution narratives and mock executions. These works – the "vulgar tongue" of law – were originally a way for early modern Anglo-American criminal law regimes to bolster their legitimacy, and, while entertaining citizens, portrayed the lives of offenders as moral signposts. Increasingly, however, execution narratives were used as vehicles for offenders at odds with the authorities. Decoding the hidden transcripts within vernacular legal cultures tells us much about how the legal imagination could work out its strategies within the framework of a received genre.

In the midst of serious contention between England and the colonies, and especially during the mid-1770s, vernacular legal literature was appropriated to debate, and often critique, more broadly the aims of criminal sanctions. This might be seen in the complex legal fictions – the narratives – surrounding the executions of felons and the controversies they engendered. As we saw in the cases of William Beadle and Joseph Mountain, transatlantic dissension about religion and race, revolutionary politics and slavery, and even financial credit and sexual mores might be acted out within the discourse of criminal law. Moreover, just as patriots used the print medium of vernacular legal culture in their struggle against England, so, too, did they employ legal language in the performance of mock trials of effigies and mock executions.

One of the core arguments of this book has been that law is imagined before it is constructed. This may be seen in the case of the American critique of England's Bloody Code. In response to English polemicists' charge that Americans were hypocrites for embracing slavery and demanding liberty at the same time, Americans turned to a critique of the central role of capital punishment in England. This imagining of England's many capital statutes as a single code, it was argued, presages America's first thrust toward codification, whereby numerous states recast their criminal codes and replaced sanguinary punishment with prisons. The shift away from public punishment coincided with a rejection of the French model of revolutionary justice as embodied in the Reign of Terror. In many ways, then, the criminal law of the Early Republic incorporated the 1780s and early 1790s critique of English and French criminal justice as imposing a violent ordering of people's lives. The contradictions in seeking to make criminal law simultaneously a system of deterrence and a reflection of republican values of citizen consent, of using the imagination as an instrument of social control and also allowing it to flourish as a well-spring of popular legal interpretation, may be seen in the case of John Young.

AN UNTIDY STORY OF LEGAL ORIGINS

When nineteenth-century Americans canonized the legal legacy of the American Revolution, it was as the historical event that gave rise to the Constitution and made court-based jurisprudence triumphant, nothing more. We set aside our truly formative period of the emergence of legal language and instead focused on the rise of Constitutional interpretation through judicial review. It is this tradition that we have tried to export as rule of law around the world. We expect foreign nations – from new democracies in Eastern Europe to potentially new democracies in the Middle East – to have an orderly regime change, institute court-based legal norms, draft a model constitution, and vest a robust supreme court or constitutional court with the ultimate power to interpret its written text.

In the late 1960s and early 1970s, law and development projects sought to export American constitutionalism to Latin America. These projects often focused upon legal education and the dissemination of legal information. During the 1990s, a second wave of American civic missionary activity took place. Rule of law was the watchword for emerging democracies, especially in Eastern Europe. Often ignoring cultural differences, American law academics, large public foundations, and government-sponsored programs fostered the adaptation of American constitutional norms. Federalism, separation of powers, and judicial review were considered critical for the grounding of a well-established legalism. America's Constitution became its most important export.

Most significantly, we exported our founding myth as well. The origins of America's rule of law began with a Constitutional Convention, civilized debates among framers, and the creation of a constitutional court with a self-confident ethos. Ultimately, through the years, this cultural affinity for rule of law trickled down to the people at large – who contract, as Tocqueville declared, "the habits and tastes of the magistrates." Myths are important for the construction of social solidarity. But under other contexts, such as what has been called "legal imperialism," these founding stories have become yardsticks for how legal systems *must* develop.[1]

Nevertheless, our own origins were singularly untidy: extraofficial legal actions – what might be called law-out-of-doors, vernacular legal storytelling, the bric-a-brac of criminal trials, and, above all, the explosion of law talk with a volatile mix of law and politics. Criminal justice stood at the core of the aspirational concerns of a revolutionary generation. In our time, when – in the words of Wallace Stevens – we have "come to the end of imagination" and "return to a plain sense of things," it is difficult for us to conceive of legal discourse not confined to the courts, of breaking down the Chinese wall between law and politics without compromising the integrity, or perhaps even the intellectual vitality, of legal doctrine. Perhaps that is precisely the point. We need to rediscover law's imagined republic.

[1] James A. Gardner, *Legal Imperialism: American Lawyers and Foreign Aid in Latin America* (Madison: University of Wisconsin Press, 1981).

Bibliography

Archival Collections

"Bill for Adding to Punishment of Atrocious Crimes the Puncturing of Forehead with Design of Gallows" (1779), Connecticut Archives, First Series, 6/100 Hartford.

"Crimes and Misdemeanors," Connecticut Archives.

Connecticut Superior Court Records, 27/147–148, August 1770, Connecticut Archives (Hartford).

Cushing Papers, Notes on Cases Decided in the Supreme Judicial Court of Massachusetts, 1772–1789, Manuscript Collection, Harvard Law School Library.

Domestic George III, Domestic Entry Book, 1771–1776, London: Public Record Office.

Edmund Trowbridge, Notes on Legal Actions, Dana Papers, Massachusetts Historical Society.

Hutchinson to Hillsborough, May 15, 1771, London: Public Records Office, CO 5, 768/198–200.

"Joseph Mountain Pardon Petition," Connecticut Archives, 2nd Series, 4/131, August 15, 1790, Hartford.

Manuscript of Moot Cases, July 26, 1774, New-York Historical Society.

February 22, 1762, 66 Massachusetts Archives.

Minute Book of the Superior Court of Judicature, 30–31 Massachusetts Archives.

Minute Book of the Supreme Court of Judicature, July 28, 1797, Manhattan County Archives, New York.

"Order of the King in Council," November 23, 1761 in O'Callahan, *New York Colonial Documents*, 7:472–476.

June 23, 1737. Pennsylvania Colonial Records.

May 24, 1754. Pennsylvania Colonial Records.

May 9, 1767, Rhode Island Archives.

Robert Treat Paine Papers, Massachusetts Historical Society.

Secretary of Commonwealth, Pardon Books, September 2, 1793, Pennsylvania State Archives (Harrisburg).

Sparks Manuscripts, Belknap Papers, Harvard University.

Vital Records of New Haven, 2 vols. Hartford: Connecticut Society, 1917, 1:428.

Newspapers, Periodicals

Aurora General Advertiser. Philadelphia, Pa.: Benjamin Franklin Bache, 1794–1824.

Columbian Centinel. Boston, Mass: Benjamin Russell, 1790–1799.

Columbian Gazetteer. New York: J. Buel & Co, 1793–1794.

Gazette of the United States, & Philadelphia Daily Advertiser. Philadelphia, Pa.: John Fenno, 1796–1800.

Greenleaf's New-York Journal and Patriotic Register. New York: Thomas Greenleaf, 1792–1800.

Maryland Gazette. Annapolis, Md.: J. Green, 1745–1813.

National Gazette. Philadelphia, Pa.: P. Freneau, 1791–1793.

Newport Mercury. Newport, R.I.: Printed by J. Franklin, 1759–1928.

New York Daily Gazette. New York: J. & A. M'Lean, 1788–1795.

Pennsylvania Chronicle and Universal Advertiser. Philadelphia, Pa.: 1767–1774.

Porcupine's Gazette. Philadelphia, Pa.: W. Cobbett, 1797–1800.

The American Herald. Boston, Mass.: Edward E. Powars, 1784–1788.

The American Mercury. Hartford, Conn: Barlow and Babcock, 1784–1833.

The Augusta Chronicle and Gazette of the State. Augusta, Ga.: John E. Smith, 1789–1806.

The Baltimore Daily Intelligencer. Baltimore, Md.: Yundt and Patton, 1793–1794.

The Boston Evening-Post. Boston, Mass.: T. Fleet, 1735–1775.

The Boston Gazette, or, Country Journal. Boston, Mass.: B. Edes and J. Gill, 1755–1793.

The Boston Post-Boy & Advertiser. Boston, Mass.: Green & Russell, 1763–1769.

The Centinel of Freedom. Newark, N.J.: D. Dodge, 1796–1823.

The Connecticut Courant. Hartford, Conn.: Hudson & Goodwin, 1791–1914.

The Connecticut Gazette. New London, Conn.: T. Green, 1787–1799.

The Connecticut Journal and New-Haven Post-Boy. New Haven, Conn.: Thomas & Samuel Green, 1767–1775.

The Essex Gazette. Salem, Mass.: E. & S. Hall, 1768–1775.

The Gazette of the State of South-Carolina, Charleston, S.C.: Peter Timothy, 1777–1785.

The Gentleman's Magazine. London, England: E. Cave, 1736–1850.

The Independent Chronicle. Boston, Mass.: Powars & Willis, 1776.

The Independent Gazetteer, or, The Chronicle of Freedom. Philadelphia, Pa.: E. Oswald, 1782–1790.

The London Chronicle. London, England: J. Wilkie, 1765–1823.

The Massachusetts Centinel. Boston, Mass.: Warden & Russell, 1784–1790.

The Massachusetts Gazette, and the Boston Post-Boy and Advertiser. Boston, Mass.: Green & Russell, 1769–1775.

The Massachusetts Gazette and the Boston Weekly News-Letter. Boston, Mass.: 1769–1776.

The Massachusetts Magazine, or, Monthly Museum of Knowledge and Rational Entertainment. Boston, Mass.: Isaiah Thomas and Co., 1789–1796.

The Massachusetts Spy. Boston, Mass.: Isaiah Thomas, 1770–1778.

The Minerva & Mercantile Evening Advertiser. New York: Hopkins, Webb & Co, 1796–1797.

The New World. Philadelphia, Pa.: Samuel Harrison Smith, 1796–1797.

The New York Daily Advertiser. New York: F. Childs & Co, 1785–1806.

The New-York Gazette and General Advertiser. New York: A. M'Lean, 1795–1820.

The New-York Gazette, or, The Weekly Post-Boy. New York: J. Parker and W. Weyman, 1753–1759.

The New-York Gazette, or, The Weekly Post-Boy. New York: James Parker, 1766–1773.

The New York Journal and Patriotic Register. New York: Thomas Greenleaf, 1790–1793.

The New-York Journal, and Weekly Register. New York: Thomas Greenleaf, 1788–1790.

The New-York Journal, or, General Advertiser. New York: John Holt, 1766–1782.

The New-York Mercury. New York: H. Gaine, 1752–1768.

The New-York Packet. New York: S. Loudon, 1785–1792.

The Norwich-Packet, or, The Country Journal. Norwich, Conn.: J. Trumbull, 1785–1790.

The Pennsylvania Gazette. Philadelphia, Pa.: B. Franklin and H. Meredith, 1729–1778.

The Pennsylvania Gazette. Philadelphia, Pa.: Printed by Hall & Sellers, 1782–1815.

The Pennsylvania Journal, or, Weekly Advertiser. Philadelphia, Pa.: William Bradford, 1742–1793.

The Pennsylvania Mercury and Universal Advertiser. Philadelphia, Pa.: D. Humphreys, 1784–1791.

The Pennsylvania Packet, and Daily Advertiser. Philadelphia, Pa.: J. Dunlap and D. C. Claypoole, 1784–1790.

The Pennsylvania Packet, or, The General Advertiser. Lancaster, Pa.: J. Dunlap, 1777–1783.

The State Gazette of South-Carolina. Charleston, S. C.: A. Timothy, 1785–1793.

The Universal Asylum and Columbian Magazine. Philadelphia, Pa.: W. Young, 1790–1792.

The Vermont Gazette. Bennington, Vt.: Haswell & Russell, 1784–1796.

The Vermont Journal and the Universal Advertiser. Windsor, Vt.: Hough and Spooner, 1783–1792.

The Virginia Gazette. Williamsburg, Va.: William Parks, 1736–1781.

The Weekly Register. Norwich, Conn.: E. Bushnell, 1791–1795.

Legislation and Law Reports

A List of Infringements & Violations of Rights (1772) in *A Report of the Record Commissioners of the City of Boston: Containing the Boston Town Records, 1770 Through 1777*. City Document No. 91. (Boston: Rockwell and Churchill, 1887), pp. 99–106.

An Act Against Adultery, Polygamy, and Fornication (February 27, 1787), *State Papers of Vermont*. XIV: 165–167.

An Act Against Dueling (June 30, 1784), *The Perpetual Laws of the Commonwealth of Massachusetts from the Commencement of the Constitution in October 1780 to the Last Wednesday in May, 1789* (Boston, 1789), p. 213.

An Act Against Impertinence, Immorality and Profaneness, and for the Reformation of Manners (1712), *Massachusetts Statutes*, pp. 395–399.

An Act Against Incest, Sodomy, and Bestiality (1700), *Statues at Large of Pennsylvania 1682–1701*. Harrisburg: C. M. Busch, 1896.

An Act Against Rape or Ravishment (1700), *Statues at Large of Pennsylvania 1682–1701*. Harrisburg: C. M. Busch, 1896.

An Act Concerning Servants and Slaves (1705) *The Statutes at Large ... of All the Laws of Virginia*, ed. William Hening (Philadelphia: Thomas DeSilver, 1823), 3:447–462.

An Act for Preventing and Punishing Burglary, and for repealing of an act entitled, An Act Against Burglary, 10 Geo. III (1770) and 1 Geo. I (1715) in *Charter and General Laws of the Colony and Province of Massachusetts Bay (Boston: T. B. Wait and Co., 1814)*, pp. 406–407 and 668–669. Early American Imprints, Series II: Shaw-Shoemaker, No. 32028.

An Act for the Better Preventing of the Horrid Crime of Murder, 25 Geo. II (1752) in *The Charters and General Laws of the Colony and Province of Massachusetts Bay* (Boston: T. B. Wait and Co., 1814), Chapter XXXVII.

An Act for the Better Preventing the Horrid Crime of Murder (25 Geo. II, c. 37, 1752), Vol. 20, Pickering, *The Statutes at Large From the 23rd to the 26th Year of King George II* (Cambridge: J. Bentham, 1765), pp. 380–382.

An Act for the Better Regulating the Choice of Petit Jurors (1760), Chapter CCLXXV, *The Charters and General Laws of the Colony and Province of Massachusetts Bay* (Boston: T. B. Wait and Co., 1814), pp. 624–627. Early American Imprints, Series II: Shaw-Shoemaker, No. 32028.

An Act for the Punishment of Certain Crimes (April 30, 1790), U.S. Statutes, chap. IX, *Acts Passed at the First Congress of the United States of America*. Philadelphia: F. Childs, 1795.

An Act for the Punishment of Crimes (March 18, 1796), *Laws of the State of New Jersey Revised and Published Under the Legislature*. Newark: 1800.

An Act for the Punishment of Diverse Capital and Other Felonies (1787), *Revised Laws of the State of Vermont*. Windsor: Hough and Spooner, 1784.

An Act for the Returning of Able and Sufficient Jurors, and for the Better Regulation of Juries, *The Colonial Laws of New York*, 5 vols. Albany: James B. Lyon, 1894, 3:185–192.

An Act for the Trial of Negroes (1700), *Statues at Large of Pennsylvania 1682–1701*. Harrisburg: C. M. Busch, 1896.

An Act to Amend the Act Entitled, An Act to Amend the Act for the Better Government of Servants and Slaves (1769), *The Statutes at Large ... of All the Laws of Virginia*, ed. William Hening, 12 vols. (Philadelphia: Thomas DeSilver, 1823) 8:358–361.

An Act to Prevent the Odious Practice of Digging Up and Removing for the Purpose of Dissection, Dead Bodies Interred in Cemeteries or Burial Places (January 6, 1789), *Laws of the State of New York*. New York: 1792.

An Act to Remedy the Evil This Colony Is Exposed to from the Great Quantities of Counterfeit Money Introduced to It (1773), *Journal of the Votes and Proceedings of the General Assembly of the Colony of New-York 1766–76*. Albany: J. Buel, 1820, pp. 50–51.

Blackwell v. Wilkinson, 1768 in Thomas Jefferson, *Reports of Cases Determined in the General Court of Virginia from 1730–1740 and 1768–1772* (Buffalo: William S. Hein, 1981), pp. 73–85.

Cushing, William. *Indictment v. Daniels*, "Notes of Cases Decided in the Superior and Supreme Judicial Courts of Massachusetts 1772–1789," Manuscripts, Harvard Law Library (Cambridge).

Domestic Entry Book, 1771–6. London: Public Records Office, September 4, 1771, III: 9.

Domestic George III. London: Public Records Office, September 4, 1771, IX: 84.

House of Representatives, Impeachment of Peter Oliver (February 12, 1774), Miscellaneous Bound Manuscripts 1765–1776, Massachusetts Historical Society.

House of Representatives *John Young v. Christian Bacher*, Mayor's Court Docket – September 8, 1796, Manhattan County Archives, New York.

House of Representatives *John Young v. Eliza Miller*, Mayor's Court Docket – January 13, 1797, Manhattan County Archives, New York.

Maryland Constitution (1776), art. XIV in *The Federal and State Constitutions, Colonial Charters, and Other Organic Laws*, ed. Francis Newton Thorpe (Washington: Government Printing Office, 1909), p. 1688. Middlesex County Probate Records, January 24, 1742/3, 1918/2.

Minutebook of Philadelphia Society for Alleviating the Miseries of Public Prisons, May 8, 1787 to October 9, 1809, Historical Society of Pennsylvania, 22.

Minutebook of Philadelphia Society for Alleviating the Miseries of Public Prisons *Minutes of the Common Council of the City of New York 1784–1831*, ed. A. Everett Peterson (New York: 1917), p. 126.

Minutebook of Philadelphia Society for Alleviating the Miseries of Public Prisons, *Rex v. Doaks*, Quincy's Mass. Repts 90 (Mass. Super. Ct. 1763).

Statute defining justifiable homicide, 1647, *The Charters and General Laws of the Colony and Province of Massachusetts Bay* (Boston: T. B. Wait, 1814), p. 150.

Suffolk County Court Records (Boston), 68: 714.

Suffolk County Court Records (Boston) "When a man doth compass or imagine the death of our Lord the King." Statue of Treasons (1351) 25 Edw. 3, c. 2.

William Wimble deposition, Arthur Lee Manuscripts, Houghton Library, Harvard University (Cambridge), I: 20–22.

William Wimble deposition *U.S. v. 7* Cranch 32, 11 U.S. 32, 3 L. Ed. 259 (1812).

Books, Articles, Reports, and Dissertations

A Dialogue Between Elizabeth Smith and John Sennet, *Who were Convicted Before His Majesty's Superior Court*. Boston, Mass.: Richard Draper, 1773.

A Few Lines on Magnus Mode, Richard Hodges, and J. Newington Clark, *Who are Sentenced to Stand One Hour in the Pillory at Charlestown*. Boston, Mass.: Zachariah Fowle, 1767.

A. H., and Margret Ryer. *Narrative of the Life, and Dying Speech, of John Ryer Who Was Executed at White-Plains, in the County of Westchester, State of New-York, on the Second Day of October, 1793, for the Murder of Dr. Isaac Smith, Deputy-Sheriff of That County*. Danbury, Conn.: Nathan Douglas, 1793.

A Monumental Inscription on the Fifth of March Together with a Few Lines on the Enlargement of Ebenezer Richardson, Convicted of Murder. Boston, Mass.: Isaiah Thomas, 1772.

A Narrative of the Unhappy Life and Miserable End of Samuel Stoddard, Late of Egg Harbor, in Beers, Andrew. The Washington Almanac, for the Year of our Lord 1806...(Philadelphia, 1806). *Early American Imprints, Series II: Shaw-Shoemaker, No. 9689.*

A Poem, Wrote Upon the Execution of a Man, Who [Was] Whipt, Cropt, and Branded at Fairfield for Burglary, the First Day of March in the Year 1769. New Haven: 1769.

A Short Account of the Life of Moses Paul. New Haven: 1772.

A Solemn Farewell to Levi Ames Being a Poem Written a Few Days Before His Execution, for Burglary, Oct. 21, 1773. Boston: Draper's Printing Office, Newbury-Street, 1773.

Acts and Laws of His Majesty's Colony of Connecticut in New England. (New London, 1715).

Adams, Eliphalet. *A Sermon Preached on the Occasion of the Execution of Katherine Garrett, an Indian-servant (who was condemned for the Murder of her Spurious Child) on May 3rd 1738*. New London: T. Green, 1738.

Adams, John. "A Dissertation on the Cannon and the Feudal Law (1765)," in Robert J. Taylor, ed., *Papers of John Adams*, 8 vols. Cambridge: Harvard University Press, 1977, 1:110–114.

  Diary and Autobiography of John Adams. L. H. Butterfield, ed., 4 vols. Cambridge: Harvard University Press, 1962.

  "John Adams to Charles Cushing, 1 April 1756," in Robert J. Taylor, ed., *Papers of John Adams*, 8 vols. Cambridge: Harvard University Press, 1977, 1:12–15.

  "On Political Faction (1763)," in L. Kevin Wroth and Hiller B. Zobel, eds., *Legal Papers of John Adams*, 3 vols. Cambridge: Harvard University Press, 1965, 1:84–90.

  "Robert Treat Paine's Minutes of the Trial," in L. Kevin Wroth and Hiller B. Zobel, eds., *Legal Papers of John Adams*, 3 vols. Cambridge: Harvard University Press, 1965, 2:417–18.

  The Works of John Adams. Charles Francis Adams, ed., 10 vols. Boston: Charles C. Little and James Brown, 1851.

Adams, Samuel. *The Writings of Samuel Adams.* Harry Alonzo Cushing, ed. 4 vols. New York: G. Putnam, 1904–1908.

Adelson, Judah. "The Vermont Press and the French Revolution." Ph.D. dissertation, New York University, 1961.

Alexander, James. *A Brief Narrative of the Trial of John Peter Zenger.* Stanley N. Katz, ed., Cambridge: Harvard University Press, 1972.

Allen, David Grayson. *In English Ways: The Movement of Societies and the Transferal of English Local Law and Custom to Massachusetts Bay in the Seventeenth Century.* Chapel Hill, N.C.: University of North Carolina Press, 1981.

Allen, John. *An Oration Upon the Beauties of Liberty or the Essential Rights of Americans.* New London, 1773.

Americanus, Junius [aka Arthur Lee]. *The Political Detection or the Treachery and Tyranny of Administration Both at Home and Abroad.* London, 1770.

Ames, Levi. *Boston, October 21, 1773. The Dying Penitent; or, The Affecting Speech of Levi Ames.* Boston: Opposite the Court-House in Queen-Street, 1773.

The Life, Last Words, and Dying Speech of Levi Ames. Boston, 1773.

An Account of the Life of Bryan Sheehan [broadside] (Portsmouth, N.H., 1772). Early American Imprints, Series I: Evans, No. 12559.

An Account of the Robberies Committed by John Morrison, and his Accomplices, in and near Philadelphia, 1750. Philadelphia, Pa.: Anthony Armbruster, 1751.

"An Act for Preventing and Punishing Burglary, and for repealing of an act entitled, An Act Against Burglary," 10 Geo. III (1770) and 1 Geo. I (1715) in *The Charters and General Laws of the Colony and Province of Massachusetts Bay* (Boston: T. B. Wait and Co., 1814), chapter CXIII, pp. 406–407; chapter CCCXI, pp. 668–669. Early American Imprints, Series II: Shaw-Shoemaker, No. 32028.

An Address to the Inhabitants of Boston, (Particulary [Sic] to the Thoughtless Youth:) Occasioned by the Execution of Levi Ames, Who so Early in Life, As Not 22 Years of Age, Must Quit the Stage of Action in This Awful Manner. He Was Tried for Burglary on the 7th of September, and After a Fair and Impartial Examination of Facts, the Jury Went Out but Soon Return'd, Who Upon Their Oaths Pronounc'd Him Guilty. Boston: Ezekiel Russell, 1773.

Anonymous. *A Short Narrative of the Horrid Massacre in Boston.* London, England: C. Dilly, 1770.

Argument against the summoning of juries by the sheriff at the Middlesex Convention, August 30–31, 1774. *The Journals of Each Provincial Congress of Massachusetts in 1774 and 1775.* (Boston, Mass.: Dutton and Wentworth, 1838), p. 612.

Appleby, Joyce. *Capitalism and a New Social Order.* New York: New York University Press, 1984.

Arasse, Daniel. *La Guillotine et L'imaginaire de la Terreur.* Paris: Flammarion, 1987.

"At a Meeting of the Merchants & Traders at Faneuil-Hall, on the 23rd of January 1770" [Broadside, 1770]. Early American Imprints, Series I: Evans, No.11576. Sparks Manuscripts, Houghton Library (Harvard University), New England Papers, March 16, 1770, 3:69.

Austin, Benjamin. *Observations on the Pernicious Practice of the Law As Published Occasionally in the Independent Chronicle, in the Year 1786, and Republished at the Request of a Number of Respectable Citizens: With an Address Never Before Published*. Boston, Mass.: Joshua Belcher, 1814.

Bacon, Francis. *The Tremulous Private Body: Essays on Subjection*. London: Methuen, 1984.

Bailyn, Bernard. *The Ideological Origins of the American Revolution*. Cambridge: Harvard University Press, 1967.

Banner, Stuart. *The Death Penalty in America*. Cambridge: Harvard University Press, 2003.

Barlow, Joel. "Advice to the Privileged Orders in the Several States of Europe," in William K. Bottorff, ed., *The Works of Joel Barlow*, 2 vols. Gainesville: Scholars' Facsimiles, 1970.

Bauman, Richard. *Let Your Words Be Few: Symbolism of Speaking and Silence among Seventeenth-Century Quakers*. Cambridge: Cambridge University Press, 1983.

Beattie, J. M. *Crime and the Courts in England, 1660–1800*. Princeton, N.J.: Princeton University Press, 1986.

Bell, Jr., Whitfield J. "Science and Humanity in Philadelphia 1775–1790." Ph.D. dissertation, University of Pennsylvania, 1947.

Bender, John. *Imagining the Penitentiary: Fiction and the Architecture of Mind in Eighteenth-Century England*. Chicago, Ill.: University of Chicago Press, 1987.

Benes, Peter. *Two Towns: Concord and Wethersfield: A Comparative Exhibition of Regional Culture 1635–1850*. Concord: Concord Antiquarian Museum, 1982.

Bentham, Jeremy. *A Fragment on Government*, J. H. Burns and H. L. A. Hart, eds., London: Athlone Press, 1977.

Bernstein, R. B. "Legal History's Pathfinder: The Quest of John Phillip Reid," in Hendrik Hartog and William E. Nelson, eds. *Law as Culture and Culture as Law*. Madison: Madison House, 2000, pp. 10–37.

Bernstein, Samuel. *Joel Barlow: A Connecticut Yankee in an Age of Revolution*. Portland: Ultima Thule Press, 1985.

Black, Barbara A. "The Constitution of Empire: The Case for the Colonists." *University of Pennsylvania Law Review* 124:5 (May 1976): 1157–1211.

"Massachusetts and the Judges: Judicial Independence in Perspective." *Law and History Review* 3:1 (Spring 1985): 101–162.

Blackstone, William. *Commentaries on the Laws of England*, Stanley N. Katz, ed., 4 vols. Chicago, Ill.: University of Chicago Press, 1979.

Blau, Alan. "New York City and the French Revolution 1789–1797: A Study in French Revolutionary Influence." Ph.D. dissertation, City University of New York, 1973.

Bloch, Ruth H. *Visionary Republic: Millennial Themes in American Thought 1756–1800.* Cambridge: Cambridge University Press, 1985.

Block, Sharon. *Rape and Sexual Power in Early America.* Chapel Hill, N.C.: University of North Carolina Press, 2006.

"Rape Without Women: Print Culture and the Politicization of Rape 1765–1815." *Journal of American History,* 89:3 (Dec. 2002): 849–868.

Bolster, W. Jeffrey. *Black Jacks: African American Seamen in the Age of Sail.* Cambridge: Harvard University Press, 1997.

Bonomi, Patricia U. *Under the Cope of Heaven: Religion, Society, and Politics in Colonial America.* Oxford: Oxford University Press, 1986.

Bosco, Ronald A. "Lectures at the Pillory: The Early American Execution Sermon." *American Quarterly* 30:2 (Summer 1978): 156–176.

Botein, Stephen. "Cicero as a Role Model for Early American Lawyers: A Case Study in Classical Influence." *The Classical Journal* 73:4 (Apr.–May 1978): 313–321.

Boyle, John. "Boyle's Journal of Occurrences in Boston." *New England Historical and Genealogical Register,* 84 (1930): 262.

Braithwaite, John. *Crime, Shame, and Reintegration.* Cambridge: Cambridge University Press, 1989.

Breen, T. H. *The Marketplace of Revolution: How Consumer Politics Shaped American Independence.* Oxford: Oxford University Press, 2004.

Brewer, Holly. *By Birth or Consent: Children, Law, and the Anglo-American Revolution in Authority.* Chapel Hill, N.C.: University of North Carolina Press, 2007.

Brewer, John. *A Sentimental Murder: Love and Madness in the Eighteenth Century.* New York: HarperCollins, 2004.

Party Ideology and Popular Politics at the Accession of George III. Cambridge: Cambridge University Press, 1976.

"The Wilkites and the Law, 1763–74: A Study of Radical Notions of Governance," in John Brewer and John Styles, eds., *An Ungovernable People: The English and Their Law in the Seventeenth and Eighteenth Centuries.* New Brunswick, N.J.: Rutgers University Press, 1980.

Brooks, Peter. *Body Work: Objects of Desire in Modern Narrative.* Cambridge: Harvard University Press, 1993.

Troubling Confessions: Speaking Guilt in Law and Literature. Chicago, Ill.: University of Chicago Press, 2000.

Brown, Irene Quenzler and Brown, Richard D. *The Hanging of Ephraim Wheeler.* Cambridge: Harvard University Press, 2003.

Brown, Richard D. *Knowledge Is Power: The Diffusion of Information in Early America, 1700–1865.* Oxford: Oxford University Press, 1989.

Revolutionary Politics in Massachusetts: The Boston Committee of Correspondence and the Towns 1772–1774. Cambridge: Harvard University Press, 1970.

Burgess-Jackson, Keith. "The Legal Status of Suicide in Early America: A Comparison with the English Experience." *Wayne Law Review* 29 (1982–83): 57–87.

Burke, Edmund. *A Philosophical Enquiry into the Origin of Our Ideas of the Sublime and the Beautiful.* James T. Boulton, ed. Notre Dame, Ind.: University of Notre Dame Press, 1968.

"Speech on Moving his Resolution for Conciliation with the Colonies (March 22, 1775)," in Charles R. Morris, ed., *Speech on Conciliation with America.* New York: Harper and Brothers, 1945.

Burke, Peter. *Popular Culture in Early Modern Europe.* New York: New York University Press, 1978.

Burt, Martha. "Cultural Myths and Supports for Rape." *Journal of Personality and Social Psychology* 38:2 (Feb. 1980): 217–230.

Butler, Jon. *Awash in a Sea of Faith: Christianizing the American People.* Cambridge: Harvard University Press, 1990.

Byles, Mather. *The Prayer and Plea of David, to be Delivered from Blood-Guiltiness...Before the Execution of a Young Negro Servant for Poisoning an Infant.* Boston, Mass.: Samuel Kneeland, 1751.

Byrne, Peter. *Natural Religion and the Nature of Religion: The Legacy of Deism.* London: Routledge, 1989.

Cadwaller Colden to the Secretary of State and Board of Trade, December 6, 1765, "Colden Letter Books, 1760–1775," 2 *Collections of New-York Historical Society* (1877): 68–71.

Cairns, J. W. "Blackstone, An English Institutionalist: Legal Literature and the Rise of the Nation-State." *Oxford Journal of Legal Studies* 4:3 (Winter 1984): 318–360.

"Blackstone, the Ancient Constitution, and the Feudal Law." *Historical Journal* 28:3 (Sept. 1985): 711–717.

Carnochan, W. B. *Confinement and Flight: An Essay on English Literature of the Eighteenth Century.* Berkeley, Calif.: University of California Press, 1977.

Chamblit, Rebekah. *The Declaration, Dying Warning, and Advice of Rebekah Chamblit....* Boston, Mass.: S. Kneeland and T. Green, 1733.

Chapin, Bradley. "Colonial and Revolutionary Origins of the American Law of Treason," *William and Mary Quarterly* 17:1 (Jan. 1960): 3–21.

The American Law of Treason: Revolutionary and Early National Origins. Seattle: University of Washington Press, 1964.

Chia-Hsia, Po. *The Myth of Ritual Murder.* New Haven, Conn.: Yale University Press, 1988.

Chipman, Nathaniel. *Reports and Dissertations, in Two Parts ... With an Appendix, Containing Forms of Special Pleadings in Several Cases, Forms of Recognizances, of Justices Records and of Warrants of Commitment.* Rutland: Anthony Haswell, 1793.

Clinton, George. *An Oration, Delivered on the Fourth of July, 1798 Before the General Society of Mechanics and Tradesmen, the Democratic Society, the Tammany Society or Columbian Order, the New York Cooper Society, and a Numerous Concourse of Other Citizens.* New York: M. L. & W. A. Davis, 1798.

Clark, J. C. D. *The Language of Liberty, 1660–1832.* Cambridge: Cambridge University Press, 1994.

Clark, Stuart. "French Historians and Early Modern Popular Culture." *Past & Present* 100 (Aug. 1983): 62–99.

Cobban, Michael. "Blackstone and the Science of Law." *Historical Journal* 30:2 (June 1987): 311–336.

Cobbett, William and T. C. Hansard. *The Parliamentary History of England from the Earliest Period to the Year 1803.* (London, 1803) vol. 26.

Cobbett, William. *Cobbett's Parliamentary History of England,* 36 vols. (London, 1806) vol. XXVII, p. 50.

History of the American Jacobin, Commonly Denominated Democrats. Philadelphia, Pa.: William Cobbett, 1796.

The Democratic Judge of the Equal Liberty of the Press. Philadelphia, Pa.: William Cobbett, 1798.

The Last Confession and Dying Speech of Peter Porcupine with an Account of his Dissection. Philadelphia, Pa.: T. Palmer, 1797.

Cohen, Daniel A. "A Fellowship of Thieves: Property Criminals in Eighteenth-Century Massachusetts." *Journal of Social History* 22:1 (Autumn 1988): 65–92.

Pillars of Salt, Monuments of Grace: New England Crime Literature and the Origins of American Popular Culture 1674–1860. Oxford: Oxford University Press, 1993.

Cole, Arthur Harrison. *Wholesale Commodity Prices in the United States 1700–1861.* Cambridge: Harvard University Press, 1938.

Colonial Society of Massachusetts. "Legal Literature in Colonial Massachusetts." in *Law in Colonial Massachusetts, 1630–1800: A Conference Held 6 and 7 November 1981.* (Boston: The Society, 1984), pp. 243–272.

Colley, Linda. *Britons: Forging the Nation, 1707–1837.* New Haven: Yale University Press, 1994.

The Ordeal of Elizabeth Marsh: A Woman in World History. New York: Pantheon Books, 2007.

Conley, John A. "Doing It by the Book: Justice of the Peace Manuals and English Law in Eighteenth-Century America." *The Journal of Legal History* 6:3 (1985): 257–298.

Connecticut. "An Act in Addition to the Law Entitled an Act Against Theft and Burglary," (1735) in Charles J. Hoadley, ed., *The Public Records of the State of Connecticut, 1636–1776,* 15 vols. Hartford: Lockwood and Brainard, 1850, 7:561.

Cook, Charles M. *The American Codification Movement: A Study of Antebellum Legal Reform.* Westport: Greenwood Press, 1981.

Coram, Robert. *Political Inquiries, To which is Added a Plan for the Establishment of Schools Throughout the United States.* Wilmington, Del.: Andrews and Brynberg, 1791.

Cosgrove, Denis and Stephen Daniels, eds., *The Iconography of Landscape: Essays on the Symbols, Representations, Design, and Use of Past Environments.* Cambridge: Cambridge University Press, 1988.

Cover, Robert. "Nomos and Narrative," in Martha Minow, Michael Ryan, and Austin Sarat, eds., *Narrative, Violence, and the Law: The Essays of Robert Cover.* Ann Arbor: University of Michigan Press, 1992, p. 141.

Crocker, Lester G. "The Discussion of Suicide in the Eighteenth Century." *The Journal of the History of Ideas* 13:1 (Jan. 1952): 47–72.

Cross, Arthur Lyon. "Benefit of Clergy in American Criminal Law." *Proceedings of the Massachusetts Historical Society* 61 (1927–1928): 154–181.

Crowley, J. E. *This Sheba. Self: The Conceptualization of Economic Life in Eighteenth-Century America.* Baltimore, Md.: The Johns Hopkins University Press, 1974.

Cushing, John D. (ed.). *The First Laws of the State of Rhode Island*, 2 vols. Wilmington, Del.: Michael Glazier, 1983.

Cushing, John D. "The Judiciary and Public Opinion in Revolutionary Massachusetts," in George A. Billings, ed., *Law and Authority in Colonial America.* Barre, Mass.: Barre Publishers, 1965, pp. 168–186.

Dabydeen, David. *Hogarth's Blacks: Images of Blacks in Eighteenth-Century English Art.* Athens: University of Georgia Press, 1987.

Dalzell, George W. *Benefit of Clergy in America and Related Matters.* Winston-Salem: John F. Blair, 1955.

Dana, James. *A Discourse Delivered at Wallingford, December 22, 1782, Occasioned by the Tragical Exit of William Beadle, His Wife, and Four Children at Wethersfield, on the Morning of the 11th Instant by His Own Hands.* New Haven, Conn.: T. and S. Green, 1778.

  The Intent of Capital Punishment. A Discourse Delivered in the City of New-Haven, October 20, 1970, Being the Day of the Execution of Joseph Mountain for a Rape. New Haven, Conn.: T. and S. Green, 1790.

Davis, David Brion. "The Movement to Abolish Capital Punishment in America 1787–1861" in *From Homicide to Slavery: Studies in American Culture.* Oxford: Oxford University Press, 1986, pp. 17–40.

  Revolutions: Reflections on American Equality and Foreign Liberations. Cambridge: Harvard University Press, 1990.

  The Problem of Slavery in the Age of Revolution, 1770–1823. Ithaca, N.Y.: Cornell University Press, 1975.

Davis, Lennard J. *Factual Fictions: The Origins of the English Novel.* New York: Columbia University Press, 1983.

  "Wicked Actions and Feigned Words: Criminals, Criminality, and the Early English Novel." *Yale French Studies* 59 (1980): 106–118.

Davis, Natalie Zemon. *Fiction in the Archives: Pardon Tales and Their Tellers in Sixteenth-Century France.* Stanford, Calif.: Stanford University Press, 1987.

  "Printing and the People" in *Society and Culture in Early Modern France: Eight Essays.* Stanford, Calif.: Stanford University Press, 1975, pp. 189–226.

  "The Reasons of Misrule: Youth Groups and Charivaris in Sixteenth-Century France." *Past & Present* 50 (Feb. 1971): 41–75.

Dawes, Menassaeh. *An Essay on Crimes and Punishments: With a View of, and Commentary Upon Beccaria, Rousseau, Voltaire, Montesquieu, Fielding, and Blackstone: In Which Are Contained Treatises of the Idea of God and Religion (As an Incentive to Virtue), Scepticism and Faith (As Conducive to Knowledge), Heresy and Toleration (As an Enemy to and a Promoter of Happiness), Religion in General (As a Support to Public Peace), of the Progress of It Since the Reformation (As Productive of Liberty), the Idea of*

Honour, Ambition, and Pride (As the Source of Criminal Offences), and of Morality (As the Source of All Good). London: C. Dilly, 1782.

Dayton, Cornelia Hughes. *Women before the Bar: Gender, Law, and Society in Connecticut, 1639–1789*. Chapel Hill, N.C.: University of North Carolina Press, 1995.

de Castro, John Paul. *The Gordon Riots*. Oxford: Oxford University Press, 1926.

DePauw, Linda Grant. *The Eleventh Pillar: New York State and the Federal Constitution*. Ithaca, N.Y.: Cornell University Press, 1966.

Desan, Suzanne. "Ritual in the Work of E. P. Thompson and Natalie Davis," in Lynn Hunt, ed., *The New Cultural History*. Berkeley, Calif.: University of California Press, 1989, pp. 47–72.

Dexter, Franklin Bowditch. *Biographical Sketches of the Graduates of Yale College, 1778–1792*, 6 vols. New York: Henry Holt and Company, 1907, 4:260–264.

Dickerson, Oliver M. *The Navigation Acts and the American Revolution*. Philadelphia, Pa.: University of Pennsylvania Press, 1951.

Dickinson, A. T. and K. Logue. "The Porteous Riot: A Study of the Breakdown of Law and Order in Edinburgh, 1736–1737." *Journal of the Scottish Labor History Society* (1976): 21–40.

Doerflinger, Thomas M. *A Vigorous Spirit of Enterprise: Merchants and Economic Development in Revolutionary Philadelphia*. Chapel Hill, N.C.: University of North Carolina Press, 1986.

Dolan, Frances E. *Dangerous Familiars: Representations of Domestic Crime in England 1550–1700*. Ithaca, N.Y.: Cornell University Press, 1994.

Drayton, John. *Letters Written During a Tour Through the Northern and Eastern States of America*. Charleston: Harrison Bower, 1794.

Dressler, Jr., John B. "The Shaping of the American Judiciary: Ideas and Institutions in the Early Republic." Ph.D. dissertation, University of Washington, 1971.

Dukett, Valentine. *The Life, Last Words, and Dying Speech of Valentine Dukett Who Was Shot for Desertion, on Boston Common, Friday Morning, Sept. 9, 1774*. Boston, Mass.: Mills and Hicks, 1774.

Dunlap, William. *André A Tragedy in Five Acts: To Which Are Added Authentic Documents Respecting Major Andre, Consisting of Letters to Miss Seward*. New York: Swords, 1798.

Eakin, John. *Fictions in Autobiography: Studies in the Art of Self-Invention*. Princeton, N.J.: Princeton University Press, 1985.

Edinburgh (Scotland). *Act of Council against Throwing Stones, &C. at the Execution of Criminals*. 1737.

Ekirch, A. Roger. *Bound for America: The Transportation of British Convicts to the Colonies 1718–1775*. Oxford: Oxford University Press, 1987.

Eliot, Andrew. *Christ's Promise to the Penitent Thief, A Sermon Preached on the Lord's Day Before the Execution of Levi Ames, Who Suffered Death for Burglary, October 21, 1773*. Boston, Mass.: John Boyles, 1773.

Eisenstein, Elizabeth L. *The Printing Press as an Agent of Change: Communications and Cultural Transformations in Early Modern Europe*. Cambridge: Cambridge University Press, 1979.

Fabricant, Carole. *Swift's Landscape*. Baltimore, Md.: Johns Hopkins University Press, 1982.

Faller, Lincoln B. *Turned to Account: The Forms and Functions of Criminal Biography in Late Seventeenth and Early Eighteenth Century England*. Cambridge: Cambridge University Press, 1987.

Fanu, W. R. "The Rewards of Cruelty." *Annals of the Royal College of Surgeons* 21:6 (Dec. 1957): 390–394.

Faugeres, Margaretta. "On seeing a Print, Exhibiting the Ruins of the Bastille," in *The Posthumous Works of Ann Eliza Bleeker in Prose Verse to which is Added a Collection of Essays, Prose, and Poetical*. New York: T. and J. Swords, 1793.

Ferguson, Frances. "Rape and the Rise of the Novel." *Representations* 20 (Autumn 1987): 88–112.

Ferguson, Robert. "Becoming American: High Treason and Low Invective in the Republic of Laws," in Austin Sarat and Thomas R. Kearns, eds., *The Rhetoric of the Law*. Ann Arbor: University of Michigan Press, 1994, pp. 103–134.

  Law and Letters in American Culture. Cambridge: Harvard University Press, 1984.

Ferrari, Giovanna. "Public Anatomy Lessons and the Carnival in Bologna." *Past & Present* 117 (Nov. 1987): 50–106.

Fitzpatrick, Peter. *The Mythology of Modern Law*. London: Routledge, 1992.

Flaherty, David H. "Law and the Enforcement of Morals in Early America." *Perspectives in American History* 5 (1971): 201–235.

Flanagan, Christopher. *The Conversation & Conduct, of the Late Unfortunate John Young, Who Was Executed for the Murder of Robert Barwick, (Deputy Sheriff) from the Time of Receiving Sentence of Death, to That of His Execution*. New York: T. Kirk, 1797.

Fliegelman, Jay. *Prodigals and Pilgrims: The American Revolution Against Patriarchal Authority 1750–1800*. Cambridge: Cambridge University Press, 1982.

Foner, Eric. *Tom Paine and Revolutionary America*. Oxford: Oxford University Press, 1976.

Fortis, Edmund. *The Last Words and Dying Speech of Edmund Fortis*. Exeter: 1795.

Fowle, Eugene Chalmers. *Descendants of George Fowle (1610/11–1682), of Charlestown, Massachusetts*, Gary Boyd Roberts and Neil D. Thompson, eds. Boston: New England Historic and Genealogical Society, 1990.

Frasier, Isaac. *A Brief Account of the Life and Abominable Thefts of the Notorious Isaac Frasier, Who was Executed at Fairfield, September 7th 1768, Penned from his Own Mouth and Signed by Him, A Few Days Before his Execution*. New Haven, Conn.: Green, 1768.

Freeman, Rhoda G. "The Free Negro in New York City in the Era Before the Civil War." Ph.D. dissertation, Columbia University, 1966.

Freneau, Philip Morin. *General Gage's Confession: Being the Substance of his Excellency's Last Conference with his Ghostly Father, Friar Francis*. New York: Hugh Gaine, 1775.

Friedman, Lawrence M. *A History of American Law*. New York: Simon and Schuster, 1973.

Fritz, Christian G. *American Sovereigns: The People and America's Constitutional Tradition Before the Civil War*. Cambridge: Cambridge University Press, 2008.

Furneaux, Philip. *Letters to the Honourable Mr. Justice Blackstone Concerning His Exposition of the Act of Toleration*. Philadelphia, 1773.

Gallagher, Catherine and Thomas Laquer. *The Making of the Modern Body: Sexuality and Society in the Nineteenth Century*. Berkeley, Calif.: University of California Press, 1987.

Galloway, Joseph. "A Letter to the People of Pennsylvania (1760); Occasioned by the Assembly's Passing that Important Act for Constituting the Judges of the Supreme Courts and Common- Pleas, During Good Behaviour," in Bernard Bailyn, ed., *Pamphlets of the American Revolution, 1750–1776*. Cambridge: Harvard University Press, 1965, pp. 256–272.

Gardner, James A. *Legal Imperialism: American Lawyers and Foreign Aid in Latin America*. Madison, Wis.: University of Wisconsin Press, 1981.

Gaskill, Malcolm. *Crime and Mentalities in Early Modern England*. Cambridge: Cambridge University Press, 2000.

Gaskins, Richard. "Changes in the Criminal Law in Eighteenth-Century Connecticut." *American Journal of Legal History* 25:4 (Oct. 1981): 309–342.

Gates, Jr., Henry Louis. *The Signifying Monkey: A Theory of Afro-American Literary Criticism*. Oxford: Oxford University Press, 1988.

Gatrell, V. A. C. *The Hanging Tree: Execution and the English People 1770–1868*. Oxford: Oxford University Press, 1994.

Geertz, Clifford. *Local Knowledge: Further Essays in Interpretive Anthropology*. New York: Basic Books, 1983.

George, Carol V. R. *Segregated Sabbaths: Richard Allen and the Rise of Independent Black Churches 1760–1840*. Oxford: Oxford University Press, 1973.

Gilje, Paul. "The Common People and the Constitution: Popular Culture in Late Eighteenth-Century New York City," in Paul Gilje and William Pencak, eds., *New York in the Age of the Constitution 1775–1800*. Rutherford, N.J.: Fairleigh Dickinson University Press, 1992, pp. 48–73.

The Road to Mobocracy: Popular Disorder in New York City 1763–1834. Chapel Hill, N.C.: University of North Carolina Press, 1987.

Ginzburg, Carlo. *The Cheese and the Worms: The Cosmos of a Sixteenth-Century Miller*. London: Routledge and Kegan Paul, 1980.

Gladfelder, Hal. *Criminality and Narrative in Eighteenth-Century England: Beyond the Law*. Baltimore, Md.: The Johns Hopkins University Press, 2001.

Gless, Alan G. "Self-Incrimination Privilege Development in the Nineteenth-Century Federal Courts: Questions of Procedure, Privilege, Production, Immunity, and Compulsion." *American Journal of Legal History* 45:4 (Oct. 2001): 391–467.

Goodman, Paul. *The Democratic-Republicans of Massachusetts; Politics in a Young Republic*. New York: Columbia University Press, 1964.

Graff, Harvey J. *The Legacies of Literacy: Continuities and Contradictions in Western Culture and Society.* Bloomington, Ind.: Indiana University Press, 1987.

Green, Johnson. *The Life and Confession of Johnson Green Who Is to Be Executed This Day, August 17th, 1786, for the Atrocious Crime of Burglary; Together with His Last and Dying Words.* Worcester: Isaiah Thomas, 1786.

Green, Thomas A. "A Retrospective on the Criminal Trial Jury, 1200–1800," in J. S. Cockburn and Thomas A. Green eds., *Twelve Good Men and True: The Criminal Trial Jury in England, 1200–1800.* Princeton, N.J.: Princeton University Press, 1988.

"The Jury and the English Law of Homicide 1200–1600." *Michigan Law Review* 74:3 (Jan. 1976): 413–499.

Verdict According to Conscience: Perspectives on the English Criminal Jury 1200–1800. Chicago, Ill.: University of Chicago Press, 1985.

Greenberg, Douglas. *Crime and Law Enforcement in the Colony of New York 1691–1776.* Ithaca, N.Y.: Cornell University Press, 1976.

Greenblatt, Stephen. *Marvelous Possessions: The Wonder of the New World.* Chicago: University of Chicago Press, 1991.

Renaissance Self-Fashioning: From More to Shakespeare. Chicago, Ill.: University of Chicago Press, 1980.

Greene, Jack P. "From the Perspective of Law: Context and Legitimacy in the Origins of the American Revolution." *South Atlantic Quarterly* 85: (1986): 56–77.

"John Phillip Reid and the Reinterpretation of the American Revolution," in Hendrik Hartog and William E. Nelson, eds., *Law as Culture and Culture as Law.* Madison: Madison House, 2000, pp. 48–57.

Grose, Francis. *A Classical Dictionary of the Vulgar Tongue.* London: S. Hooper, 1785.

Gustafson, Thomas. *Representative Words: Politics, Literature, and the American Language 1776–1865.* Cambridge: Cambridge University Press, 1992.

Halbert, Henry. *The Last Speech and Confession of Henry Halbert who was Executed at Philadelphia, October 19, 1765 for the Inhuman Murder of the Son of Jacob Woolman.* Philadelphia, Pa.: Anthony Armbruster, 1765.

Hall, David D. *Worlds of Wonder, Days of Judgment: Popular Religious Belief in Early New England.* New York: Alfred A. Knopf, 1989.

Harris, Jonathan. "The Rise of Medical Science in New York 1720–1820." Ph.D. dissertation, New York University, 1971.

Harris, Trudier. *Exorcising Blackness: Historical and Literary Lynching and Burning Rituals.* Bloomington, Ind.: Indiana University Press, 1984.

Hartog, Hendrik. "Distancing Oneself from the Eighteenth Century: A Commentary on Changing Pictures of American Legal History," in Hendrik A. Hartog, ed., *Law in the American Revolution and the Revolution in the Law.* New York: New York University Press, 1981, pp. 229–257.

Hay, Douglas. "Property, Authority, and the Criminal Law," in Douglas Hay et al., eds., *Albion's Fatal Tree: Crime and Society in Eighteenth-Century England.* New York: Pantheon Books, 1975, pp. 17–64.

"The Class Composition of the Palladium of Liberty: Trial Jurors in the Eighteenth Century," in J. S. Cockburn and Thomas A. Green, eds., *Twelve Good Men and True: The Criminal Trial Jury in England 1200–1800*. Princeton: Princeton University Press, 1988, pp. 305–357.

Hazen, Charles Downer. *Contemporary American Opinion of the French Revolution*. Baltimore, Md.: Johns Hopkins University Press, 1897.

Heaton, Claude. "Body Snatching in New York City." *New York State Journal of Medicine* 43 (1943): 1861–1865.

Herrnstein-Smith, Barbara. "Narrative Versions, Narrative Theories." *Critical Inquiry* 7:1 (Autumn 1980): 213–236.

Herskovits, Melville J. *The Myth of the Negro Past*. Boston: Beacon Press 1958.

Heyrman, Christine Leigh. *Commerce and Culture: The Maritime Communities of Colonial Massachusetts 1690–1750*. New York: W. W. Norton, 1984.

Hickey, Thomas. *The Last Speech and Dying Words of Thomas Hickey (a soldier in the Continental Army) who was Executed in a Field Near the City of New York, on Friday June 28, 1776....* Newport, R.I.: Solomon Southwick, 1776.

Hill, Christopher. "The Norman Yoke," in Christopher Hill, ed., *Puritanism and Revolution*. London: Secker and Warburg, 1958, pp. 50–122.

Hindus, Michael S. *Prison and Plantation: Crime, Justice, and Authority in Massachusetts and South Carolina, 1767–1878*. Chapel Hill: University of North Carolina Press, 1980.

Hirsch, Adam. "From Pillory to Penitentiary: The Rise of Criminal Incarceration in the New Republic." Ph.D. dissertation, Yale University, 1987.

Hobart, Noah. *Excessive Wickedness, the Way to an Untimely Death, a sermon preached at Fairfield, in Connecticut, September 7th, 1768*. New Haven, Conn.: Thomas and Samuel Green, 1768.

Hoerder, Dirk. *Crowd Action in Revolutionary Massachusetts 1765–1780*. New York: Academic Press, 1977.

Hoffer, Peter Charles. "Disorder and Deference: The Paradoxes of Criminal Justice in the Colonial Tidewater," in David J. Bodenhammer and James W. Ely, Jr., eds., *Ambivalent Legacy: A Legal History of the South*. Jackson, Miss.: University Press of Mississippi, 1984, 187–201.

Law and People in Colonial America. Baltimore, Md.: Johns Hopkins University Press, 1992.

Hoffer, Peter Charles and N. E. H. Hull. *Murdering Mothers: Infanticide in England and New England, 1558–1803*. New York: New York University Press, 1981.

Holcraft, Thomas. *A Plain and Succinct Narrative of the Late Riots and Disturbances in the Cities of London and Westminster and Borough of Southwark*. London: Fielding and Walker, 1780.

Horwitz, Morton J. "The Rule of Law: An Unqualified Human Good?" *Yale Law Journal* 86:3 (Jan. 1977): 561–566.

The Transformation of American Law 1780–1860. Cambridge: Harvard University Press, 1977.

How, Joshua and Seth Hudson. *A Serious-Comical Dialogue Between the Famous Dr. Seth Hudson and the noted Joshua How, Who Were Lately Tried in*

Boston and Convicted of Counterfeiting. Boston, Mass.: Benjamin Mecom, 1762.

Howell, T. B. *A Complete Collection of State Trials*, 34 vols. London: T. C. Hansard, 1816–28.

Hudson, Seth and Nathaniel Hurd. *H-DS-N's Speech from the Pillory.* Boston, Mass.: N. Hurd, 1762.

Hudson, Seth. *The Humble Confession of that Notorious Cheat, Doctor Seth Hudson.* Boston: 1762.

Humphrey, David C. "Dissection and Discrimination: The Social Origins of Cadavers in America 1760–1915." *Bulletin of the New York Academy of Medicine* 49:9 (Sept. 1973): 819–827.

Hunt, Lynn Avery. *Politics, Culture, and Class in the French Revolution.* Berkeley, Calif.: University of California Press, 1984.

Hunter, J. Paul. *Before Novels: The Cultural Contexts of Eighteenth-Century English Fiction.* New York: W. W. Norton, 1990.

Hurst, James Willard. *The Law of Treason in the United States: Collected Essays.* Westport: Greenwood Publishing Company, 1971.

Hutchinson, Thomas. *The History of the Colony and Province of Massachusetts-Bay*, Lawrence Shaw Mayo ed., 3 vols. Cambridge: Harvard University Press, 1936, 3:67–69.

Ignatieff, Michael. *A Just Measure of Pain: The Penitentiary in the Industrial Revolution 1750–1850.* New York: Pantheon Books, 1978.

Ingram, Martin. "Ridings, Rough Music, and the 'Reform of Popular Culture' in Early Modern England." *Past & Present* 105 (Nov. 1984): 79–113.

Inhuman Cruelty: Or Villainy Detected, Being a True Relation of the Most Unheard-of, Cruel and Barbarous Intended Murder of a Bastard Child Belonging to John and Anne Richardson. Boston: Richard Draper, 1773.

Innes, Joanna and John Styles. "The Crime Wave: Recent Writing on Crime and Criminal Justice in Eighteenth-Century England." *Journal of British Studies* 25:4 (Oct. 1986): 380–435.

Isaac, Rhys. "Books and the Social Authority of Learning: The Case of Mid-Eighteenth-Century Virginia," in William L. Joyce et al., eds., *Printing and Society in Early America.* Worcester: American Antiquarian Society, 1983, pp. 228–249.

The Transformation of Virginia 1740–1790. Chapel Hill, N.C.: University of North Carolina, 1982.

Jefferson, Thomas. "A Bill for Proportioning Crimes and Punishment" (1779) in Julian P. Boyd, ed., *The Papers of Thomas Jefferson*, 18 vols. Princeton, N.J.: Princeton University Press, 1950, 2: 492–507.

A Summary View of the Rights of North America. Philadelphia, Pa.: John Dunlap, 1774.

"Thomas Jefferson to James Madison, 17 February 1826," in Paul Leicester Ford, ed., *The Works of Thomas Jefferson*, 12 vols. New York: G.P. Putnam, 1905.

Johnson, Edward F. *Woburn Records of Births, Deaths, and Marriages from 1640–1873.* Woburn: Andrews, Cutler & Co., 1890.

Johnson, Herbert A. *Imported Eighteenth-Century Law Treatises in American Libraries, 1700–1799.* Knoxville: University of Tennessee Press, 1978.

Johnson, Marmaduke. *The Cry of Sodom Enquired Into.* Cambridge, 1674.

Johnson, William Samuel. *The Superior Court Diary of William Samuel Johnson, 1772–1773: With Appropriate Records and File Papers of the Superior Court of the Colony of Connecticut for the Terms, December 1772 Through March 1773.* John T. Farrell, ed., American legal records, v. 4. Washington, D.C.: American Historical Association, 1942.

Jones, Douglas Lamar. "The Strolling Poor: Transiency in Eighteenth-Century Massachusetts." *Journal of Social History* 8:2 (Winter 1975): 28–54.

Jones, John. *The Surgical Works of the Late John Jones.* Philadelphia, 1795.

Jones, William. *An Inquiry into the Legal Mode of Suppressing Riots with a Constitutional Plan of Future Defense.* London: C. Dilly, 1780.

Jordan, Cynthia S. *Second Stories: The Politics of Language, Form, and Gender in Early American Fictions.* Chapel Hill, N.C.: University of North Carolina Press, 1989.

Jordan, Winthrop D. *White Over Black: American Attitudes Towards the Negro, 1550–1812.* Chapel Hill, N.C.: University of North Carolina Press, 1968.

Journal of the House of Representatives of Massachusetts (1770), 44: 197–280.

Journals of the House of Representatives of Massachusetts 1772–1773, 50 vols. Boston, Mass.: Massachusetts Historical Society (1980) 49: 280–282. Early American Imprints, Series I: Evans, No.12458.

Kann, Mark E. *Punishment, Prisons, and Patriarchy: Liberty and Power in the Early American Republic.* New York: New York University Press, 2005.

Katz, Stanley N. "Republicanism and the Law of Inheritance in the American Revolution." *Michigan Law Review* 76:1 (Nov. 1977): 1–29.

"The Politics of Law in Colonial America: Controversies over Chancery Courts and Equity Law in the Eighteenth Century," in *Perspectives in American History* Cambridge: Harvard University Press, 1971, 5: 257–287.

Kay, Marvin L. Michael. "The North Carolina Regulation, 1766–1776: A Class Conflict," in Alfred F. Young, ed., *Beyond the American Revolution: Explorations in the History of American Radicalism.* DeKalb: Northern Illinois University Press, 1976, pp. 71–124.

Kaye, J. M. "The Early History of Murder and Manslaughter." *Law Quarterly Review* 83 (1967): 365–394.

Kelman, Mark. *A Guide to Critical Legal Studies.* Cambridge, Mass.: Harvard University Press, 1987.

Kennedy, Duncan. "Structures of Blackstone's Commentaries." *Buffalo Law Review* 28 (1978–1979): 205–382.

Kenneth, Campbell. "The Origins and Development of a Philosophy for the Protection of Opinion in Defamation Law." Ph.D. dissertation, University of North Carolina, 1990.

Kent, James. *An Introductory Lecture to a Course of Law Lectures, delivered November 17, 1794.* New York: Francis Childs, 1794.

Commentaries on American Law. Birmingham, Ala.: Legal Classics Library, 1986.

Kittrie, Nicholas N. and Eldon D. Wedlock, Jr. (eds.). *The Tree of Liberty: A Documentary History of Rebellion and Political Crime in America.* Baltimore, Md.: Johns Hopkins University Press, 1986.

Klein, Milton M. "Prelude to Revolution in New York: Jury Trials and Judicial Tenure." *William and Mary Quarterly* Third Series 17:4 (October 1960): 439–463.

Konig, David Thomas. *Law and Society in Puritan Massachusetts, Essex County 1629–1692.* Chapel Hill, N.C.: University of North Carolina Press, 1979.

"Legal Fiction and the Rule(s) of Law," in Christopher L. Tomlins and Bruce H. Mann, eds., *The Many Legalities of Early America.* Chapel Hill, N.C.: The University of North Carolina Press, 2001, pp. 97–117.

Kramer, Larry D. *The People Themselves: Popular Constitutionalism and Judicial Review.* Oxford: Oxford University Press, 2005.

Kramer, Michael P. *Imagining Language in America: From the Revolution to the Civil War.* Princeton, N.J.: Princeton University Press, 1992.

Krumbhaar, Edward B. "Early History of Anatomy in the United States." *Annals of Medical History* 4 (1922): 271–286.

Kulikoff, Alan. "The Progress of Inequality in Revolutionary Boston." *William and Mary Quarterly* 28:3 (Jul. 1971): 375–412.

Kushner, Howard I. *American Suicide: A Psychocultural Exploration.* New Brunswick: Rutgers University Press, 1991.

Laden, Marie-Paul. *Self-Imitation in the Eighteenth-Century Novel.* Princeton, N.J.: Princeton University Press, 1987.

Ladenheim, Julius Calvin. "The Doctors' Mob of 1788." *Journal of the History of Medicine and Allied Sciences* 5 (1950): 23–43.

Langbein, John H. "Albion's Fatal Flaws." *Past & Present* 98 (Feb. 1983): 96–120.

"Shaping the Eighteenth-Century Criminal Trial: The View from the Ryder Sources." *Chicago Law Review* 50 (1983): 1–136.

Langdon, Timothy. *A Sermon Preached at Danbury, November 8th, 1798, Being the Day of the Execution of Anthony.* Danbury: Douglas & Nichols, 1798.

Laqueur, Thomas. "Crowds, Carnival, and the State in English Executions 1604–1868," in A. C. Beier, David Cannadine, and James M. Rosenheim, eds., *The First Modern Society: Essays in English History in Honor of Lawrence Stone.* Cambridge: Cambridge University Press, 1989, pp. 305–356.

Lathrop, John. *Innocent Blood Crying to God from the Streets of Boston. A Sermon Occasioned by the Horrid Murder on the 5th of March, 1770.* Boston: Edes and Gill, 1771.

Lavie, Smadar. *The Poetics of Military Occupation: Mzeina Allegories of Bedouin Identity Under Israeli and Egyptian Rule.* Berkeley, Calif.: University of California Press, 1990.

Laws of the State of New York: Comprising the Constitution and the Acts of the Legislature since the Revolution, From the First to the Twelfth Session, Inclusive. New York: Hugh Gaine, 1789.

Lawson-Peebles, Robert. *Landscape and Written Expression in Revolutionary America: The World Turned Upside Down.* Cambridge: Cambridge University Press, 1988.

Leland, John. *A View of the Principal Deistical Writers That Have Appeared in England in the Last and Present Century.* London: 1757.

Lemisch, Jesse. "Jack Tar in the Streets: Merchant Seamen in the Politics of Revolutionary America." *William and Mary Quarterly* Third Series 25:3 (July 1968): 371–407.

Lewis, Jan. "The Republican Wife: Virtue and Seduction in the Early Republic." *William and Mary Quarterly* 44:4 (Oct. 1987): 687–721.

The Pursuit of Happiness: Family and Values in Jefferson's Virginia. Cambridge: Cambridge University Press, 1983.

Lieberman, David. "Blackstone's Science of Legislation." *Journal of British Studies* 27:2 (Apr. 1988): 117–149.

The Providence of Legislation Determined: Legal Theory in Eighteenth-Century Britain. Cambridge: Cambridge University Press, 1989.

Lindemann, Barbara S. "'To Ravish and Carnally Know': Rape in Eighteenth-Century Massachusetts." *Signs: Journal of Women in Culture and Society* 10:1 (Autumn 1984): 63–82.

Linebaugh, Peter. *The London Hanged: Crime and Civil Society in the Eighteenth Century.* Cambridge: Cambridge University Press, 1991.

Linebaugh, Peter and Marcus Rediker. *The Many-Headed Hydra: Sailors, Slaves, Commoners, and the Hidden History of the Revolutionary Atlantic.* Boston, Mass.: Beacon Press, 2000.

Linebaugh, Peter. "The Ordinary of Newgate and his Account," in J. S. Cockburn, ed., *Crime in England 1500–1800.* Princeton, N.J.: Princeton University Press, 1977, pp. 246–270.

"The Tyburn Riot Against the Surgeons," in Douglas Hay, ed., *Albion's Fatal Tree: Crime and Society in Eighteenth-Century England.* New York: Pantheon Press, 1975, pp. 65–118.

Link, Eugene Perry. *Democratic-Republican Societies 1790–1800.* New York: Columbia University Press, 1942.

Linsey, William. *The Dying Speech and Confession of William Linsey to be Executed at Worcester, October 25th 1770.* Boston: 1770.

Lockridge, Kenneth A. *Literacy in Colonial New England: An Enquiry into the Social Context of Literacy in the Early Modern West.* New York: W. W. Norton, 1974.

Lovejoy, David S. "Rights Imply Equality: The Case Against Admiralty Jurisdiction in America, 1764–1776." *William and Mary Quarterly* Third Series 16:4 (October 1959): 459–484.

Lovey, John Wall. *The Last Speech, Confession, and Dying Words of John Wall Lovey Who was Executed at Albany, on Friday the 2d of April, 1773 for Counterfeiting the Currency of the Province of New-York.* Albany: Alexander and James Robertson, 1773.

Lynde, Jr., Benjamin. *Diaries of Benjamin Lynde and Benjamin Lynde, Jr.* Boston, Mass.: private printing, 1880.

Maccarty, Thaddeus. *The Rev. Maccarthy's* [sic] *Account of the Behavior of Mrs. Spooner after her Commitment and Condemnation for Being an Accessory in the Murder of Her Husband.* Boston: 1778.

MacDonald, Michael and Terence R. Murphy. *Sleepless Souls: Suicide in Early Modern England.* Oxford: Oxford University Press, 1990.

MacDonald, Michael. "The Secularization of Suicide in England 1600–1800." *Past & Present* 111 (May 1986): 52–57.

MacLeod, Duncan J. *Slavery, Race, and the American Revolution.* Cambridge: Cambridge University Press, 1974.

Maier, Pauline. *From Resistance to Revolution: Colonial Radicals and the Development of American Opposition to Britain, 1765–1776.* New York: Alfred A. Knopf, 1972.

Maine, Jackson Turner. *Society and Economy in Colonial Connecticut.* Princeton, N.J.: Princeton University Press, 1985.

Malone, Dumas (ed.). *Dictionary of American Biography,* 10 vols. New York, 1931.

Mandeville, Bernard. *An Enquiry into the Causes of the Frequent Executions at Tyburn: And a Proposal for Some Regulations Concerning Felons in Prison, and the Good Effects to Be Expected from Them.* London: J. Roberts, 1725.

Mann, Bruce. "A Great Case Makes Law, Not Revolution," in Hendrik Hartog, ed., *Law in the American Revolution and the Revolution in the Law.* New York: New York University Press, 1981, pp. 3–19.

Republic of Debtors: Bankruptcy in the Age of American Independence. Cambridge: Harvard University Press, 2003.

Neighbors and Strangers: Law and Community in Early Connecticut. Chapel Hill, N.C.: University of North Carolina Press, 1987.

Many Federalists and John Jay. *To the Independent Electors of the City of New-York There Was a Time When a Majority of the Citizens of New-York Were so Opposed to Lawyers As Members of the Legislature, That a Single Gentleman of That Profession … Could Not Obtain a Majority of Suffrages … But the Times Are Changed.* New York: s.n, 1788.

Margaretta v. Faugeres, *The Ghost of John Young the Homicide who was Executed the 17th of August Last, for the Murder of Robert Barwick, a Sherifs Officer.* (New York, 1797), p. 4.

Marietta, Jack D. *Troubled Experiment: Crime and Justice in Pennsylvania, 1682–1800.* Philadelphia, Pa.: University of Pennsylvania Press, 2006.

Marsh, John. *The Great Sin and Danger of Striving With God: A Sermon Preached at Wethersfield, December 13th 1782 at the Funeral of Mrs. Lydia Beadle and their Four Children who were all Murdered by his Own Hands on the Morning of the Eleventh Instant.* Hartford: Hudson and Goodwin, 1783.

Martin, James P. "When Repression Is Democratic and Constitutional: The Federalist Theory of Representation and the Sedition Act of 1798." *University of Chicago Law Review* 66:1 (Winter 1999): 117–120.

Martin, Margaret E. *Merchants and Trade of the Connecticut River Valley 1750–1820.* Northampton: Smith College Studies in History, 1939.

Massachusetts. "An Act Taking Away the Benefit of Clergy," March 11, 1785. *The General Laws of Massachusetts from the Adoption of the Constitution to February 1822,* 2 vols. Boston: Wells & Lilly, 1823, 1: 183–184.

Masur, Louis. *Rites of Execution: Capital Punishment and the Transformation of American Culture 1776–1865*. Oxford: Oxford University Press, 1989.

Mather, Samuel. *Christ Sent to Heal the Broken Hearted, A Sermon Preached at the Thursday Lecture in Boston on October 21st, 1773 when Levi Ames, A Young Man Under Sentence of Death for Burglary was Present to Hear the Discourse*. Boston, Mass.: William M'Alphine, 1773.

Mathews, Albert. "Early Autopsies and Anatomical Lectures." *Publications of the Colonial Society of Massachusetts, Transactions* (1916–1917): 273–290.

Mazzio, Carla. *The Body in Parts: Fantasies of Corporeality in Early Modern Europe*. London: Routledge, 1997.

McGowen, Randall. "He Beareth Not the Sword in Vain: Religion and the Criminal Law in Eighteenth-Century England." *Eighteenth-Century Studies* 21:2 (Winter 1987–88): 192–211.

McLennan, Rebecca M. *The Crisis of Imprisonment: Protest, Politics, and the Making of the American Penal State, 1776–1941*. Cambridge: Cambridge University Press, 2008.

McLynn, Frank. *Crime and Punishment in Eighteenth-Century England*. Oxford: Oxford University Press, 1989.

McManners, John. *Death and the Enlightenment: Changing Attitudes to Death Among Christians and Unbelievers in Eighteenth-Century France*. Oxford: Oxford University Press, 1981.

McNamara, Martha J. *From Tavern to Courthouse: Architecture and Ritual in American Law, 1658–1860*. Baltimore, Md.: The John Hopkins University Press, 2004.

Meranze, Michael. *Laboratories of Virtue: Punishment, Revolution, and Authority in Philadelphia, 1760–1835*. Chapel Hill, N.C.: University of North Carolina, 1996.

"The Penitential Ideal in Late Eighteenth-Century Philadelphia." *Pennsylvania Magazine of History and Biography* 108:4 (Oct. 1984): 419–450.

Meskell, Mathew W. "The History of Prisons in the United States from 1777–1877." *Stanford Law Review* 51:4 (Apr. 1999): 839–865.

Minnick, Wayne C. "The New England Execution Sermon, 1639–1800." *Speech Monographs* 35:1 (Mar. 1968): 77–89.

Mitchell, Stephen. *A Narrative of the Life of William Beadle of Wethersfield, Connecticut*. Bennington: Anthony Haswell, 1794.

Mitnick, John M. "From Neighbor-Witness to Judge of Proofs: The Transformation of the English Civil Juror." *American Journal of Legal History* 32 (1988): 201–235.

Moglen, Eben. "Settling the Law: Legal Development in New York 1664–1776." Ph.D. dissertation, Yale University, 1993.

Monaghan, E. Jennifer. "Literacy Instruction and Gender in Colonial New England." *American Quarterly* 40:1 (Mar. 1988): 18–41.

Monod, Paul. *Jacobitism and the English People 1688–1788*. Cambridge: Cambridge University Press, 1989.

Moore, Frank. *Songs and Ballads of the American Revolution*. New York: D. Appleton, 1856.

Morais, Herbert M. *Deism in Eighteenth-Century America*. New York: Russell and Russell, 1960.

Morgan, Edmund S. *The Challenge of the American Revolution*. New York: Norton, 1976.

The Gentle Puritan: A Life of Ezra Stiles 1727–1795. New Haven, Conn.: Yale University Press, 1962.

Morgan, Edmund S. and Helen M. Morgan. *The Stamp Act Crisis: Prologue to Revolution*. New York: Collier Books, 1963.

Morris, Richard B. *Select Cases of the Mayor's Court of New York City 1764–1784*. Washington: American Historical Association, 1935.

Morris, Robert. *A Letter to Sir Richard Aston ... and Some Thoughts on the Modern Doctrine of Libels*. London, 1770.

Mount, Thomas. *The Confession, &c. of Thomas Mount Who was Executed at Little-Rest, in the State if Rhode-Island, on Friday the 27th of May, 1791, for Burglary*. Newport, R.I.: Peter Edes,1791.

Mountain, Joseph. *Sketches of the Life of Joseph Mountain, A Negro Who was Executed at New-Haven on the 20th Day of October 1790*. New Haven, Conn.: David Daggett, 1790.

Muchembled, Robert. *Culture Populaire et Culture des Elites dans La France Moderne*. Paris: Flammarion, 1978.

Murrin, John M. "Anglicizing an American Colony: The Transformation of Provincial Massachusetts." Ph.D. dissertation, Yale University, 1966.

Murrin, John. "The Great Inversion, or Court versus Country: A Comparison of the Revolutionary Settlements in England (1699–1721) and America (1776–1816)," in J. G. A. Pocock, ed., *Three British Revolutions*. Princeton, N.J.: Princeton University Press, 1980, pp. 368–453.

Nash, Gary and Jean R. Soderlund. *Freedom by Degrees: Emancipation in Pennsylvania and Its Aftermath*. New York: Oxford University Press, 1991.

Nash, Gary. "Forging Freedom: The Emancipation Experience in the Northern Seaport Cities 1775–1820" in Ira Berlin and Ronald Hoffman, eds., *Slavery and Freedom in the Age of the American Revolution*. Charlottesville, Va.: University of Virginia Press, 1983, pp. 3–48.

Forging Freedom: The Formation of Philadelphia's Black Community 1720–1840. Cambridge: Harvard University Press, 1988.

Race, Class, and Politics: Essays on Colonial and Revolutionary America. Champaign: University of Illinois Press, 1986.

"Slaves and Slaveholders in Colonial Philadelphia," *William and Mary Quarterly* Third Series 30:2 (Apr. 1973): 223–256.

The Urban Crucible: Social Change, Political Consciousness, and the Origins of the American Revolution. Cambridge: Harvard University Press, 1979.

Navas, Deborah. *Murdered by His Wife: An Absorbing Tale of Crime and Punishment in Eighteenth-Century Massachusetts*. Amherst, Mass.: University of Massachusetts Press, 1999.

Nelson, William E. *The Americanization of the Common Law: The Impact of Legal Change on Massachusetts Society, 1760–1830*. Cambridge: Harvard University Press, 1975.

"The Eighteenth-Century Background of John Marshall's Constitutional Jurisprudence." *Michigan Law Review* 76:6 (May 1978): 893–960.

"The Legal Restraint of Power in Pre-Revolutionary America: Massachusetts as a Case Study 1760–1775." *American Journal of Legal History* 18:1 (Jan. 1974): 1–32.

Niles, Hezekiah. *Principles and Acts of the American Revolution.* Baltimore, Md.: W. O. Niles, 1822.

Nobles, Gregory. *Divisions Throughout the Whole: Politics and Society in Hampshire County, Massachusetts 1740–1775.* Cambridge: Cambridge University Press, 1983.

Nolan, Dennis R. "Sir William Blackstone and the New American Republic: A Study of Intellectual Impact." *New York University Law Review* 51 (1976): 731–768.

O'Beirne, Thomas Lewis. *Considerations on the Late Disturbances.* London: J. Almon, 1780.

O'Donnel, Charles and Simon Cochrun. *The Life and Confession of Charles O'Donnel, Who Was Executed at Morgantown, June 19, 1797, for the Wilful Murder of His Son: Though He Had Murdered a Woman About 27 Years Before That Time.* Lancaster, Pa.: W. & R. Dickson, 1798.

Offutt, Jr., William M. "Law and Social Cohesion in a Plural Society: The Delaware Valley 1680–1710." Ph.D. dissertation, Johns Hopkins University, 1987.

Oliver, Peter. *Origin and Progress of the American Rebellion.* Stanford, Calif.: Stanford University Press, 1961.

Otis, James. "A Vindication of the British Colonies (1765)," in Bernard Bailyn, ed., *Pamphlets of the American Revolution, 1750–1776.* Cambridge: Harvard University Press, 1965, pp. 560–561.

Brief Remarks on the Defence of the Halifax Libel, on the British American Colonies. Boston, Mass.: Edes and Gill, 1765.

"Rights of the British Colonies Asserted and Proved (1764)," in Bernard Bailyn, ed., *Pamphlets of the American Revolution, 1750–1776.* Cambridge: Harvard University Press, 1965.

Outram, Dorinda. *The Body and the French Revolution: Sex, Class, and Political Culture.* New Haven, Conn.: Yale University Press, 1989.

Packer, Joseph Bill. *A Journal of the Life and Travels of Joseph-Bill Packer.* Albany: 1773.

Paine, Thomas. "Common Sense," in Eric Foner, ed., *Thomas Paine: Collected Writings.* New York: Library of America, 1995, pp. 5–59.

Palmer, Bryan. "Discordant Music: Charivaris and Whitecapping in Nineteenth-Century North America." 3 *Labour/Le travail* (1978): 5–62.

Palmer, Robert C. "The Federal Common Law of Crime." *Law & History Review* 4:2 (Autumn 1986): 267–323.

Parker, James. *Conductor Generalis or the Duty and Authority of Justices of the Peace.* New York, 1788.

Patten, Jonathan K. van. "Magic, Prophecy, and the Law of Treason in Reformation England." *American Journal of Legal History* 27:1 (Jan. 1983): 1–32.

Pestritto, Ronald J. *Founding the Criminal Law: Punishment and Political Thought in the Origins of America.* DeKalb: Northern Illinois University Press, 2000.

Pocock, J. G. A. *The Ancient Constitution and the Feudal Law*. Cambridge: Cambridge University Press, 1957; reprinted., 1987.

Poem Occasioned by the Most Shocking and Cruel Murder was ever Represented on the Stage or the Most Deliberate Murder that Ever was Represented in Human Life. Boston, Mass.: Ezekiel Russell, 1782.

Post, Albert. "Early Efforts to Abolish Capital Punishment in Pennsylvania." *Pennsylvania Magazine of History and Biography* 68:1 (Jan. 1944): 38–53.

Powers, Thomas. *The Narrative and Confession of Thomas Powers, a Negro, Formerly of Norwich in Connecticut*. Norwich: John Trumbull, 1796.

Preyer, Kathryn. "Jurisdiction to Punish: Federal Authority, Federalism, and the Common Law of Crimes in the Early Republic." *Law & History Review* 4:2 (Autumn 1986): 223–265.

"Penal Measures in the American Colonies: An Overview." *American Journal of Legal History* 26:4 (Oct. 1982): 326–352.

Proceedings in the Case of John Wilkes, esq. on Two Informations for Libels, (1763–1770) in T. B. Howell, ed., *A Complete Collection of State Trials and Proceedings for High Treason and Other Crimes and Misdemeanors From the Earliest Period to the Present Time*, 21 vols. (London: T. C. Hansard, 1813), 19:1075–1138.

Quincy, Josiah. *Reports of cases argued and adjudged in the Superior Court of Judicature of the Province of Massachusetts Bay, between 1761 and 1772*. Boston, Mass.: Little, Brown, and Company, 1865.

Radin, Margaret J. "Reconsidering the Rule of Law." *Boston University Law Review* 69 (1989): 781–819.

Radzinowicz, Leon. *A History of Criminal Law and Its Administration from 1750: The Movement for Reform 1750–1833*, 4 vols. New York: Macmillan Company, 1948.

Ragon, Michel. *L'Espace de la Mort: Essai sur 1 'architecture. la decoration et l'urbanisme funeraires*. Paris: Albin Michel, 1981.

Randall, Adrian. *Riotous Assemblies: Popular Protest in Hanoverian England*. Oxford: Oxford University Press, 2007.

Rogan, Michael. *The Space of Death: A Study of Funerary Architecture, Decoration, and Urbanism*. Translated by Alan Sheridan. Charlottesville, Va.: University of Virginia Press, 1983.

Readex. *A Council of six churches, Conven'd at Woburn, upon the request of the Rev. Mr. Jackson Pastor and the First Church in said town, to hear and advise upon the great and uncommon difficulties among them*. Boston: s.n, 1747.

Rediker, Marcus. *Between the Devil and the Deep Blue Sea: Merchant Seamen, Pirates, and the Anglo-American Maritime World 1700–1750*. Cambridge: Cambridge University Press, 1987.

"Good Hands, Stout Hearts, and Fast Feet: The History and Culture of Working People in Early America." *Labour/Le Travail* 10 (Fall/Automne1982): 123–144.

"The Anglo-American Seaman as Collective Worker, 1700–1750," in Stephen Innes, ed., *Work and Labor in Early America*. Chapel Hill, N.C.: University of North Carolina Press, 1988, pp. 252–286.

The Slave Ship: A Human History. New York: Viking Press, 2007.

Reid, John Phillip. *A Constitutional History of the American Revolution*, 4 vols. Madison: University of Wisconsin Press, 1986, 1:179–181.

"Civil Law as a Criminal Sanction," in Edward M. Wise and Gerhard O. W. Mueller, eds., *Studies in Comparative Criminal Law*. Springfield: Charles Thomas Publisher, 1975.

In a Defiant Stance: The Conditions of Law in Massachusetts Bay, the Irish Comparison, and the Coming of the American Revolution. University Park: Pennsylvania State University Press, 1979.

In a *Rebellious Spirit: The Argument of Facts, the Liberty Riot, and the Coming of the American* Revolution. University Park: Pennsylvania State University Press, 1979.

In Defiance of the Law: The Standing-Army Controversy, The Two Constitutions, and the Coming of the American Revolution. Chapel Hill, N.C.: University of North Carolina Press, 1981.

Reid, John Philip (ed.). *The Briefs of the American Revolution: Constitutional Arguments Between Thomas Hutchinson, Governor of Massachusetts Bay and James Bowdoin for the Council and John Adams for the House of Representatives, 1773*. New York: New York University Press, 1981.

Revere, Paul. *The Speech of Death to Levi Ames Who Was Executed on Boston-Neck, October 21, 1773, for the Crime of Burglary*. Boston, Mass.: John Boyle, 1773.

Rice, James D. "The Criminal Trial Before and After the Lawyers: Authority, Law, and Culture in Maryland Jury Trials 1681–1837." *American Journal of Legal History* 40:4 (Oct. 1996): 455–475.

Richards, George. *An Oration on the Independence of the United States of Federate America Pronounced at Portsmouth, New-Hampshire, July 4, 1795*. Portsmouth, N. H.: John Melcher, 1795.

Richardson, Ruth. *Death, Dissection, and the Destitute*. London: Weidenfeld and Nicolson, 2001.

Richetti, John. *Popular Fiction Before Richardson: Narrative Patterns 1700–1739*. Oxford: Oxford University Press, 1992.

Roeber, A. G. *Faithful Magistrates and Republican Lawyers: Creators of Virginia Legal Culture 1680–1810*. Chapel Hill, N.C.: University of North Carolina Press, 1981.

Roediger, Daniel R. "And Die in Dixie: Funerals, Death, and Heaven in the Slave Community 1700–1865." *Massachusetts Review* 22:1 (Spring 1981): 163–183.

Rogers, Nicholas. *Crowds, Culture, and Politics in Georgian Britain*. Oxford: Oxford University Press, 1998.

Root, Jesse. *Reports of Cases Adjudged in the Superior Court and the Supreme Court of Errors from July 1789....* Hartford: Hudson & Goodwin, 1798.

Rosen, Lawrence. *The Anthropology of Justice: Law as Culture in Islamic Society*. Cambridge: Cambridge University Press, 1989.

Rosenberg, Norman L. *Protecting the Best Men: An Interpretive History of the Law of Libel*. Chapel Hill, N.C.: University of North Carolina Press, 1986.

Rosencrantz, Herman. *The Life and Confession of Herman Rosencrantz Executed in the City of Philadelphia, on the 5th day of May 1770 for Counterfeiting and Uttering the Bills of Credit of the Province of Pennsylvania.* Philadelphia, Pa.: Crukshank, 1770.

Ross, Richard J. "The Commoning of the Common Law: The Renaissance Debate Over Printing English Law, 1520–1640." *University of Pennsylvania Law Review* 146:2 (Jan. 1998): 323–461.

"The Legal Past of Early New England: Notes for the Study of Law, Legal Culture, and Intellectual History." *William & Mary Quarterly* 50:1 (Jan. 1993): 28–41.

"The Memorial Culture of Early Modern English Lawyers: Memory as Keyword, Shelter, and Identity 1560–1640." *Yale Journal of Law & the Humanities* 10:2 (Summer 1998): 229–326.

Rothman, David J. *The Discovery of the Asylum: Social Order and Disorder in the New Republic.* Boston, Mass.: Little, Brown and Company, 1971.

Rous, George. *A Letter to the Jurors of Great Britain.* London: G. Pearch, Numb. 12, Cheapside, 1771.

Rowe, Gary D. "The Sound of Silence: United States v. Hudson & Goodwin: The Jeffersonian Ascendancy and the Abolition of Federal Common Law of Crimes." *Yale Law Journal* 101:4 (Jan. 1992): 919–948.

"Constitutionalism in the Streets." *Southern California Law Review* 78:2 (Jan. 2005): 401–455.

Rowe, John. *Letters and Diary of John Rowe*, Anne Rowe Cunningham, ed. Boston, Mass.: W.B. Clarke Co., 1903.

Rowsome, Beverly Z. "How Blackstone Lost the Colonies: English Law, Colonial Lawyers, and the American Revolution." Ph.D. dissertation, Indiana University, 1971.

Royster, Charles. "'The Nature of Treason': American Revolutionary Virtue and American Reactions to Benedict Arnold." *William & Mary Quarterly* Third Series 36:2 (Apr. 1970): 163–193.

Rudé, George. "The Gordon Riots: A Study of the Rioters and Their Victims." *Transactions of the Royal Historical Society*, 6 (1956): 93–114.

Rudiments of Law and Government Deduced from the Law of Nature, Particularly Addressed to the People of South Carolina. Charleston: John M'Iver, 1783.

Rush, Benjamin. *An Enquiry into the Effects of Public Punishments upon Criminals and upon Society.* London: C. Dilly, 1787.

Considerations on the Injustice and Impolicy of Punishing Murder by Death Extracted from the American Museum; with Additions. Philadelphia, Pa.: M. Carey, 1792.

Russell, Peter Edmund. "His Majesty's Judges: The Superior Court of Massachusetts, 1750–1774." Ph.D. dissertation, University of Michigan, 1980.

Salinger, Sharon V. *To Serve Well and Faithfully: Labor and Indentured Servants in Pennsylvania 1682–1800.* Cambridge: Cambridge University Press, 1987.

Sappol, Michael. *A Traffic in Dead Bodies: Anatomy and Embodied Social Identity in Late Nineteenth-Century America.* Princeton, N.J.: Princeton University Press, 2002.

Scarry, Elaine. *The Body in Pain: The Making and Unmaking of the World.* Oxford: Oxford University Press, 1985.

Schadt, Richard Schuyler. "The French Revolution in Contemporary American Thought." Ph.D. dissertation, Syracuse University, 1960.

Schlesinger, Arthur Meier. *The Colonial Merchants and the American Revolution 1763–1776.* New York: Frederick Ungar, 1957.

Schultz, William E. *Gay's Beggar's Opera.* New Haven, Conn.: Yale University Press, 1923.

Schwarz, Philip J. *Twice Condemned: Slaves and the Criminal Laws of Virginia, 1705–1865.* Baton Rouge: Louisiana State University Press, 1988.

Scott, James C. *Domination and the Arts of Resistance: Hidden Transcripts.* New Haven, Conn.: Yale University Press, 1990.

Weapons of the Weak: Everyday Forms of Peasant Resistance. New Haven, Conn.: Yale University Press, 1985.

Scott, Kenneth. *Counterfeiting in Colonial America.* New York: Oxford University Press, 1957.

Counterfeiting in Colonial New York. New York: The American Numismatic Society, 1953.

Seaberg, B. B. "The Norman Conquest and the Common Law: The Levellers and the Argument from Continuity." *Historical Journal* 24:4 (Dec. 1981): 791–806.

Sewall, Samuel. *The History of Woburn, Middlesex County, Mass. From the grant of its territory to Charlestown in 1640.* Boston, Mass.: Wiggin and Lunt, 1868.

Shalhope, Robert E. "Towards a Republican Synthesis: The Emergence of an Understanding of Republicanism in American Historiography." *William and Mary Quarterly* 29:1 (Jan. 1972): 49–80.

Shapiro, Barbara J. *"Beyond Reasonable Doubt" and "Probable Cause": Historical Perspectives on the Anglo-American Law of Evidence.* Berkeley, Calif.: University of California Press, 1991.

Sharpe, J. A. "'Last Dying Speeches': Religion, Ideology, and Public Executions in Seventeenth-Century England." *Past and Present* 107 (May 1985): 144–167.

Shaw, Peter. *American Patriots and the Rituals of Revolution.* Cambridge: Harvard University Press, 1981.

Shearman, John. *I am now to finish a life, which, long since....* Boston, Mass.: Z. Fowle, 1764.

Sheridan, Charles. *Observations on the Doctrine Laid Down by Sir William Blackstone Respecting the Extent of the Power of the British Parliament in Relation to Ireland.* Dublin, 1779.

Shoemaker, Robert. *Prosecution and Punishment: Petty Crime and the Law in London and Rural Middlesex, c. 1660–1725.* Cambridge: Cambridge University Press, 1991.

Shyllon, F. O. *Black Slaves in Britain.* Oxford: Oxford University Press, 1974.

Silverman, Kenneth. *A Cultural History of the American Revolution: Painting, Music, Literature, and Theatre in the Colonies and the United States from the Treaty of Paris to the Inauguration of George Washington 1763–1789.* New York: Columbia University Press, 1987.

Silverman, Lisa. *Tortured Subjects: Pain, Truth, and the Body in Early Modern France*. Chicago, Ill.: University of Chicago Press, 2001.

Simpson, A. W. B. "The Rise and Fall of the Legal Treatise: Legal Principles and Forms of Legal Literature." *University of Chicago Law Review* 48:3 (Summer 1981): 632–679.

Simpson, David. *The Politics of American English 1776–1850*. Oxford: Oxford University Press, 1986.

Smith, Barbara Clark. *After the Revolution: The Smithsonian History of Everyday Life in the Eighteenth Century*. New York: Pantheon Books, 1985.

Smith, Billy G. and Richard Wojtowicz. *Blacks Who Stole Themselves: Advertisements for Runaways in the Pennsylvania Gazette 1728–1790*. Philadelphia, Pa.: University of Pennsylvania Press, 1989.

Smith, John. *The Last Speech, Confession, and Dying Words of John Smith who was Executed at Albany, on the Fifth Day of February 1773....* New Haven, Conn.: Thomas and Samuel Green, 1773.

Smith, Joseph H. "An Independent Judiciary: The Colonial Background." *University of Pennsylvania Law Review* 124:5 (May 1976): 1104–1156.

Smith, Maurice Henry. *The Writs of Assistance Case*. Berkeley, Calif.: University of California Press, 1978.

Smith, Olivia. *The Politics of Language, 1791–1819*. Oxford: Oxford University Press, 1984.

Smith, Steven R. "The London Apprentices as Seventeenth-Century Adolescents." *Past & Present* 61 (Nov. 1973): 149–161.

Smith, William. *The Convict's Visitor: Or, Penitential Offices in the Antient Way of Liturgy, Consisting of Prayers, Lessons, and Meditations with Suitable Devotions Before and at the Time of Execution*. Newport, R. I.: Peter Edes, 1791.

Soderlund, Jean R. *Quakers and Slavery: A Divided Spirit*. Princeton, N.J.: Princeton University Press, 1985.

Spindel, Donna J. *Crime and Society in North Carolina, 1663–1776*. Baton Rouge: Louisiana State University Press, 1989.

St. John de Crèvecoeur, J. Hector. *Letters from an American Farmer: Describing Certain Provincial Situations, Manners, and Customs Not Generally Known; and Conveying Some Idea of the Late and Present Interior Circumstances of the British Colonies in North America*. London: T. Davies, 1783.

Staves, Susan. "British Seduced Maidens." *Eighteenth-Century Studies* 14:2 (Winter 1980–81): 109–134.

Stearns, Asahel and Lemuel Shaw. "An Act Taking Away the Benefit of Clergy (11 March 1785)" in Theron Metcalf, ed., *The General Laws of Massachusetts from the Adoption of the Constitution to February 1822*, 2 vols. Boston, Mass.: Wells and Lilly, 1823, 1:183–184.

Steenburg, Nancy H. "Murder and Minors: Changing Standards in the Criminal Law of Connecticut, 1650–1853." *Connecticut History* 41: 2 (Fall 2002): 125–143.

Stiles, Ezra. *A History of Three of the Judges of Charles I: Major-General Whalley, Major-General Goffe, and Colonel Dixwell*. Hartford: Elisha Babcock, 1794.

Stiles, Henry R. *The History of Ancient Wethersfield, Connecticut*, 2 vols. New York: Grafton Press, 1904.

Stillman, Samuel. *Two Sermons ... Delivered the Lord's-Day Before the Execution of Levi Ames, who was Executed at Boston, Thursday October 21, 1773 for Burglary*. Boston, Mass.: John Kneeland, 1773.

Stimson, Shannon. *The American Revolution in the Law*. Princeton, N.J.: Princeton University Press, 1990.

Stokes, I. and N. Phelps. *The Iconography of Manhattan Island, 1498–1909*, 6 vols. New York: Arno Press, 1967.

Stout, Harry S. *The New England Soul: Preaching and Religious Culture in Colonial New England*. Oxford: Oxford University Press, 1986.

Strong, Nathan. *The Reasons and Design of Public Punishments a Sermon, Delivered Before the People Who Were Collected to the Execution of Moses Dunbar*. Hartford: Ebenezer Watson, 1777.

Stuckey, Sterling. *Slave Culture: Nationalist Theory and the Foundations of Black America*. New York: Oxford University Press, 1987.

Sullivan, James. *The Altar of Baal Thrown Down or the French Nation Defended Against the Pulpit Slander of David Osgood, A. M. Pastor the Church in Medford a Sermon*. Boston, Mass.: Chronicle Press, 1795.

Sullivan, Owen. *A Short Account of the Life of John*****, Alias Owen Syllavan, Alias John Livingston, Alias John Brown: by which Names he stood Indicted by the Grand Jury and Was Found Guilty ....* New York: 1756.

Sullivan, Robert R. "The Birth of the Prison: The Case of Benjamin Rush." *Eighteenth-Century Studies* 31:3 (Spring 1998): 333–344.

Surrency, Edwin C. "The Beginnings of American Legal Literature." *American Journal of Legal History* 31:3 (July 1987): 207–220.

Sweeting, Whiting. *The Narrative of Whiting Sweeting Who was Executed at Albany, the 26th of August 1792 [i.e., 1791]*. Albany: 1791.

Swift, Zechariah. *A System of the Laws of Connecticut*. Windham, Conn.: John Byrne, 1795.

Tavuchis, Nicholas. *Mea Culpa: A Sociology of Apology and Reconciliation*. Stanford, Calif.: Stanford University Press, 1991.

Teeters, Negley K. "Public Executions in Pennsylvania: 1682–1834." *Journal of the Lancaster County Historical Society* 64: 2 (Spring 1960): 85–165.

Thatcher, B. B. *Traits of the Tea Party: Being a Memoir of George R. T. Hewes, One of the Last of Its Survivors: With a History of That Transaction, Reminiscences of the Massacre, and the Siege, and Other Stories of Old Times*. New York: Harper & Bros., 1835.

"The Diary of Mr. Thomas Newell." *Proceedings of the Massachusetts Historical Society* 15 (1876–77): 335–363.

The Dying Speech of the Effigy of a Wretched Importer which was Exalted Upon a Gibbet and Afterwards Committed to the Flames at New York. New York: 1770.

The Life, and Dying Speech of Arthur, a Negro Man, Who was Executed at Worcester, October 20th 1768. Boston: 1768.

The Life, and humble confession, of Richardson, the Informer. Boston: s.n, 1770.

The People the Best Governors: or a Plan of Government Founded on the Just Principles of Natural Freedom. United States, 1776.

The Perpetual Laws of the Commonwealth of Massachusetts from the Commencement of the Constitution. Boston, Mass.: Adams and Nourse, 1789.

The Society for Alleviating the Miseries of Public Prisons. *Extracts and Remarks on the Subject of Punishment and Reformation of Criminals.* Philadelphia: Zachariah Paulson, 1790.

The Speech of the Statute, of the Right Hon. William Pitt, Earl of Chatham to the Virtueous [sic] and Patriotic Citizens of New York. New York: Hugh Gaine, 1770.

The Tom-Cod Catcher. On the Departure of an Infamous B-R – T. Boston: 1769.

The Trial of Alice Clifton for the Murder of her Bastard-child.... Philadelphia: 1787.

Theft and Murder! A Poem on the Execution of Levi Ames, Which Is to Be on Thursday, the 21st of October Inst. for Robbing the H[o]use of Mr. Martin Bicker, and Was Convicted of Burglary. Boston, Mass.: Isaiah Thomas, near the Mill-Bridge, 1773.

Thomas, Elisha. *The Last Words, and Dying Speech of Elisha Thomas who was Executed at Dover, on the 3rd June 1788.* Portsmouth, N. H.: 1788.

Thompson, Edward P. "Patrician Society, Plebeian Culture." *Journal of Social History* 7:4 (Summer 1974): 382–405.

"'Rough Music': Le charivari anglais." *Annales: Economies, sociétés, civilisations* 27: 2 (1972): 285–312.

Whigs and Hunters: The Origins of the Black Act. New York: Pantheon Press, 1975.

Thorpe, Francis Newton. *The Federal and State Constitutions, Colonial Charters, and Other Organic Laws of the State, Territories, and Colonies Now or Heretofore Forming the United States of America,* 7 vols. Washington, D.C.: G. P. O., 1909.

Tocqueville, Alexis de (trans. & eds. Harvey C. Mansfield and Delba Winthrop). *Democracy in America.* Chicago, Ill.: University of Chicago Press, 2000.

Tomlins, Christopher. "The Legal Cartography of Colonization: The Legal Polyphony of Settlement: English Intrusions on the American Mainland in the Seventeenth-Century." *Law and Social Inquiry* 26:2 (Spring 2001): 315–372.

"The Many Legalitites of Colonization: A Manifesto of Destiny for Early American Legal History," in Christopher L. Tomlins and Bruce H. Mann, eds., *The Many Legalities of Early America.* Chapel Hill, N.C.: University of North Carolina Press, 2001, pp. 1–24.

Towers, Joseph. *An Enquiry into the Question whether Juries are, or are not Judges of Law as well as of Fact.* London, 1764.

Towner, Lawrence W. "True Confessions and Dying Warnings in Colonial New England," in Frederick S. Allis, ed., *Sibley's Heir: A Volume in Memory of Clifford Kenyon Shipton.* Boston, Mass.: Colonial Society of Massachusetts, 1982, pp. 523–540.

Tryon, William. *The Speech of William Tr[yo]n, Esq, who was Executed on Thursday the 18th if March, 1776.* New York: 1776.

Tully, Alan. "Literacy Levels and Educational Development in Rural Pennsylvania, 1729–1775." *Pennsylvania History,* 39: 3 (July 1972): 301–312.

Turnbull, Robert J. *A Visit to the Philadelphia Prison*. Philadelphia, Pa.: T. Phillips and Sons, 1797.

Ubbelohode, Carl. *The Vice-Admiralty Courts and the American Revolution*. Chapel Hill, N.C.: University of North Carolina Press, 1960.

Ulrich, Laurel Thatcher. *A Midwife's Tale: The Life of Martha Ballard, Based Upon her Diary, 1785–1812*. New York: Alfred A. Knopf, 1990.

U. S. Census Bureau, *A Century of Population Growth from the First Census of the United States to the Twelfth, 1790–1900*. (1909).

Veall, Donald. *The Popular Movement for Law Reform, 1640–1660*. Oxford: Oxford University Press, 1970.

Vermont. *Statutes of the State of Vermont Revised and Established*. Bennington: Anthony Haswell, 1791.

Vinton, John Adams. *The Richardson Memorial, Comprising a Full History and Genealogy of the Three Brothers Ezekiel, Samuel, and Thomas Richardson*. Portland, Maine: B. Thurston & Co., 1876.

Virginia. "An Act for Altering the Method of Trial" (1738), in William Henning, ed., *The Statutes at Large Being of All the Laws of Virginia*, 12 vols. Philadelphia: Thomas DeSilver, 1823, 3:447–462.

Waite, Frederick C. "Grave Robbing in New England." *Bulletin of the Medical Library Association* 33:3 (July 1945): 272–294.

"The Development of Anatomical Laws in the States of New England." *New England Journal of Medicine* 233:24 (Dec. 13, 1945): 716–726.

Wall, Rachel. *Life, Last Words and Dying Confession, of Rachel Wall Who, with William Smith and William Dunogan, Were Executed at Boston, on Thursday, October 8, 1789, for High-Way Robbery*. Boston: s.n, 1789.

Warner, Michael. *The Letters of the Republic: Publication and the Public Sphere in Eighteenth-Century America*. Cambridge: Harvard University Press, 1990.

Warren, Mercy Otis. *The Adulateur A Tragedy, As It Is Now Acted in Upper Servia*. Tarrytown, N. Y.: W. Abbatt, 1918.

Waters, John J. and John A. Schutz. "Patterns of Massachusetts Colonial Politics: The Writs of Assistance Case and the Rivalry between the Otis and Hutchinson Families." *William and Mary Quarterly* 24:4 (Oct. 1967): 543–567.

Watson, Alan. "The Structure of Blackstone's *Commentaries*." *Yale Law Journal* 97:5 (Apr. 1988): 795–822.

Welch, William. *The Last Speech and Dying Words of William Welch, 23 Years of Age Who was Executed at Boston in New-England, on the 11th day of April 1754 for the Murder of Darby O'Brian, on the Evening of the 19th day of November, 1753*. Boston: 1754.

Welsh, Alexander. *Strong Representations: Narrative and Circumstantial Evidence in England*. Baltimore, Md.: The Johns Hopkins University Press, 1992.

Wharton, Francis. *State Trials of the United States During the Administrations of Washington and Adams*. Philadelphia, Pa: Cary and Hart, 1849.

Wheatley, Phillis. "On the Death of Mr. Snider Murder'd by Richardson (1770)," in Julian D. Mason, Jr., ed., *The Poetry of Phillis Wheatley*. Chapel Hill, N.C.: University of North Carolina Press, 1989, p. 131–132.

White, James Boyd. *Justice as Translation: An Essay in Cultural and Legal Criticism*. Chicago, Ill.: University of Chicago Press, 1990.

White, Shane. *Somewhat More Independent: The End of Slavery in New York City 1770–1810.* Athens: University of Georgia Press, 1991.

"'We Dwell in Safety and Pursue Our Honest Callings': Free Blacks in New York City 1783–1810." *Journal of American History* 75:2 (Sept. 1988): 445–470.

Wilentz, Sean. *Chants Democratic: New York City & the Rise of the American Working Class, 1788–1850.* New York: Oxford University Press, 1984.

Wilf, Steven. "Anatomy and Punishment in Late Eighteenth-Century New York." *Journal of Social History* 22:4 (Summer 1989): 507–530.

"Imagining Justice: Aesthetics and Public Executions in Late Eighteenth-Century England." *Yale Journal of Law & the Humanities* 5:1 (Winter 1993): 51–78.

"The First Republican Revival: Virtue, Judging and Rhetoric in the Early Republic." *Connecticut Law Review* 32 (Summer 2000): 1675–1698.

The Law Before the Law. Lanham: Rowman and Littlefield, 2008.

Williams, Daniel E. *Pillars of Salt: An Anthology of Early American Criminal Narratives.* Madison: Madison House, 1993.

Williams, Samuel. *The Natural and Civil History of Vermont.* Walpole, N. H.: Isaiah Thomas and David Carlisle, Jr., 1794.

Willman, Robert. "Blackstone and the 'Theoretical Perfection' of English Law in the Reign of Charles II." *Historical Journal* 26:1 (March 1983): 39–70.

Wilson, Elizabeth. *A Faithful Narrative of Elizabeth Wilson who was Executed at Chester, January 3d, 1786 Charged with the Murder of Her Twin Infants.* Philadelphia: 1786.

Wilson, James. "Charge to the Grand Jury of the Circuit Court for the District of Virginia, 23 May 1791 (Richmond)," in Maeva Marcus and James R. Perry, eds., *The Documentary History of the Supreme Court, 1789–1800.* New York: Columbia University Press, 1986.

"Considerations on the Nature and Extent of the Legislative Authority of the British Parliament (1772)," in Robert Green McCloskey, ed., *The Works of James Wilson,* 2 vols. Cambridge: Harvard University Press, 1967, vol. II, pp. 721–746.

"Lectures on Law," in Robert Green McCloskey, ed., *The Works of James Wilson,* 2 vols. Cambridge: Harvard University Press, 1967. vol. I, pp. 105–125.

Winterbotham, William. *An Historical, Geographical, Commercial, and Philosophical View of the United States,* 4 vols. London: J. Ridgway, 1795.

Withington, Ann Fairfax. *Toward a More Perfect Union: Virtue and the Formation of American Republics.* New York: Oxford University Press, 1991.

Wolkins, G. G. "Daniel Malcom and the Writs of Assistance." *Proceedings of the Massachusetts Historical Society* Third Series 58 (1924–25): 5–84.

Wood, Gordon. "Conspiracy and the Paranoid Style: Causality and Deceit in the Eighteenth Century," *William and Mary Quarterly* 39: 2 (Apr. 1982): 401–444.

"A Note on Mobs in the American Revolution," *William & Mary Quarterly* 23:4 (Oct. 1966): 635–642.

Creation of the American Republic, 1766–1787. Chapel Hill, N.C.: University of North Carolina Press, 1969.

The Radicalism of the American Revolution. New York: Alfred A. Knopf, 1992.

Worcester, Noah. *A Sermon Delivered at Haverhill, New Hampshire, July 28, 1796, at the Execution of Thomas Powers*. Haverhill: N. Coverly, 1796.

Wrigley, E. A. and R. S. Schofield. *The Population History of England 1541–1971: A Reconstruction*. London: Edward Arnold, 1981.

Young, Alfred. "English Plebeian Culture and Eighteenth-Century American Radicalism," in Margaret and James Jacobs, eds., *The Origins of Anglo-American Radicalism*. London: Allen and Unwin, 1989, pp. 185–212.

"George Robert Twelve Hewes (1742–1840): A Boston Shoemaker and the Memory of the American Revolution." *William and Mary Quarterly* 38:4 (Oct. 1981): 562–623.

"Pope's Day, Tar and Feathers, and Cornet Joyce, Jun.: From Ritual to Rebellion in Boston, 1745–1775." *Bulletin of the Society for the Study of Labour History* 27 (1973): 27–59.

The Democratic Republicans of New York: The Origins 1763–1797. Chapel Hill, N.C.: University of North Carolina Press, 1967.

Young, Robert. *The Dying Criminal: A Poem*. Worcester, Mass.: Isaiah Thomas, 1779.

Zilversmit, Arthur. *The First Emancipation: The Abolition of Slavery in the North*. Chicago, Ill: University of Chicago Press, 1967.

Zubly, John J. *The Law of Liberty*. Philadelphia for J. Almon, 1775.

Index